BASIC LOGIC

The Author

RAYMOND J. MCCALL received his doctorate in
Philosophy from Fordham University and his doctorate in Psychology from Columbia University.
At present, he is Professor of Psychology at Marquette University. Previously, he was Chairman of
the Department of Psychology at De Paul University, Chicago. For fifteen years (1936 to 1951) he
was associated with St. John's University, Brooklyn,
and was Chairman of the Department of Philosophy
and Psychology in the School of Commerce for five
years. Also he has lectured at Columbia and New
York Universities.

For two years (1949 to 1951), Dr. McCall was
associated with the Departments of Research Psy-
chiatry and Research Psychology at the New York
Psychiatric Institute. He has had articles pub-
lished in the *Commonweal*, the *New Scholasticism*,
and other periodicals and reports. He is a member
of the American Psychological Association, the
American Philosophical Association, Sigma Xi, the
American Catholic Philosophical Association, and
the American Catholic Psychological Association,
of which he is past president. He is a former secretary of the Wisconsin Psychological Association.

BASIC
LOGIC

The Fundamental Principles
of Formal Deductive Reasoning

RAYMOND J. McCALL, Ph.D.

PROFESSOR OF PSYCHOLOGY
MARQUETTE UNIVERSITY

Second Edition

BARNES & NOBLE BOOKS

A DIVISION OF HARPER & ROW, PUBLISHERS

New York, Hagerstown, San Francisco, London

for Betty

PREFACE TO THE FIRST EDITION

The present work is intended to form the basis of an introductory course of one semester in logic. It does not presuppose in the student any special classical or scientific training, and it regards the course in logic as preparatory to further courses in philosophy. I have striven to make the exposition of elementary principles sufficiently detailed and replete with examples so that the student or other interested person with no previous scientific or logical training will have no great difficulty in mastering them. I have sought, at the same time, to avoid simplifications and schemas which distort the true nature of logic as a science, and to treat as adequately and profoundly of the forms involved in deductive reasoning as the purposes of an elementary course permit. And since the work is intended for students who will go from logic to the study of philosophy, I have not hesitated at times to invoke philosophical principles for the purpose of clarifying certain issues which the study of formal logic raises, and the misunderstanding of which can vitiate the approach to the subject. If at times, too, I have ventured into the field of material logic, this was with a view to rounding out a discussion of principles that are basically formal. In those instances, I have endeavored to make clear that the problem in question belongs properly to material or major logic, and that it is being discussed briefly only for the light it casts on a cognate formal principle. If this book is written *against* anything, it is against the confusion of formal with material logic, and the confusion of logical with mathematical thinking, which are at the root of so much bad doctrine in contemporary books of logic.

To say that the present state of textbooks in the field is confused is an understatement. The author can only hope that in a minor way he has helped to lessen, and not worse confound, this confusion. To those who know something of the history of logical thought since the Middle Ages, the villain of the piece is Christian Wolff (1679–1754), whose mediocre abilities as a thinker are no gauge of his influence on nearly all subsequent writers in logic and philosophy.

Wolff was responsible for many errors, but none worse to the logician than his merger and confusion of material and formal logic (which had been clearly distinguished by Aristotle in the *Prior Analytics* and *Posterior Analytics*), and his attempt, following Leibniz, to reduce logical genera to mathematical classes. Since Wolff muddied the waters of scientific classification, logic has sought in vain to find its true image in the Wolffian system. And though many modern writers have no consciousness of their debt to Wolff, they are willy-nilly influenced and contaminated by his perversion of the ancient and medieval scheme of the sciences. For the "traditional logic" that many modern thinkers discard is chiefly the tradition of Wolff, and has little to do with the logical synthesis of Aristotle and Thomas Aquinas.

Moreover, where modern logic is most faithful, however unwittingly, to the tradition of Wolff it has become less and less an explanation of the laws of thought, a true logic, and more and more a set of algebraic combinations in which thinking is "explained away" and a mechanical substitution of symbols takes the place of the play of concepts in judgment and inference. Nor has the influence of the Wolffian tradition left unaffected many authors who would regard themselves as, on the whole, faithful to Aristotle. Thus the majority of contemporary writers on logic in the "Scholastic" tradition do little to mitigate the Wolffian perversion, for they are themselves prey to its confusion of material with formal logic, and to some extent to its mathematicism and its materialization of logical predication. In this regard, the influence of Wolff extends far beyond the field of logic, for the very design of the philosophical curriculum in most schools where the "Scholastic" philosophy is taught stems directly from Wolff, and nothing like it can be found in Thomas Aquinas or Aristotle. Since, however, our present interest is in the science of logic, we shall confine our criticisms to that field.

If the contemporary proponents of "logical positivism," "logistics," "semanticism," "symbolic logic," and the "logic of scientific method" wish to approach the subject in a manner quite different from the Aristotelian, that is their privilege, and every sincere thinker would wish them well in their efforts. That does not mean that we must subscribe to the total reduction of logic to mathematics or semantics or scientific method, and to the simple dismissal of Aristotelian logic as outmoded and unscientific. If the point of departure of the modern logician is to be the rejection of the "traditional" approach, let him be sure that he fully understands that tradition. And when he rejects Aristotle, let him be sure that it is an authentic Aristotle, and not an Aristotle of straw who never lived except between the pages of "manuals" in the corrupt and decadent Wolffian tradition.

Few college students, however, will have the inclination or the opportunity to go directly to the works of Aristotle and St. Thomas Aquinas and their commentators for the fundamentals of logic. Many would be disappointed if they did, for the logical doctrine of these thinkers is scattered through many treatises, and, brilliant and profound though it is, it is often couched in a manner that is tedious to the modern student who has no special scholarly interest, and for whom logic is only one subject in a large curriculum. Fortunately, there are some modern works which, while faithful to the authentic Aristotelian tradition, are sufficiently relevant and orderly in their presentation of the subject to command the student's interest. Chief among these valuable modern presentations of Aristotelian logic is the *Petite Logique* of Jacques Maritain, translated into English under the title, "An Introduction to Logic." [1]

My own indebtedness to Maritain's great work should be evident in the analyses on almost every one of the pages which follow. If they, by their very incompleteness, should send the reader to Maritain, they will have served some purpose. If, in certain instances, I have been led to approach problems from a different point of view, that in no way diminishes the extent of my obligation to the writings of the eminent French philosopher. Maritain, in truth, is the kind of thinker who stimulates independent thinking in his readers, and though I have found his book a perfect wellspring of sound logical principle, I have nevertheless deemed a much more elementary approach than his necessary in presenting the fundamentals of formal logic to students in the first two years of college, whose educational background is principally commercial and practical, rather than classical or scientific. If, in this effort of presentation, I have been guilty of any errors or imprecisions, the responsibility is mine alone.

Of the many persons to whom I am indebted for direct or indirect assistance in the preparation of this work, I should mention first my

[1] New York: Sheed and Ward, 1937.

students. To one of these, Robert C. Chilton, I owe a clearer understanding of certain aspects of the hypothetical proposition, and to
many others the benefit of interest and cooperation in a subject that
is often complex and exacting. 1 should also like to thank Prof. J. G.
Scully, of St. John's, who, from his long experience as a teacher, has
given me several important insights into presentation.

R. J. M.

PREFACE TO THE SECOND EDITION

This book has been completely re-written, though the essential plan and purpose remain unaltered. In four years of using the original edition as a text, I have become increasingly aware of certain of its deficiencies, and I have sought to modify many sections in the direction of greater clarity for the student and greater precision for the instructor.

Users of the earlier edition will note a new system of classifying the indefinite and the singular proposition, and an attempt to accord the latter its just due as a unique and important form, while retaining the traditional recognition of its kinship to the universal proposition. I have also attempted to bring the "circumstantially quantified" proposition under the traditional principles governing quantity and quality. The treatments of the modal proposition and of eductive implication have also been considerably extended.

In the final chapter, the rules of the categorical syllogism have been regrouped under three very simple headings (terminology, quantity, and quality). This should, I feel, facilitate student understanding. I have also ventured to suggest the use of obversion as a substitute for indirect reduction and I have given greater consideration to chain arguments and the power of the exclusive particle "only" to alter the direction of deductive statements. More space has likewise been given the oblique syllogism and a brief attempt has been made to show more clearly its distinction from the direct syllogism, especially in its exemption from the rule requiring that the middle term be distributed at least once. As a "bridge" between Aristotelian and relational logic, the oblique syllogism deserves much greater consideration than it has so far received. I have felt that its inclusion in the elementary course might, despite its complexity, help to awaken interest in this important form.

It is a pleasure to recall here my debt to many friends and colleagues at St. John's and De Paul universities and to several members of the Department of Philosophy at St. Bonaventure University for stimulating criticism. I have not always been able to agree with their criticisms, but I trust that the present edition will give evidence of considerable benefit from them.

This revision was undertaken in the midst of many other responsibilities, and its completion has been greatly aided by my secretary, Mary Frances Schroeder. Miss Schroeder has coped nobly with bad handwriting and an author's whimsical penchant for making endless alterations in apparently perfect copy.

My wife, Betty, who has borne and foreborne, sustained and encouraged, protected my little leisure, and placated our children with quiet heroism, undoubtedly deserves coauthor status. Since she might, however, regard this as a doubtful honor, she may be better pleased that this book is for, rather than by, her.

RAYMOND J. McCALL

Feast of St. Thomas Aquinas

TABLE OF CONTENTS

Chapter 1

SIMPLE APPREHENSION AND TERM

Chapter 2

JUDGMENT AND PROPOSITION

Chapter 3

DEDUCTION AND THE SYLLOGISM

LOGIC EXERCISES

INTRODUCTION

Logic in general is the science and art of right thinking. Unlike physical science, or social science, or philosophy, it is not concerned with the *reality* about which we are thinking but only with the *operation of thinking* itself. Until recent years, however, it has displayed a natural gravitation toward philosophy, and academically it is still usually included in the philosophical curriculum. This situation is, in all likelihood, as it should be. For if logic is not part of philosophy, it is a study that is a natural and necessary preparation for philosophy.

The ancients considered logic as preparatory to all science, and for this reason they called it the *organon,* or instrument, of science. It was that which no science included, and which every science presupposed. In our own day, it is doubtful that this holds in any strict sense with respect to the physical, biological, or social sciences, at least in their primary stages. It seems, nevertheless, to be as true as ever of philosophy, and of all efforts to determine the larger implications of scientific laws and principles.

The biologist, or the physical or the social scientist, is ordinarily interested in more than the restricted portion of reality that his science governs. He is concerned at least to know the place of his science in the general scheme of knowledge (a problem in *epistemology* and *material logic*), and the bearing of his researches on the problems of human nature and destiny, problems which pertain respectively to *philosophical psychology* and *ethics*. The scientist, in short, like every other thinking man, requires a philosophy and will inevitably develop one, deliberately or willy-nilly. The thinking man indeed never has the choice whether or not he shall philosophize. His choice is rather whether he shall philosophize openly and critically on the one hand or in a naive and surreptitious and half-baked fashion on the other. And if his philosophizing is to be more than a generalization of self-interest and local prejudice, it must spring from a rigorous and profound logic. That the brilliant sociologist or physicist should

xvii

betray crudity in logical reasoning, and be guilty of gross paralogisms when he comes to consider questions concerning ultimate meaning and value, is a distressing phenomenon, but unfortunately not uncommon. Much of the philosophizing of scientists is, in fact, simply an uncritical extrapolation of scientific methods into an alien field, like the sociologist Durkheim's attempt to refute the doctrine of free will by *statistics,* or the pious assumption of certain contemporary physicists that the same doctrine of free will can be safeguarded by the "indetermination principle" of nuclear physics. To anyone who reads the philosophical *obiter dicta* in which many scientific books abound, it must be obvious that competence, even excellence, in the techniques of controlled observation and experiment, in the formulation of scientific hypotheses and the methods of mathematical deduction, is by itself insufficient guarantee of respectable philosophical thinking. Not the least of the added requirements, we should say, is a thorough grounding in the laws of logic.

But, someone is certain to ask, if you know the facts, is not common sense enough to insure your drawing the right conclusions from those facts and developing a sound philosophy? And if common sense is sufficient, why bother to study logic?

The answer is not far to seek. Though common sense is a necessary prerequisite to all effective thinking, it is not sufficient by itself to insure correct procedure, particularly when the matters under consideration are profound and complicated. Common sense is the guide of our workaday existence. It is unreasonable, however, to expect it to guide us equally well along the tortuous and thorny paths of science and wisdom. For so exalted a purpose common sense is too unreflective and uncritical, and, when relied on exclusively, is certain, as history proves, to lead to the most enormous errors. Common sense, unchecked by logical criticism or scientific investigation, is the mother of superstition and folklore, assuring us that the earth is fixed and the sun moves, that spirit is breath, that everything which moves is alive, and that only the palpable is real. It confuses cause with antecedent, overgeneralizes a limited experience, erects the postulates of local culture into self-evident principles, and, as Zeno showed 2400 years ago, is quite inadequate to justify its belief in the very existence of an elementary fact like motion.

Common sense is not entirely illogical, of course, for one of its components is *natural logic,* which is our native or inborn facility in judgment and reasoning. This natural logic in some sense stands to the developed art and science of logic as any native ability (for instance, singing) stands to that same ability as perfected by training and criticism. By natural logic we are able to perform correctly and readily those primary acts of judgment and inference without which our later scientific and philosophical reasoning could not be valid. It seems to be, in truth, what St. Thomas called the "habit of first principles" as applied to the operation of reason itself. Just as we recognize naturally that a thing cannot both be and not be at the same time, that a physical whole is equal to the sum of its parts, that if something happens it requires a cause, so we recognize readily and without special training that it is wrong to contradict ourselves, that affirmative premises require an affirmative conclusion, that what is true of a given universal is true of a particular coming under that universal, and the like. Given that

"Every plant is living"

and that

"Every bush is a plant"

you do not require a course in logic to recognize the appropriate conclusion as "Every bush is living," rather than "No bush is living" or "Only some bushes are living" or "Some bush is not a plant." If as much were not evident by natural logic, the science of logic would have no foundation.

Just as the primitive data of ordinary or natural experience by which we know the existence of a physical world of colors and sounds and extended bodies must be supplemented with controlled observation and measurement and by the use of special instruments like microscopes, balances, telescopes, photometers, and the like, before we can have an exact science of nature, so the native power of judgment and inference, which is natural logic, must be deepened and systematized by reflective analysis and criticism before we can have a fitting instrument for philosophical thinking. This is precisely the task of logic as a science. Scientific, or *acquired,* logic does not, we should repeat, dispense with natural logic. It presupposes it, and proceeds reflectively and critically to raise its insights to the level of general principles and to codify its laws.

Everybody philosophizes, but we cannot really *think* philosophically unless we first make ourselves proficient logicians. We must learn to organize our concepts and our judgments and our inferences, to express them precisely, and to extract from our own thoughts and experiences, as well as from those of others as expressed in words, their complete and exact meaning. We must learn to detect beneath the flesh of rhetoric the sinews of argument. A good logician will never mistake a platitude for a principle, or a generality for a universal. He will recognize that while "Man is rational" expresses a truth which is proper matter for philosophical consideration, "Woman is fickle" expresses a half-truth, suitable for exploitation upon the operatic stage.

Good logicians are not made, however, in a day—or a semester. The present text does not essay to cover the entire field of logic but only its most basic and elementary division, viz., formal deductive logic. Do not be misled by that word "elementary," for formal deductive logic is by no means simple. It is, nonetheless, truly fundamental, so that if it is grasped adequately the more advanced aspects of the science can be readily mastered by the student (*rara avis,* indeed!) who is minded to continue his studies on his own initiative.[1]

Formal as Distinguished from Material Logic. What is this formal deductive logic? We have seen that logic in general is the *art and science* of right thinking. As a science it is a *speculative* science, that is, it is concerned simply with *what is* right reasoning and *why* it is right. As an art it is a *liberal* art, that is, it seeks to develop in us a stable habit by which in the act of reasoning we can proceed in *ordered, easy,* and *errorless* fashion. The function of

---

[1] The student interested in the practical application of logic to social problems and political controversy, will find Fr. Thomas Gilby's *Barbara Celarent,* A Description of Scholastic Dialectic (Toronto, Longmans, Green, 1949), witty, erudite, and eminently readable. Two works, now available in inexpensive reprint editions, should also prove interesting and helpful. They are *How to Think Straight* by Robert H. Thouless (New York, Simon and Schuster, 1945) and *Thinking to Some Purpose* by L. S. Stebbing (New York, Penguin Books, 1939).

These books are principally concerned with material logic, and with fallacies present in everyday thinking. As such, they are much more immediately practical in scope than the present text, and belong to what certain scholastics would call *logica utens* or applied logic, rather than to *logica docens,* or principles of logic.

the art of logic, then, is to equip our minds for a certain action, the principles of which the science of logic enables us to understand. This action is right thinking. But right thinking can be considered under two distinct aspects, the aspect of *form* and the aspect of *matter*. Reasoning can be right with respect to *correctness* or *sequence* on the one hand, or with respect to *content* or *truth* on the other. If I argue

> Every cat is animal
> Every tiger is animal
> Therefore, every tiger is cat

every one of the propositions involved is *true*—that is, every proposition is a statement which is *in agreement with reality*. The argument is, nevertheless, totally *incorrect* or *formally invalid,* because the conclusion alleged *does not follow from* the premises stated. It is true that every tiger is cat, but this does not follow from the fact that both cat and tiger are animal. The pig is animal, too; but we obviously cannot argue:

> Every cat is animal
> Every pig is animal
> Therefore, every pig is cat.

If, on the other hand, I reason as follows:

> Every animal is vertebrate
> Every cabbage is animal
> Therefore, every cabbage is vertebrate

it is clear that both premises and the conclusion of this syllogism are *false;* yet the argumentation is *correct,* or *in form,* because, supposing the premises to be true, the *conclusion really does follow from them.* If it were true that every animal is vertebrate and that every cabbage is animal, then it would be consequently true that every cabbage is vertebrate. From the standpoint of *formal logic,* this syllogism is perfectly valid. Formal logic, then, is interested in the form or structure of reasoning, that is to say its correctness, irrespective of whether or not the elements of this reasoning agree with reality. Consequently, a syllogism of the sort

Every M is P
Every S is M
Therefore, every S is P

is, from the viewpoint of formal logic, a good syllogism, no matter what equivalents we use for M, P, and S.

The branch of logic that is concerned primarily with the content of argumentation, its truth, is called *material,* or *major,* logic. Presupposing formal validity, material or major logic goes on to inquire what are the conditions necessary for reasoning to be *totally* valid. It considers such problems as logical definition and division, the requirements of the various kinds of demonstration, and the methods of avoiding material fallacies like *begging the question, arguing in a vicious circle, confusing cause with antecedent,* and the like. In our own day, the tremendous growth of the sciences of nature has provided a powerful stimulus toward a corresponding development within material logic of a logic of scientific method. Advances in the mathematics of probability and statistical theory, and in the investigation of language as a medium of communication (*semantics* or *semeiotics*) have also enriched—and complicated—the work of the material logician. Yet practically no additions to the principles of *formal* logic have emerged since the time of Aristotle, who was the first man to write a treatise on the subject.

Our interest will be confined almost exclusively to this *formal* or *minor* logic. We shall deal with certain elementary principles of *material* or *major* logic only to the extent that they cast light upon the formal principles of thinking. Aside from the pedagogical justification of this procedure, we may argue in its defense that it is precisely because so many contemporary logicians, scholastic and other, have confused or glossed over the distinction between formal and material logic, that they have failed to appreciate the intrinsic autonomy of formal logic and the almost perfectly definitive character of Aristotle's treatment of the *forms* of reasoning. In what follows, the organization and examples may be fairly modern, but the substance is almost entirely Aristotle.

Induction and Deduction.   Even formal logic, however, may be understood in a somewhat broader sense than we shall take it here, for formal logic may be considered to include the formal principles of induction (complete and incomplete) as well as those of deductive reasoning, and we shall not find it necessary or convenient to treat at length of induction. Both the *complete* induction, or exhaustive enumeration of possibilities, treated by Aristotle, and the *incomplete* induction, so widely used in the descriptive phases of the biological and social sciences, derive their conditions of validity almost entirely from the material or content with which they deal, so that it would be quite inadequate to consider them from a purely formal point of view.

Incomplete induction is important in the determination of general facts or laws in the natural sciences, but even here it is more important as a method of discovery than as a method of demonstration in the strict sense, for it never as such gives reasons for, or explanations of, the generalizations it achieves. When the biologist, or the chemist, or the social scientist attempts to give the *reason* for any general statement he must make use of deduction. It is on this account that the sciences of nature are constantly drawn to mathematics and philosophy, which employ a primarily deductive mode of reasoning. The forms of reasoning employed in political and literary debate are also preponderantly deductive. For the beginning student, therefore, who is not seeking from logic preparation for a career in the biological or social sciences, deduction is much more important than induction. We shall illustrate the distinction between the two forms of reasoning by contrasting incomplete or scientific induction with the syllogism, and thereafter concentrate on the analysis of the deductive mode.

Deduction argues from the universal to the particular, or from the more to the less universal, by way of a middle term. We might, for example, from the general principle that "Every organism is destructible," conclude that "Every animal is destructible" (by way of the middle term "organism"), our thought thus resting in a less general truth. We might go further and argue that since "Clark Kent is animal," he too is destructible, thereby proceeding to the still less universal (in this case, individual) by way of the middle term "animal." This is an instance of deductive reasoning, and its formal expression is called a *syllogism*.

If, on the contrary, we start with a series of observations bearing on the individual or particular, and argue *up to* a general principle, our reasoning is said to be inductive. In scientific or incomplete induction we may note that this spermatophyte (string bean) has a flower, and this spermatophyte (cactus) has a flower, and this spermatophyte (buckwheat) has a flower, and so on, until we conclude finally from a *sufficient enumeration without exception* that "Every spermatophyte has a flower." Note that in induction there is no middle term, but instead an enumeration of particulars. In scientific induction the enumeration of particulars upon which the inference rests can never be total—hence the name "incomplete induction"— and the possibility is often present that our conclusion is *too general*. If, for example, from the enumeration of all the familiar plants, we should conclude that "Every plant has a flower," our conclusion would be too broad, for certain types of plant, such as bacteria and fungi, do not have flowers. Similarly, inductive generalizations like the following, "Every mammal is viviparous," "All solids expand when heated," must be narrowed somewhat before they can be said to express truth precisely. Incomplete induction is thus essentially imperfect as a mode of reasoning, though invaluable as a means of fixing general data or laws amid the succession of individuals given in experience.

The Elements Involved in Deductive Reasoning. Deduction, then, should be of primary interest to the beginner in logic who is concerned to know the principles of demonstration. Now if we look at a specimen of deductive reasoning:

> Every changeable thing is imperfect,
> But, every material thing is changeable,
> Therefore, every material thing is imperfect

we can see that it is a complex structure, and therefore analysable into simpler elements. The deductive argument has two aspects, which must be clearly distinguished: (A) It is an act of the *mind;* (B) it is a definitely structured combination of verbal symbols or *words*. The ancients called the act of the mind *syllogism,* and its verbal expression an *argumentation,* while in modern usage the term *syllogism* is customarily employed for the verbal statement. The act of the mind is called a deduction or a *deductive inference*. It would seem best to adhere to the modern terminology, and to reserve the term *syllogism* for the verbal expression of the mental act of deduction.

In the syllogism we note that there are three statements or *propositions*. These propositions are the verbal expression of mental acts called *judgments*, so that judgment can be said to be a more fundamental act of the mind implied in reasoning. We judge when we think something *is* something else (or negatively that something *is not* something else). Thus:

Every changeable being is imperfect
or
No earthworm is mammal.

In deduction, from the comparison of two such judgments we infer a third judgment as necessarily implied by the first two. But the judgment itself can be resolved still further. We judge when we affirm or deny mentally that something *is* something else: "Some rose is red" or "This lecture is boring." Obviously, before we can think "Some rose is red," we must know the *meaning* of "rose" and the meaning of "red." Judgment, too, therefore, implies a simpler and more fundamental act of the mind, and this act of the mind we call *conception,* or *simple apprehension.* It is by means of what this act produces, a *concept* or *simple apprehension,* that I know the meaning of "rose," "red," "lecture," "boring." Such concepts or simple apprehensions are expressed verbally by a *term.* Do not confuse the mental and intangible representation by which I apprehend the meaning of "rose" or "lecture" with the *word* "rose" or "lecture" which expresses verbally that apprehension.

We are now in a position to distinguish the various mental operations involved in deductive reasoning and their verbal expressions. The following table will serve as a kind of blueprint of all that we shall study in formal deductive logic:

Mental Act	*Verbal Expression*
Deductive Inference	Syllogism
Judgment	Proposition
Simple Apprehension	Term

It should be clear that, if we wish to understand thoroughly deduction and the syllogism, we shall have to study carefully the simpler operations and products which they involve. Just as we could not hope to understand adequately the operation of the motor in a car without understanding the separate functions of carburetor, distributor, transmission, and pistons, so it is only when we have understood the nature and properties of *judgment* and *proposition, simple apprehension* and *term,* that we shall be in a position to deal effectively with reasoning itself.

Though certain contemporary psychologists may deceive themselves into thinking that they can deal adequately with mental operation by considering it simply as a form of "verbal behavior," the logician should admit that his primary interest is in the operations of the mind, rather than in their verbal expressions. For purposes of logical analysis, however, we can get at the mental act only through its verbal statement, so that even when we are treating of the most impalpable process of thought, we must *begin* with words. But there is no reason why we must end there. Let us grant that for the purposes of logic the imperfect translucencies of language are the only windows of the mind, and that to a great extent words are the instruments as well as the expressions of thought; but to become preoccupied with the words themselves without always striving to penetrate through them to the mental act itself, would make of logic only a more subtle grammar, a glorified anagram or verbal gymnastic, without real significance.

In our study of the logical processes and their verbal concomitants, we shall begin with the simplest of these: *simple apprehension* and *term;* pass on to *judgment* and *proposition;* and conclude with an analysis of the act of *deductive reasoning* as expressed in the *syllogism.*

BASIC LOGIC

Chapter 1

SIMPLE APPREHENSION AND TERM

SECTION 1: SIMPLE APPREHENSION

The first and most fundamental operation of the intellect is conception, or simple apprehension. It is not, however, our first source of knowledge, for the operation of the senses, both external and internal, is prior to any action of the mind. The human intellect is open only from below, so that all it receives must come, in some way, from the sense faculties.

Vision, hearing, somesthesis, and the other *external* senses give us our first presentation of objects as visible, audible, or tangible. The *internal* sense of perception, or *sensus communis*, co-ordinates the data of the external senses in such a way as to give us a concrete percept of a physical object; and another *internal sense*, the imagination or fancy, can *re*-produce or *re*-present a previously experienced object. If you endeavor to recall the appearance of your mother, there will usually arise in your fancy a definite visual *image*, or picture, of a familiar face and figure, which can represent only your mother. We can also imagine such qualities as the sound of a voice or a melody, the feel of silk or cold water, and in imagination we can renew the sensations of falling in space—we do often in dreams —and of warmth and pain. All this is to be classified as *internal sensation*, rather than thinking. In very young childhood, the external and internal senses are apparently operative without calling the intellect into play; and even in maturity, intellection presupposes the prior action of the senses.

The intellect begins to function at the time when we first apprehend the *abstract or general meaning* of the things about us. It is at this time that the difference between man and the other animals in the physical world asserts itself, for while other animals can respond to *concrete* meanings or connections (like that between the rattle of

1

a dish and being fed, or between the sound "sit" and the action of sitting) there is no evidence that any animal other than man is responsive to *general* meanings, such as that of "chair" (a movable seat with a back) or "dish" (a concave vessel with a rimmed edge).

Animal "generalization," of which there has been much loose talk by psychologists, is a generalization of *confusion* or *indiscrimination* rather than a simple apprehension or grasp of a general meaning. A laboratory animal may be conditioned to give a certain response—say pushing a bar—to the musical note C, and he may then proceed to give the same response to the note A or the note F, simply responding indiscriminately to any tone in a certain range; or he may be further conditioned by associative reward and punishment to discriminate between two notes. Neither the confusion nor the discrimination is generalization in any proper sense of the term, for both are indissolubly wedded to the concrete stimulus, now experienced vaguely, now more clearly. Man, on the other hand, can derive from the individual and concrete data of his sensible experience their *abstract* or *general* significance, and it is upon this ability that all his superior intellectual development is based. Perhaps this capacity is, as Piaget suggests, largely dormant in the very young, so that when the four-year-old says "chair," the word relates more closely to a concrete object (his chair) or to a cluster of individual images (corresponding to the chairs of which he has had actual experience) than it does to the general meaning, symbolized by the dictionary definition of "chair." Be that as it may, the normal human eventually comes to develop general concepts, which, though based on experience, are independent of any particular experience. It is to these we refer in logic by the term *simple apprehension*.

Definition of Simple Apprehension. Let us define simple apprehension as

an act by which the mind grasps the general meaning of an object without affirming or denying anything about it.

When I understand what is meant by "triangle," "man," "isosceles," "stupid," this understanding is a simple apprehension. If I think something *about* the apprehended triangle or man: "Some triangle is isosceles," "This man is not stupid," then I no longer simply apprehend. Rather I *affirm* or *deny* something *about* what I have apprehended. This affirmation or denial is called a *judgment*. It is an act distinct from simple apprehension, though it presupposes simple apprehension. Simple apprehension, then, is distinguished from judgment in that it neither affirms nor denies: it simply lays hold of, or grasps. What results from this intellectual apprehension or conception or seizing of the essence of an object—the product of the act—is also referred to as a *concept, notion,* or *mental term.* Concept is the synonym most frequently used for simple apprehension, regarded as the *product* of an act.

Distinction of Concept and Image. It is necessary to distinguish carefully the simple apprehension, or concept, from the image which so often seems to accompany it. This distinction belongs properly to philosophical psychology, but it is of capital importance for the logician to understand it.

Study this word MAN for a moment. Think what it means. You understand the meaning of the term clearly; you know the kind of thing which the term stands for. Notice that when you think "man," there is likely to arise before your inner eye a certain image, or picture. Vague, perhaps, but likely to be present if you attend carefully in your reflection. This image has at least two physical qualities: a certain color, however difficult to specify; a certain shape, however fluid. It may be like an evanescent photograph of some individual human being whom you do not recognize clearly. Though we have auditory, tactile, kinesthetic, olfactory, and other images, visual images seem clearest and most fundamental in most persons, and most readily confused with concepts. Because of their relative stability and their tendency to occupy the focus of consciousness, we are more likely to "see" visual images when we introspect than any other. It is necessary to stress, however, that though some kind of image *may accompany* our simple apprehensions, it is not the same psychic entity as the simple apprehension which it accompanies. Unless we distinguish the image from the concept, we have no notion of what thinking really is.

The image, however vague, is *physically* or *materially* representative; while the simple apprehension is the grasp of something *intangible* and *immaterial*—a universal meaning—which has neither color nor shape nor any other physical quality. Yet a percept *or* an image has to be present in order that we may have a concept, for the concept is an abstraction or withdrawing of the *general* meaning from an *individual* thing presented to the mind in a percept or in an image. The percept *presents,* the image *represents,* an individual. The intellect, by an activity which is at once illuminative and separative, lays bare the universal (the essence or meaning) potentially resident within the individual.

What of so-called "imageless thought"? Certainly this is a reality, as any number of psychological investigations and our own introspections show. In many cases it is unnecessary to form an image in order to have a simple apprehension, since the concept may be derived *directly from a percept,* as when we grasp a general meaning directly from the auditory perception of a spoken word without any intervening image. Nevertheless, an image is often evoked *after* the concept is formed, as an illustration or example of the meaning conceptualized. If, for example, we are called on to think about properties of a certain nature, let us say "parallelogram," it is extremely difficult to hold the meaning in mind without an accompanying image. The fact that the relatively more tangible and vivid image continues in such cases to coexist with the concept is a further reason why it may be easily taken for the concept. Yet it is the concept which is the *thought,* the instrument of judgment and reasoning, that in which the intellect *lives the meaning* of the object. The image is only a prop which is required in order to hold our sensual nature up in the realm of the intelligible. If there were no more to thinking than forming images, reasoning would not be essentially different from dreaming, and logic a form of *folie raisonnante,* a well-organized and self-conscious phantasmagoria. Perhaps, in truth, the nightmare which it seems to some students!

The act by which the intellect derives the meaning from the phantasm (percept or image) is called *abstraction,* and the quality of being abstracted or withdrawn from the contingencies and limitations of sense experience is most characteristic of the concept as distinguished from the image. It is abstraction which lifts objects from the plane of mere sensibility to the level of intelligibility; it is abstraction which dematerializes images and percepts so that the intellect may apprehend the meaning or essence of the thing perceived or imagined. To neglect abstraction is to neglect the most characteristic and revealing function of the human intellect. It is small wonder that those philosophers, psychologists, and logicians who have done so have found it easy to reduce human thinking to association of images, or to weak motor responses in the pharyngeal musculature, or, finally, to a kind of verbal geometry which the logician systematizes by means of a set of arbitrary algebraic symbols.

Notice that in judgment, as when I think that "Man is animal," the images are purely auxiliary. In making this judgment I am conscious introspectively of a faint tableau, involving a whiskered human and honey-colored bear. But surely this is not what I am *thinking about!* Rather my thought concerns the *nature* "man," and the *meaning* or *essence* "animal," which my judgment affirms are united in existence. Of course, there is a *similarity* between physically existing or imagined men and bears, or the judgment "Man is animal" would not be true. It is the very capacity to *mark this similarity* between physically distinct things that is the basis of conception and judgment. We know that the intellectual representation is derived from, and therefore related to, some sort of sensory presentation or representation. Yet the *particular* sensory qualities represented in the image of a man (fair-complexioned, red-haired, tall, let us say), do not adequately symbolize the meaning "man," for the next time I think "man," the accompanying image máy represent quite different particular characteristics (dark-skinned, brown-haired, short, for example). Though the image varies from one individual to another, and for the same individual on different occasions, the concept, representing the meaning and held within the limits of the definition, remains constant. If the concepts varied with the images, we would not know that the identical judgment referred to the same thing, yesterday and today.

Notice, too, that no image of "man" can apply to *all men.* Try to form an image of "man" which applies equally to Caucasian and Negro, fat man and thin man, tall man and short man, male and female, infant and octogenarian. The *universal* concept which expresses the meaning "man," however, applies equally and perfectly to any and every man, for each man is an "animal capable, under normal circumstances, of abstract thought" or a "rational animal."

Every man has a nature, corresponding to the meaning "man" represented in the concept. The image is always *particular* (or better, *individual*), while the concept is *universal*.

We may summarize the differences noted between concept and image in the following table.

Image	*Concept*
Material	Immaterial
Concrete	Abstract
Variable	Constant
Individual	Universal

Distinction from Judgment. It has already been remarked that a concept, or simple apprehension, unlike a judgment, neither affirms nor denies. For this reason, the concept by itself is an incomplete or imperfect act: the mind does not rest in it, but must go on to think something *about* the thing apprehended, to make a judgment. It is for this reason, too, that a concept, or simple apprehension, cannot be said to be either *true* or *false*. If I think "fish" or "polygon," my thinking is neither true nor false, precisely because I have neither affirmed nor denied anything of these entities. If, on the other hand, I *say something mentally* (I do not mean merely or principally *verbally*) about the object of my conception: "The polygon is a fish" or "The polygon is a plane," my thought can be denominated *true* or *false*, false in the first case and true in the second. We may say in summary, therefore, that the simple apprehension, unlike the judgment, is incomplete; it neither affirms nor denies, and on this account the simple apprehension, though it may be clear or confused, adequate or inadequate, can never be either true or false. Let us tabulate the differences noted.

Simple Apprehension	*Judgment*
Incomplete, imperfect	Complete or perfect act in which the intellect rests
Neither affirms nor denies	Must affirm or deny
Neither true nor false	Must be either true or false [1]

---

[1] The so-called "future contingent" judgment: "I shall be at home tomorrow," "There will be no major war in the next thirty years," is not true or false *determinately* but only *indeterminately;* that is to say, it becomes true or

SECTION 2: PROPERTIES OF SIMPLE APPREHENSION

The Comprehension of Concepts. We have seen that in the simple apprehension the intellect knows the essence or meaning of a certain object. This meaning can be expressed in the definition. Now most objects that we consider do not have a perfectly simple essence or meaning, and cannot therefore be expressed in a concept or in a corresponding definition which is in all respects simple. You cannot, for example, say in a single word what "man" is. What man is (his "quiddity" or "whatness" or meaning) is something complex. In logic, the parts or elements of that complex meaning are called the *notes* represented by the concept, and the sum total of these notes, when articulated in proper order, is called the *comprehension* or *connotation* of the concept. This very important property of a concept or simple apprehension may be defined as follows:

> *The comprehension or connotation is the completely articulated sum of the intelligible aspects, or elements, or notes represented by a concept.*

We are familiar with the definition of man as "rational animal." This definition, however, or any other definition, does not make explicit all the notes in the essence "man." This is because the concept "animal" is itself not simple, but capable of being resolved into several simpler notes. "Animal" means a *material substance* of a certain kind, namely, living; but more than this, an animal is *sentient* (capable of sensation). If, then, we were asked to give the comprehension or connotation of the concept "animal," we should arrange these notes in proper order, from most to least general, and say:

| *Substance* | *Material* | *Living* | *Sentient* |

Add one more note, and we have the comprehension of "man":

| *Substance* | *Material* | *Living* | *Sentient* | *Rational* |

---

false at the appropriate time, upon the realization or non-realization of the event predicted. *Doubtful* judgments are actually either true or false, though it may be impossible for us to decide which.

The note "rational," we learn in major logic, is the *specific difference* of "man," because it is the note which distinguishes the *logical species* "man" from any other species. The most general note is the *category* "substance," for that is the most general class of being to which man belongs. Between the most general *category* and the *specific difference* of "man," there occur the *generic differences*, "material," "living," "sentient." The first four notes, as we have seen, constitute the comprehension of "animal," and "animal" is said to be the *proximate genus* of "man." "Material substance" (body) and "living material substance" (organism) are called *remote genera* of "man." The third-century logician, Porphyry, used a diagram based on logical division by contradiction, or *dichotomous division*, to illustrate these relationships. Here is an adaptation of this diagram, since known as the *Porphyrian Tree:*

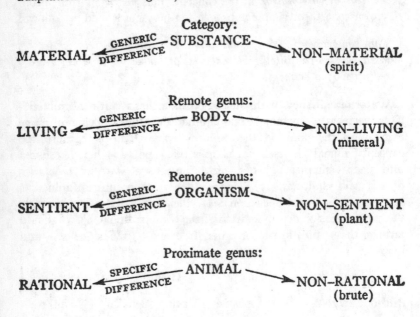

Category:
SUBSTANCE
MATERIAL ← GENERIC DIFFERENCE — SUBSTANCE → NON–MATERIAL (spirit)

Remote genus:
BODY
LIVING ← GENERIC DIFFERENCE — BODY → NON–LIVING (mineral)

Remote genus:
ORGANISM
SENTIENT ← GENERIC DIFFERENCE — ORGANISM → NON–SENTIENT (plant)

Proximate genus:
ANIMAL
RATIONAL ← SPECIFIC DIFFERENCE — ANIMAL → NON–RATIONAL (brute)

Logical species:
MAN

The notes in the comprehension of "man" are read from this illustration by beginning with the category, adding the generic differences, and concluding with the specific difference. If we start at the bottom of the Porphyrian Tree, we can see that the comprehension makes explicit all that the definition, or *logical species*, leaves implicit. When we explicate the definition "rational animal," we derive the comprehension: *substance, material, living, sentient, rational.*

We cannot give all the notes in the comprehension of most concepts, because the number of real beings of which we can formulate a logical definition in terms of "proximate genus" and "specific difference" is extremely limited. As a matter of fact, "man" is the only essence corresponding to an actual being that we can so define, for man is the only actual being whose *specific difference* is known to us. For the entire animal, vegetable, and mineral kingdoms, we have to be content with *generic* definitions, to which we add certain constant sensible *marks* or *characteristics,* which serve more or less satisfactorily to distinguish one kind of animal or plant or mineral substance from another. In endeavoring to define "horse," for example, we can give a generic definition of the horse as animal (sentient organism), and make explicit the various notes involved (substance, material, living, sentient); but instead of the specific difference, we have to be satisfied with stating certain *descriptive characteristics* (vertebrate, mammal, ungulate, herbivorous, having a mane and tail, etc.). No one of these qualities is exclusively characteristic of "horse," but the sum total of them serves to distinguish "horse" from "sheep" or "antelope."

It is part of the office of sciences like biology and chemistry to render such "descriptive definitions" as exact as possible, by means of careful observation and measurement. Though the adequate resolution of the problems raised by these "descriptive definitions" belongs properly to major logic, it is sufficiently important to the proper understanding of the notion of comprehension for the formal logician to consider at least the basic principles involved. Moreover, since these principles are widely misunderstood, they should be attended to carefully.

In the logical sense, such descriptive definitions are not definitions at all. They are substitutes, in terms of sensible characteristics, for an intelligible characteristic (the specific difference) which we do not know. By the same token, many so-called sensible "properties" are not properties in the original sense of that term. Strictly, a property is a characteristic which "flows from the essence" of a thing—that is, either it can be deduced from the very nature or meaning of the thing, or at least its logical connection with the nature as known is evident. Not only is it found invariably wherever this essence is found, but, if it is a *specific* property, it can be true of *no other* kind of thing. Such sensible characteristics as "cloven-footed" in the sheep, or "solid-hoofed" in the horse, cannot be deduced from the meaning of "horse" or "sheep"; nor is their logical connection with the essences in question manifest. If they are observed to be present whenever "horse" or "sheep" is given in sense experience, they are nevertheless not truly *specific*, since there are animals other than sheep which are cloven-footed, and animals other than horses which are solid-hoofed. Such characteristics, therefore, cannot be said to be satisfactory substitutes for the unknown specific difference. In the case of creatures other than man, rarely if ever do we find a sensible quality which is uniquely characteristic, that is, true of this one kind of thing and of no other. What is taken to be specific is the particular *collection* or *sum* of such constant sensible characteristics, or the *amount* of some single characteristic, like the neck of the giraffe or the trunk of the elephant.

Even deducible properties, or characteristics logically connected with the essence, are not part of the comprehension of a concept. Characteristics of "man" like "having the power of free choice," "endowed with natural rights," are not strictly part of the comprehension of "man," but are said to flow from the comprehension as specific properties, because they can be deduced from the specific difference. From the fact that man is rational, for example, we can deduce the necessity of his being free. There are other characteristics which observation discovers and reason certifies as specific properties. Wherever man is found, you find a being capable of speech, of fashioning tools, of laughter. There are many such properties which we may classify as truly *specific*, because they are discovered in no other animal. If such properties are not, absolutely speaking, deducible from the essence of man, at least their natural and fitting connection with his rationality can be readily understood. It is quite otherwise with qualities like "cloven-footed" or "warm-blooded" or "ruminant." In the first place, they are generic rather than specific characteristics; and in the second place, their connection with the essence of the thing which has these characteristics is always obscure. We know *that* the sheep is cloven-footed and ruminant, as sensible facts. The *intelligible reason* for these facts, that is, *why* the sheep should be ruminant and cloven-footed, remains a mystery. Thus these descriptive characteristics may better be referred to as "rightful accidentals" or "proper accidents" than as properties. Qualities like "tall" or "shortsighted" in man, or "gray" or "two years old" in sheep might then be called *pure accidentals*. Pure accidentals are neither part of the essential comprehension, nor necessarily connected with it, nor are they always found where a given nature is found. They are discovered by experience and assigned to one individual or to some individuals—to this man or some men, to this sheep or some sheep—never to man and sheep as such and universally. In the following tables (pp. 12, 13) these distinctions are illustrated.

Though neither properties nor accidentals are part of the comprehension of a concept, we sometimes speak as though they were. When we predicate any characteristic of a *subject* in a judgment, we are said to place the predicate in the comprehension of the subject. If we judge, for example, that "This man is tall," we are said to place "tall" (an accidental) in the comprehension of "this man." This is true, we should remember, only in a very broad sense of the term "comprehension," and it is said only of a concept which is *functioning as the subject of a judgment,* never of a concept taken in itself. "Tall" is in no sense part of the comprehension of "man," taken universally or in itself. Only those notes which are explicitly or implicitly in the essential definition are rightfully considered part of the comprehension of any concept.

There is one class of entities that can be readily defined in terms of proximate genus and specific difference, and which therefore offers opportunity for exercises in determining the comprehension of concepts. These entities are plane geometrical figures. *Triangles, circles, parallelograms,* and the like do not, needless to say, exist as such in the physical order. Yet they do represent a type of real (possible) being, for they are all modes of quantity, and quantity is by no means a mere intellectual figment. Thus mathematical entities usually stand for real being—not substance but quantity—though

MAN

Essential Comprehension	Properties (specific)	Descriptive Characteristics (true of all)	Pure Accidentals (true of only some)
substance material living sentient rational	powers of laughter free choice natural rights speech toolmaking, etc.	mammal, vertebrate, upright, biped, opposable thumb, etc.	tall, slender brown-eyed fair-haired talkative, etc.

OTHER ANIMALS

Essential Comprehension (generic)	Properties (generic)[2]	Descriptive Characteristics (true of all)	Pure Accidentals (true of only some)
Sheep substance material living sentient	occupying space divisible, powers of growth nutrition, reproduction, movement, etc.	mammal, vertebrate, herbivorous, quadruped, ruminant, cloven-footed, valuable for food and wool, etc.	gray or black fat or thin old or young, etc.
Horse substance material living sentient	occupying space divisible, powers of growth nutrition, reproduction, movement, etc.	mammal, vertebrate, herbivorous, quadruped, solid-hoofed, having mane and tail, trainable for human use, etc.	roan or bay fast or slow gentle or fiery, etc.
Beetle substance material living sentient	occupying space divisible, powers of growth nutrition, reproduction, movement, etc.	invertebrate, oviparous, six-legged, exoskeletonic, segmented, one pair of antennae, etc.	black or brown small or large, crawling or resting, etc.

[2] As animal, "man" has the same *generic properties* as any other animal. In the original Aristotelian meaning of the term "prop-

PLANTS AND MINERALS

	Essential Comprehension (generic)	Properties (generic)	Descriptive Characteristics (true of all)	Pure Accidentals (true of only some)
Violet	substance material living	occupying space divisible, powers of nutrition, growth, reproduction	phaenogamous (flowering) dicotyledonous (2 seed-leaves), angiosperm (seeds enclosed), having 5 separated petals, 5 sepals, 5 stamens, ovary and pod one-celled, etc.	actually flowering, having a bird-foot leaf, fading, of a purplish or yellow color, etc.
Edible Mushroom	substance material living	occupying space divisible, powers of nutrition, growth, reproduction	reproducing by sporulation, devoid of chlorophyll, deriving food from other organisms, having a frilled cap and stem, gills free from stem, dark-colored spores, etc.	growing in a meadow or underground, young or old, cap 4 inches in diameter, etc.
Carbon	substance material	occupying space divisible	solid, non-metallic element, atomic number 6, atomic weight 12, inert, insoluble, giving off characteristic gas (CO_2) when burned, powerful reducing agent, etc.	existing in particular allotropic form of diamond or graphite, weighing approximately 1 gram, derived from coal, etc.
Benzene	substance material	occupying space divisible	liquid, organic compound, chemical formula C_6H_6, hexagonal structural formula, useful as a solvent, readily compounds with halogens and acids, important in manufacture of dyes, etc.	derived from this particular quantity of coal tar, to be used to manufacture aniline or medicine, relatively free from impurities, etc.

erty," only qualities *deducible* from the *specific difference* are properties. It would, nonetheless, seem permissible analogically to extend the meaning of the term to qualities deducible from or necessarily implied by generic notes and to speak of "generic properties."

13

they represent quantity in an ideally perfect manner, without the irregularities and complications which the quantities we experience sensibly always have. Plane geometry deals with flat surfaces, and in the real world there are surfaces which approximate flatness, but in the real world there are no plane figures because surfaces never exist apart from the three-dimensional objects of which they are surfaces. Similarly, there are edges to objects, but no edges *without* objects, or perfectly straight lines; there are more or less round objects, but no perfect circles, as in geometry. By considering these quantities apart from the variations and unevenness of sense experience, we can define them exactly and establish their comprehension by explicating these definitions.

Let us take the example of "triangle," which is definable as a "three-sided polygon." In this definition, "polygon" is the proximate genus, "three-sided" the specific difference. We now "break down" the proximate genus, stopping when we come to the category "quantity," in order to obtain the comprehension of the concept "triangle." "Polygon" might be defined as an "enclosed plane," but the term is not usually applied to partially or wholly curvilinear figures, so that we should probably include "rectilinear" (enclosed by straight lines) as a generic difference.[3] A "plane" is a *flat* (as opposed to a spherical) *surface,* and a surface is a *two-dimensional magnitude.* "Magnitude" is the general name for any geometrical figure, and may be defined as a *continuous quantity* (as opposed to a *discontinuous quantity,* which is a *multitude* or *number*). We have now arrived at the *ultimate genus* or *category,* "quantity," so that the comprehension of "triangle" is complete. Arranging these in

[3] The restriction of the term "polygon" to rectilinear plane figures is not necessary, since we might think of the spherical triangle (which is not a plane) and the semicircle (which is partly curvilinear) as polygons, but for our purposes this restriction is convenient. It would seem, moreover, that when we think of "triangle," we do not ordinarily include the so-called "spherical triangle" in that meaning; and when we think of "polygon," we need not embrace the "curvilinear polygon" in the concept. There is a certain arbitrariness in the *terminology* of mathematical definitions which need not especially concern us here. If our concepts are clear and distinct and our use of terms consistent, we can safely leave the adjudication of the ideal terminology to the grammarians and the mathematical philosophers. In any event, the definitions given are, I believe, perfectly correct for what is meant here by "triangle" and "polygon."

proper order, from most to least general, we have a one sided Porphyrian Tree, as follows:

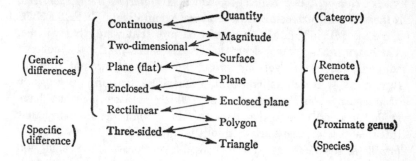

Adding the *differentiae* to the category, we have the comprehension: *quantity, continuous, two-dimensional, plane, enclosed, rectilinear, three-sided.*

Noting only that the term "plane" stands for either the adjective (as in "plane surface") or the noun (as in "enclosed plane") and that the English language does not seem to have a single noun for "enclosed plane," we may say that "triangle" is a perfectly definable entity, and that each of the notes involved in its comprehension is clear. These five notes

quantity   continuous   two-dimensional   plane   enclosed

are common to all the figures with which plane geometry deals, so that, with the help of a good dictionary, we should have little difficulty in determining proximate genus and specific difference for parallelogram, rhombus, rectangle, circle, ellipse, and the like. For "circle," for example, we add to the five notes above the generic difference "curvilinear" and the specific difference "all points equidistant from a fixed point," to complete the comprehension. Doing this for all the familiar geometrical figures should prove a valuable exercise in determining and understanding the comprehension of concepts.

Extension of Concepts. Of equal importance with the comprehension of concepts is the reciprocal property of *extension* or *denotation.* The comprehension is the sum total of notes that constitute the *essence.* Extension is that property by which the concept refers to the *sum of real things* (*both actual and possible*) *to which the essence can be applied.* The comprehension of "man," what "man" *connotes,* is a *substance,* which is *material, living, sentient, rational.* So the extension of the concept "man" is its REFERENCE TO ALL POSSIBLE MEN, those that are, that were, that will be. These are what "man" *denotes.* By the same token, the concept "animal" denotes *all possible animals,* of the past, present, and future, rational as well as irrational. Primarily extension is a *property of a concept*—and this is a point which modern logicians have tended to overlook—so that it is only by a kind of metonymy that this *reference of a concept* to things is identified with the *things referred to,* the referents. It is permissible to speak of the extension of a concept as the things coming under that concept, provided we recognize that this is not an exact way of speaking, and do not attempt to build any theory thereon.

It is evident that the extension of the concept "animal" is greater than that of the concept "man," because "animal" refers *both* to men and to irrational animals. Even though the extension of "man" embraces an indefinitely great multitude of individuals, the extension of "animal" is *greater,* because it *includes* this indefinitely great multitude of men (for men are animals), plus the indefinitely great multitude of animals other than men.

Notice, too, that even if man were the only kind of animal *actually existing,* the extension of "animal" would still be *greater* than that of "man," because it would include: (A) all actual and possible men, (B) all other possible animals as well. The extension of a concept implies not a *number,* but an indefinitely great *multitude* of individuals in possible existence to which this concept *extends.*

If we add a note to the comprehension of a concept—say "rational" to "animal"—we automatically exclude from the extension of that concept those beings which lack the added note. By adding "rational" to "animal" we exclude irrational animals from the extension. We can thus appreciate the truth of the principle:

COMPREHENSION AND EXTENSION VARY INVERSELY.

If you increase the comprehension, you decrease the extension, and *vice versa.* This is illustrated in the table on the opposite page.

Comprehension	Extension
Man (5 notes)	All possible men
Animal (4 notes)	All possible men plus all possible other animals (lions, dogs, fish, insects, etc.).
Organism (3 notes)	All possible men plus all possible other animals plus all possible plants (oak trees, tomato vines, fungi, bacteria, etc.).
Body (2 notes)	All possible men plus all possible other animals plus all possible plants, plus all possible nonliving bodies (air, carbon, gold, stones, etc.).

Remember that the extension of a concept is not affected by the coming-to-be or ceasing-to-be of individuals, because extension refers to possible, as well as to actual, existence. In other words, because one of us dies, there is no reason to subtract one from the extension of the concept "man." When logicians forget that extension is a *property of a concept,* referring to *possible* existence, and treat extension as an *actual number of things,* they turn an important aspect of the logic of concepts into a rather pointless arithmetical exercise. We shall avoid this undesirable simplification if we bear in mind: (A) that our concepts represent essences or general meanings; (B) that when these essences are analyzed into their logical constituents and reunited in proper order, they give us the property of comprehension; and (C) that when our concepts are referred to the possible existing things possessing this essence or meaning, they give us the property of extension.

SECTION 3: DIVISIONS OF CONCEPTS

Concrete and Abstract Concepts. Perhaps the greatest difficulty attaching to the understanding of this distinction is that the terms "abstract" and "concrete" have in logic a different (and much more limited) significance from what they have in everyday con-

versation. Many terms which are "abstract" in the popular sense
stand for what logic calls "concrete concepts," and *vice versa,* so
that, unless we resolutely lay aside the popular notion of what
these terms mean, we are pretty certain to have difficulties in understanding the logical meaning of their distinction. It might even
be desirable to invent new terms in logic—like *choristic* for "abstract" and *hypostatic* for "concrete"—but until such inventions are
sanctioned by at least a sizable minority of logicians, we shall have
to make the best of terminology that is both antiquated and confusing.

We have seen that every concept presents to the mind a general
meaning. The ancient logicians frequently referred to this meaning
as a "form." It is according to the way in which a concept presents this meaning or form that it is classified as "concrete" or
"abstract." If the concept presents the meaning *of* a subject or *in*
a subject, it is said to be *concrete.* Thus the concept "man" is a representation of the meaning of a (universal) subject, and is concrete. The concept "humanness" represents the same meaning, but
apart from any subject as though "humanness" were itself a thing,
as "man" is. The concept "humanness" is thus abstract. But it is
not only concepts of subjects which are concrete, but also concepts
of qualities or characteristics which represent these characteristics
in and with a subject. Thus "red" is concrete, "redness" abstract.
Why? Because "red" presents the meaning or form "to be colored
in a certain way" *in and with* a certain subject, a thing which is red;
while "redness" represents the same meaning apart from any subject,
as though this meaning were a thing existing in itself, instead of (as
it is) a *quality of* a thing. When I think of the quality of stop
lights, I think "red." When I think of that same quality apart
from stop lights, autumn leaves, bandannas, or any other subject,
I think "redness." If you ask me *what* this object is, I shall say it
is "man" or "horse," "intelligent" or "strong," all concrete. If you
ask me *what makes* this object what it is, I shall say "humanness,"
"equine-ness," "intelligence," "strength," all abstract. *What a thing
is,* is its nature and characteristics in the concrete. *That by which*
a thing is what it is, is its nature and characteristics in the abstract.

Plato thought that the abstract term, such as "beauty," "equality,"
represented not merely a manner of conception but a real entity,

existing apart from the imperfectly "beautiful" or "equal" things which we perceive in the world around us. However sublime this conception, we are pretty well agreed today that it is false, and that it is the concrete concept which represents more nearly the reality as it is, and the abstract concept which represents meanings in a way that they are never found in reality. In other words, there is no real "redness-in-itself," but only red objects; no real "human-ness-as-such," but only human beings, whose characteristic, "human," the intellect can consider *as though* it were an entity existing in itself.

Speaking in very general terms, we can say that everything we can think of is either a being (subject) or a state of being. If we think of a being or subject, the concept is concrete. If we think of a state of being *as* a state of being (that is *in* a subject), our concept is also concrete. It is only when we think of a state of being *as though the state of being were itself a being or subject* that we have an abstract concept. It follows that common nouns—names of *things*, including humans—generally stand for concrete concepts. Examples are numerous: "dog," "man," "book," "centaur," "angel," "space-ship," etc. Notice that it does not matter whether the *thing* in question is real or imaginary, singular or universal, actual or possible, material or immaterial. As long as the concept represents a *subject*, it is concrete. It follows also that adjectives in general stand for concrete concepts, because an adjective stands for a concept representing a characteristic or condition *of* something, and this something, the subject, is either mentioned or understood. The adjectival concept, then, must represent a state of being *in* or *with* a subject.

Nouns or substantives formed from adjectives, on the other hand, are invariably the expressions of abstract concepts, for they express an adjectival characteristic in a substantive manner, that is, as though it were a thing in itself, or subject—"stupidity," "devotion," "thickness." The same abstract reference attaches to nouns derived from *verbs*, or expressing *activity* substantivally, for activities, too, are states of being rather than subjects. Thus "attention," "deed," "walking," "call," etc. are all abstract.

The most difficult case for which to formulate a rule is the adjective whose implied substantive is an abstract term, like "ephemeral" implying "ephemeral thought," or "commutative" implying "commutative justice," or "isosceles" implying "isosceles trapezoid." In such cases, it might be argued that the concept for which the adjective stands is *formally* concrete, since it connotes a subject; but *materially* abstract, since the subject connoted is itself abstract. If, however, we supply the missing substantive, then the adjective is not by itself a term but only part of a term, and the whole term will be classified as abstract or concrete according as the substantive is abstract or concrete. Thus "just distribution" is an abstract term, "just man" a concrete one. In discourse, the substantive implied by an adjective should always be clear, so that we should have no special difficulty in deciding whether a term in an argument is concrete or abstract. In those cases, therefore, where the implied substantive is abstract, it is probably best to think of the adjective as expressing an abstract concept.

Mathematical terms, for the most part, stand for abstract concepts. In this category we must place "sixty-two," "triangle," "rhombus," "square root." "Triangle," for example, is the abstraction "triangularity," derived from physical objects which are three-sided, and considered by the mind as though it were an object existing in itself. The mathematician sometimes tends to neglect the origin of his concept, and to treat of "triangle" as though it were an individual thing. But there are no individual triangles, for no matter how detailed you make your description of "a" triangle, it has an indefinitely great multitude of possible inferiors or singulars, and is, therefore, universal. Geometrical entities are like angels: each individual is a species.

We should not in logic entertain the notion that abstract concepts are always vague and intangible, and concrete concepts always clear and readily exemplified in sensible existence. This would be an instance of confusing the popular with the ancient and technical meanings of these terms. Since the following concepts represent a characteristic apart from a subject, they are all abstract:

> *color   odor   disgust   muscularity   sensation*

while the following concepts, since (however vague they may be) they represent either a subject or a characteristic-with-a-subject, are concrete:

> *soul divine* (being) *temperamental* (dragon) *supernatural* (being)

One last (somewhat sad) note on the ancient terminology. The use of the terms "concrete" and "abstract" with respect to concepts is not above exception *logically,* because in the strict sense every direct concept is abstract, and there is no such thing as a direct concrete concept. Every concept immediately represents a meaning abstracted by the mind from the data provided by the senses; a *universal* meaning, moreover, which abstracts from the individualizing qualities of the objects we experience. The concept "man" does not have any concrete or individual qualities which would confine its application to "this man," and prevent its application to any other. "Man," as well as "humanness," is thus truly abstract; only humanness is *more* abstract since its prescinds from (leaves out) not only individual sensible qualities, but even the universal subject itself. We can by-pass the difficulty which the terminology involves, therefore, if for "concrete" we mentally substitute "less abstract," and if for "abstract" we mentally substitute "more abstract."

Collective and Divisive Concepts. "Abstract" and "concrete" are divisions of concepts in relation to the manner in which their comprehension is conceived. But concepts can also be divided according to extension—that is, in relation to the subjects or things for which they stand or denote. The subjects for which a concept stands are called the *singulars* of that concept. Every direct concept represents an essence or meaning which is applicable to an indefinitely great multitude of singulars. Hence we say that every direct concept is *universal.* The following are examples:

> *man   magistrate   player   team   jury   flotilla*

But notice the difference between the *singulars* of the first three concepts and those of the latter three. "Man," "magistrate," and "player" are *divisive* concepts because their ultimate singulars are *individual* beings: this man (President Lincoln), this magistrate (Justice Taney), this player (second baseman Keeler). "Team," "jury," and "flotilla," on the other hand are *collective* concepts because their ultimate singulars are not individual beings but *collections or groups* of individual beings. *A* team is many beings, as is *a* jury, and *a* flotilla.

Do not make the mistake of thinking that the collective concept is naturally singular. The concept "army," for example, is a universal concept because it can be applied to any and every army: the United States Army, Napoleon's army, the *Wehrmacht*. The concept is *collective*, since the many to which it can be applied are many *groups* or *collections* of individuals, not many individuals taken *divisively* or one by one. The concept "soldier," on the other hand, is not only universal but *divisive*, since its singulars are not groups but individuals.

Abstract concepts may be said to be *divisive* if the subjects in which the abstracted characteristic ultimately resides are individuals. Thus "color," "strength," "courage," etc. would be considered divisive concepts. The abstract concept which stands for *collections* of characteristics, on the other hand—like "spectrum" (an aggregation of colors), "complex" (a group of feelings), or "concert" (a group of musical activities)—would probably best be thought of as collective.

Remember that it is the character of its singulars which determines whether a given (universal) concept is to be designated *collective* or *divisive*. If the singular consists of many items held together in a functional or artistic unity, the singular is regarded as one, and the corresponding concept as divisive. Thus "stone wall," "chain," "newspaper," "necklace," "textbook," are divisive rather than collective. We must acknowledge, nonetheless, that many "units" of everyday thought and speech are really *aggregates*, having only *nominal* unity. Though it is convenient to think of "bag of sugar," "glass of water," or "pound of coffee" as units, it does not require much thought to realize that each of these "things" is really an aggregate of many things. Perhaps a coffee bean is a unit, or a coffee molecule. The logician can leave that problem to the philosopher of nature, but even on the evidence of common sense he would know that a concept like "pound of coffee" is really collective. To insist that common thought and speech, however, adhere to this technicality would be pedantry, especially since such arbitrary and nominal unities ordinarily play little or no role in argument, which is the logician's proper concern.

Singular and Particular Concepts. The ancient logicians further divided concepts into *singular* and *particular*. A "singular concept" might be defined as one whose extension is limited to *one* singular, whether a single group or a single individual, e.g., "this man," "the Globe Trotters Basketball Team." Do not confuse "singular concept" with "singulars *of* a concept." A singular concept is a kind of *concept;* the singulars of a concept are the *things* to which the concept extends. Every concept has singulars. It is the distinctive characteristic of a singular concept that it has for its singular only one definite individual or group, while a universal concept has an indefinitely great multitude of singulars. A *"particular* concept" is one whose extension is limited to some *indefinite* or indeterminate individual or individuals, e.g., "some man," "certain dogs." The concept is regarded not as communicable to all the singulars, but as not limited to one definitely.

Here again we must acknowledge that the accepted terminology is somewhat misleading, for, taken in itself, no proper concept is singular or particular. *In itself* every direct concept is applicable to *all* the singulars which possess the meaning which it represents, and is *universal*. It is only *in relation to another concept* (to a certain predicate in the context of a proposition), or in relation to a certain image or percept, that a concept can be said to be "singular" or "particular." Thus, the concept "man" *in itself* is always *universal;* but taken in relation to the predicate "bald," for example, it cannot be rightly understood in the full universality of its extension. I cannot judge *"Every* man is bald," but must say rather "Some man is bald." The concept "man" is still as universal as ever in itself, but in relation to the predicate "bald" its extension is limited to some indefinite individual or individuals. The ancients were well aware of the looseness of the expression "particular concept," and preferred to call it a *universal concept taken particularly*. This is what is properly meant by the so-called "particular concept."

The same may be said respecting what we call today the "individual concept." The universal concept "man" in relation to the predicate "my best friend," or in relation to a certain image or percept, cannot be extended to all the individual subjects who are men, but only to this one individual who happens to be my best friend. Thus, too, the concept "father" is universal, but in relation to that congeries of distinctive qualities in the image or percept of "my father," its natural universality is restricted or "taken individually." We then designate it "an individual concept."

Be careful not to confuse *singular* with *particular* concepts. In ordinary speech, "singular" and "particular" are pretty much synonymous, while in logic they are poles apart. In logic, "singular" means "restricted to one *definite* individual"; "particular" means "restricted to an *indefinite* individual or individuals"—as in *"Some* textbook is needed in the course"; *"Certain* nations are authoritarian."

If we bear in mind that a concept expresses primarily a certain *meaning* (made explicit by the comprehension); that secondly it has the property of standing for an indefinite multitude of singulars (its extension) which possess this meaning, we shall be in possession of the major co-ordinates in relation to which all the important divisions of concepts are made. The manner in which the mind considers the general meaning gives rise to the distinction of *concrete* and *abstract* concepts; the character of the concept's *singulars* (individuals or groups) gives rise to the distinction of *collective* and *divisive* concepts; the restriction of the concept's universal extension (to one or some of its natural multitude of singulars) gives rise to the distinction of *singular* and *particular* concepts.

It cannot be too often stressed that what the concept represents is the *general meaning*—an essence that is capable of being found in many. It is for this reason that there is no *direct* concept of the individual. Though we have direct sensible experience of individuals, our *concept* of the individual is only a reflex or indirect concept. My concept of a certain man, for example, is a product of the mind's reflection upon the universal concept "man" in association with the image or sense-percept of this individual.

The universal concept "man" stands for "every man," because it stands for human nature in its naturally unlimited extension. It does not stand for "all men" in the sense of an enumeration or collection of individuals. That is why, as we shall see, it is better in logic to say "Every man is mortal," rather than "All men are mortal." The latter expression is too well sanctioned by popular usage to be altogether avoided, but if it is taken merely as a statement about a certain *sum* of subjects, it is of little logical value or significance. Unless a proposition tells us something about the *nature* of a subject, it cannot be used as a basis for inferring anything about other subjects which may have that nature. I may count all the x's and find that they are y's, but unless y pertains in some way to the nature of x, the next x I come upon may or may not be a y. I can never be sure. It is thus that propositions like "All students in this class are American citizens"—mere *enumerative* universals, arrived at simply by counting heads—can never give rise to a genuine deductive inference.

SECTION 4: TERMS

Terms and Words. *A term is a word or a group of words which expresses verbally a concept or simple apprehension.* As concepts enter into judgments and reasoning, so terms enter into propositions and syllogisms. The term is the simplest unit into which the proposition and syllogism can be logically resolved.

Not every word is a term, for not every word by itself is the expression of a concept. Words such as "all," "but," "some," "because," "quickly"—adverbs, prepositions, conjunctions, articles—are called *syncategorematic* (*co-significant*) words. By themselves syncategorematic words do not express a concept, but may be required *in conjunction with* (*syn*) another word or words to express a new meaning. For example, "walking" is a *categorematic* (significant) word or a *term;* "quickly" is not a term, but "walking quickly" expresses a concept which the term "walking" by itself does not. Do not imagine for a moment that syncategorematic words are of small significance in discourse—consider "if" and "but." The nuances of human conversation and argument, the actual movement of thought as reflected in speech, the artful joining that removes the neat turn of speech a thousand miles from the platitude or banality "that says the same thing"—all these may owe much to the syncategorematic word.

In logic, the syncategorematic words are construed with the categorematic, so as to constitute together a single term. In the proposition, "The next installment is due promptly on the fifteenth of the month," the predicate-term is not simply "due," but "due promptly on the fifteenth of the month." Where grammar separates modifiers from object for the purposes of its analysis, logic does not, since it is the *total* concept expressed that is of logical moment.

A term *immediately* expresses a concept, and *mediately* (by means of this) it stands for the *things* which have the meaning that a concept represents. The term "man" is the immediate expression of the *concept* "man," but mediately it stands for the real nature "man," and still more mediately for all the individuals who possess this nature. A term has a certain being of its own. Usually, it has a history, an etymology, a distinctive pronunciation and spelling, its own niche in the kingdom of *verbal existence*. Yet it stands not only for itself as a verbal existent, but for a *mental* existent (a concept), and for a *real* existent (a nature) and, ultimately, for the really existing things which have this nature. Because it is possible for the same word or words to express different meanings, and because a term can, without changing meaning, stand for different orders of existence—verbal, mental, or real—the proper use of terms in logical discourse is by no means easy. Certainly, the imprecise, ambiguous use of terms is the rule rather than the exception in everyday life, and even thinkers of competence may sometimes be hard put to keep from "stretching" a term (changing the meaning of a term in the course of an argument) or confusing their idea of a thing with the thing itself (thinking the term stands for real existence when it only stands for mental existence).

The Signification of Terms. The division of terms according to signification into "univocal," "equivocal," and "analogous" belongs properly to major logic. Certain implications of this distinction are, however, of considerable importance in the theory of the syllogism, so that it will be worth our while to treat briefly of it here.

Univocal terms are terms which always have exactly the same single meaning; for example "isotope," "photoelectric cell," "anthropology," "six thousand nine hundred and fifty-eight," "shoe lace," "cuff button," "desoxycorticosterone." Univocal terms for the most part are either technical or scientific terms, or compound terms standing for highly specialized *manufactured* or similar articles: thus "shoe lace" and "cuff button." *Equivocal terms* are terms which, though spelled and pronounced alike, have a radically different and *unrelated* meaning. Thus, "pitcher," "mean," "bit," "mark," "plane." Equivocal terms have proved a fecund source of puns and other bad jokes in English, from Shakespeare to the modern television comedian (or his writers). The reminder that one can "make book" without being a publisher, "make hay" without being a farmer, and that there are at least two senses in which a German engraver might "make his mark," can be sometimes counted on to make people laugh. If the implied comparison is sufficiently outlandish, the antiquity of the theme does not seem to detract much from the humor. For the purposes of spoken humor, in fact, it is not necessary that the similar-sounding words be *spelled* alike, or be actually equivocal; similar pronunciation is sufficient, as in the chestnut about the vicious canine with a tendency to disappear from time to time: on such occasions someone altered the sign BEWARE THE DOG to read WARE BE THE DOG.

The majority of simple terms in common usage, however, are neither univocal nor equivocal, but *analogous*. Analogous terms might be described as terms which, when applied to *different* things, have a *related* (and thereby partly *similar*) meaning. Thus the "head" of an organization has a function relative to the organization similar to the function of the *head* with respect to the body of an animal. The flexible and graphic quality of our native tongue undoubtedly owes much to the fact that so many of its words permit of this analogical extension to a variety of objects. Consider the opening words of our most famous political document:

> When, in the *course* of *human events*, it *becomes necessary* for one *people* to *dissolve* the *political bands* which have *connected* them with another, and to *assume*, among the *powers* of the *earth*, the *separate* and *equal station* to which the *laws* of *nature* and *nature's God entitle* them, a *decent respect* to the *opinions* of *mankind requires* that they should *declare* the *causes* which *impel* them to the *separation*.

Without exception, each of the terms used has more than one precise significance. This in no way detracts from the political and social meaning of the statement. In fact, the "physical" and common association of words like "dissolve," "bands," and "decent" adds "color" to the language and helps render its meaning clearer and more memorable. An unabridged dictionary will show that some of these italicized terms have a dozen or more related (analogous) meanings, and some that are virtually unrelated (equivocal), like "respect" meaning "honor" and "respect" meaning "refer."

Terms are not fixed, once and for all, in one or another of these classifications. Many words which were originally analogous are, in their present usage, equivocal. Probably this is because the original relation of proportion or similarity is no longer consciously held in mind when the term is used in one of its derived senses. The word "bit," for example, in all its various meanings, is connected with the Anglo-Saxon "bite," so that some underlying similarity is involved. Yet that similarity is so slight, and so little thought of today when we speak of a "bit of sunshine" or a carpenter's "bit," that "bit" here is for all actual purposes equivocal. Moreover, as analogous terms may become equivocal, so univocal terms may take on additional meanings which render them analogous or equivocal. Most slang terms, for example, are not new words but old and reasonably respectable terms—like "alligator" and "dig"—to which some currently fanciful significance is attached. If most of these coinings are counterfeit, and disturbing to older people who have lost the zest for new experience, we must admit, nonetheless, that a certain percentage of today's slang will be tomorrow's idiom. Language is not a static and accomplished artifact but an historically living and adjustive instrument, and slang has a role to play in the constant effort of language to express novel experience and new ways of viewing reality.

The logician, at any rate, has no objection to equivocal and analogous terms, *provided their ambiguity or ambivalence is recognized*. It is not the equivocal term but the equivocal *use* of terms that is illogical. The word "seal" is quite equivocal, but in the following argument its use is logically unexceptionable:

> Every mammal is warm-blooded
> The seal is mammal
> Therefore, the seal is warm-blooded.

It is not possible to employ only univocal terms in argument, but if we take care so to phrase our statements that from the context the meaning of any possibly ambiguous term is *single* and *clear*, there can be no actual *equivocation*. By the same token, if a term is employed in two *widely different* senses, there is equivocation, but no one is likely to be fooled by it. We should be unlikely to argue, this side of schizophrenia, that:

> Every plane is a tree
> Every polygon is a plane
> Therefore, every polygon is a tree.

But subtler ambiguities and variations in meaning that are ever so slight may take us in, and we may fall victim to the fallacy of "weasel-wording." When we are told, for example, that a certain piece of legislation would restrict individual *liberty* and is therefore *undemocratic*, we must ask *in what sense* it would restrict liberty, and whether restriction of liberty *in this same sense* is undemocratic, and we must ask as well the precise meaning of "undemocratic" in this context. If there is the faintest variation in the meaning of either of these terms, the argument is entirely invalid. So when we are told that "retailing" is a "science," based on "logic" and "psychology," we may be sure that the terms "science," "logic," and "psychology" are being used in restricted and analogous senses, and we should hesitate on the basis of this premise to classify *retailing* with *physiological chemistry* or *vertebrate anatomy*, sciences in a narrower and stricter sense of the term. The substance of popular thinking in political and other controversial matters seems attached to certain terms of a truly hallowed ambiguity. Terms like "democracy," "science," "psychology," "practical," "academic," "socialism," "liberty," "fascism," "bureaucracy," "totalitarianism," "theoretical," "equality," are not only "weasel words" which are seldom precisely defined or univocally employed in argument; they are also "loaded words," for each of them has a certain emotional charge or valence which tends to arouse visceral rather than cerebral reactions in the hearer or reader. Because of the ambiguity of these terms, arguments involving them are likely to degenerate into parallel monologues, and because of the emotions engendered such arguments are more likely to lead to physical than logical conclusions. When we employ these and similar terms in debate—as we must, since these terms relate to problems of great importance—we should resolutely refuse to allow their emotional implications to interfere with their univocal employment. We must endeavor to define them as precisely as possible and to adhere rigidly to the definition given throughout the course of the argument. "Stretching" the meaning of a term in order to identify its connotation and associations with those of another term, thereby attaching to one term the emotional charge of the other—as in the attempt to identify "democracy" with "complete absence of government regulation," or "racial equality" with "intermarriage between whites and Negroes," or in the advertisers' frantic effort to label their products with the talismanic associations of such terms as "scientific proof" and "medical recommendation"—is a tempting rhetorical trick against which the student of logic should be always on guard. Ample exercise in exposing this fallacy can be had by anyone who takes the time carefully to read advertising copy, political speeches, or partisan editorials.

The Supposition of Terms. *Supposition* is without doubt the most neglected of all the properties of terms. Its neglect, in fact, has resulted in a gap in a good deal of logical theory, and an inability to cope with certain types of problems arising in regard to the syllogism and the proposition. Let us begin by defining the supposition of a term as:

> *the mode of existence for which the term stands.*

Secondly, let us note that supposition is never a property of a term taken *in itself* but only

> *of a term taken in relation to another term in a proposition.*

Why is this? Because a term *in itself* (e.g., "man") does not stand for *existence,* it stands simply for a meaning or essence, which may or may not exist. If all existing strawberries or inkwells were annihilated this instant, the *meaning* of "strawberry" or "inkwell" would not be changed one jot or tittle. It is only in a proposition that I assert *existence,* that something *is* something, e.g., "Man is animal." Only with respect to the proposition, therefore, can I ask: What mode of existence does the term stand for? What, for example, is the supposition of the term "man" in the proposition *"Man* is animal?"

There are *three* general answers to the question of what mode of existence a term in a proposition stands for, and therefore three general kinds of supposition. The medieval logicians analyzed each of these general types into several subtypes, but with most of these we need not be concerned in an elementary course.

In the first place, we may consider the case where the term stands for a *merely verbal existence,* for itself as a word, as when I say:

> "Man is three-lettered."

In this case the supposition is *material.* The *meaning* "man" is not three-lettered, nor are the *real beings,* men, three-lettered. This predicate obviously can be applied only to the *word* "man," so that in material supposition the "is" of the proposition indicates a merely verbal manner of existence.

In the second place, we may consider a proposition like:

"Man is universal."

Here the predicate "universal" indicates that the mode of existence asserted of the subject "man" is *ideal*, or *mental*, existence. It is only the concept "man," "man" as it exists in the mind's manner of conception, that is *universal*. As they exist in the real order, natures or essences are individualized. They become universal only because of the way in which the human intellect abstractively conceives them. Whenever a predicate says something of a subject that can be true of that subject *only by virtue of the manner in which the mind conceives it*, the "is" of the proposition in question asserts only ideal, or mental, existence, and the subject-term is said to be in *logical supposition*. If I judge:

"Man is a species"

or

"Man is a type of animal"

or

"Man is abstract"

in each of these cases the predicate can be said of "man" only insofar as "man" is conceived abstractly and as "man" exists in the mind, so that in each of these cases the term "man" is in logical supposition.

In the third place, in a proposition like:

"Man is animal"

we have a very different situation. Here what is asserted of "man" applies to it not only as a word, nor as an abstract meaning conceived by the mind, but to "man" as a *real nature*, and to the *really existing singulars of that nature*. The mode of existence which the verb "to be" asserts of the subject here, then, is *real* existence, and the supposition of the term "man" in this proposition is *real supposition*.

Whenever a predicate can be passed on from the universal nature to the *singulars* partaking of that nature, we have a sign of real supposition. Thus, not only can I say that *"Man* is animal," but that *"This man* (Peter) is animal," and *"This man* (Edward) is animal," and so for each and every one of the singulars of the concept "man." Similarly, in the proposition "Some man is ignorant," which places its subject-term in real supposition, the predicate "ignorant" can be applied to any and all of the singulars included in the indeterminate extension of "some man." In the case of logical supposition, on the other hand, even though the subject-term may in itself have many singulars, I *cannot* apply the predicate to these singulars. Though it is permissible to say "Man is universal," I cannot say consequently that "Peter is universal" or "Edward is universal," though Peter and Edward are men.

There is little difficulty in distinguishing material (verbal) supposition from both logical and real supposition, since in material supposition the *concept is really different* from what it is in the other two cases. In the proposition:

"Man is one-syllabled"

the concept to which the term "man" corresponds is not immediately the concept of the meaning or nature "man," but the concept of the *word* "man." The meaning or nature "man" is present only on the margin of thought, and what the term immediately stands for is the concept of *itself as a word*.

No such readily discovered difference exists between real and logical supposition. In the two propositions:

"Man is a vertebrate" (real supposition)
and
"Man is a species of animal" (logical supposition)

the concept "man" is the same. The term "man" expresses, in the two cases, *exactly the same meaning or nature*. Its signification is *univocal*. The difference is that in the first case (real supposition) it expresses that nature not only as it exists in the mind in a state of abstraction, but as it exists in reality—as communicable to the individuals having that nature. The term "man" stands for the concept "man" *not only in its comprehension but in its extension*. In the second case (logical supposition), the term "man" stands for the nature "man" only as it exists in a state of abstraction in the mind, in a manner in which it is not found in reality. If the supposition of a term is logical, the predicate which it receives cannot be passed on to the individuals which have the nature expressed by the term. The term still stands for the concept in its comprehension, but not in its normal extension. As in the case noted above, though it is true that

"Man is a species of animal"

it cannot be concluded therefrom that *this* man or *that* man is a species of animal. This or that man is not a species, but an individual.

Where the subject of a proposition is a concrete term (like "man," "plant," "book") the best procedure to follow to distinguish real from logical supposition is the following: Determine whether or not what is said of the subject in the original proposition can be ascribed to the singulars having the nature which the subject expresses. If this predicate cannot be rightly assigned to the singulars, you may be sure that the subject-term is not in real supposition. For example, in the proposition:

"Man is the most intelligent animal"

the term "man" stands for the nature "man" as an *abstract unity, existing as such only in the mind,* and not for the nature "man" as existing in the singulars of the concept "man"; for I cannot say that "Paul Garfield" or "Roger Flood" is the "most intelligent animal," even though each is man.

We should note that for real supposition the term does not have to be a *concrete* term, nor the real existence referred to *physical* existence. In the propositions:

"Justice is a virtue"
and
"Truth is good for the intellect"

the supposition of the subject-term in each case is *real,* for truth and justice are realities, even if not tangible ones. Justice is a real quality or habit, truth a real relation. A proposition with an abstract subject-term places that term in logical supposition only if the predicate must be applied to *the concept of the characteristic or relation* rather than to the characteristic or relation itself. In the proposition "Justice is a virtue" the predicate "virtue" applies to the real quality "justice," and not merely to the concept of that quality. In the proposition "Justice is abstract to the second degree," on the other hand, the predicate "abstract to the second degree" applies only to the *concept* of "justice" and not to the quality "justice" itself. The supposition of the term "justice" in this second case is, therefore, *logical supposition*.

It is not even necessary that the existence denoted by real supposition be *actual* existence. Thus most simple mathematical propositions, like

"The triangle is a polygon"
or
"Seven is the sum of four and three"

place their subjects in *real* supposition, though the *triangle* and the number *seven* exist neither in the sensible nor the actual order. "Triangle" or "seven" are not abstract classifications *created* by the mind, like "species" or "genus," but like many other mathematical terms they stand for real quantity in the *pure* state, a state in which quantity *could* exist but actually does not. Such mathematical terms ordinarily stand, then, for an order of *real, in the sense of possible existences*. Like other abstract terms, these simple mathematical terms will be in logical supposition when what is said of them applies to the *concept* of the quantity rather than to the quantity *itself*. Thus

"Triangle is an abstract notion"

has its subject-term in *logical* supposition, because it is the concept "triangle" which is an "abstract notion," rather than the quantitative entity "triangle" itself.

When the subject of a mathematical proposition is a purely *imaginary* or *fictive* (rather than a *real*) quantity, like "the square root of minus one" or "a negative number" or "zero," then the supposition is necessarily *logical*. This applies not only to the useful fictions of mathematics; it applies wherever a term in a proposition stands for a purely imaginary entity. When we predicate something of "Superman" or "the centaur," as well as of "minus eleven," the "is" of our proposition indicates not real existence, actual or possible, but only the sort of existence in the fancy that a mental construct has.

The supposition of the subject-term in these propositions is logical:

> "Minus eleven is a negative number"
> "i is the square root of minus one"
> "The centaur is vertebrate"
> "A two-sided polygon is a figural"
> "A self-caused being is eternal"
> "Cyclops is limited to monocular vision."

Terms standing for imaginary entities may be singular (like "Superman"), and they may be quantified by the signs of universality, "Every," "All," "No." They remain, nevertheless, in logical supposition. In most other cases, where the term is singular or where it can be preceded by a universal sign like "every," the supposition is real, but this never applies to purely fictional entities. Terms standing for imaginary entities may be in *material* supposition, as in:

> "Superman in German is *Uebermensch*"
> or
> "Self-caused being is a complex term."

English usage ordinarily requires that a term in material supposition be set off by quotes or italicized, but this *presupposes* that we recognize its supposition when we use the term, and in any case does not apply to the *spoken* term, nor enable us always to distinguish the term in material supposition from the term in logical supposition, which may also often be set off by quotation marks.

Some consistent and *logical* rule is required which will enable us always to distinguish one kind of supposition from another. Where, as is usual, the term in question is the subject-term of a proposition, it is possible to formulate such a rule rather simply. Given the proposition "S is P," to determine the supposition of the subject-term, "S," we ask the following questions:

1. Is it the *word* "S" that is "P"? If so, the supposition is *material*.
2. Is "S" an imaginary being? If so, the supposition is *logical*.
3a. (Where "S" is a *concrete* term) Can "P" be applied to the *singulars* of "S"? If so, the supposition is *real;* if not, the supposition is *logical*.

3b. (Where "S" is an *abstract* term) Is it the real characteristic or relation "S" that is "P," or only the concept of "S" that is "P"? If the former, the supposition is *real;* if the latter, the supposition is logical.

In some cases, it may be prudent to distinguish real supposition referring to *possible* existence ("The trapezoid is quadrilateral") from real supposition which includes *actual* existence ("Babies are irresponsible"). This can be done by writing a subscript ("p" for possible or "a" for actual) with the R (for real supposition) in designating terms in real supposition. The two examples above could thus be labelled R_p and R_a respectively. It is always necessary, in any case, to distinguish carefully the statement in logical supposition from the one in real supposition. Much of the to-do in the 17th century about the ontological argument (which sought to prove the *actual existence* of God from the *concept* "perfect being"), and much of the loose talk in our own century about the *existential* implications of theories in mathematical physics (like the *relativity* and *indetermination* theories which are based on useful mathematical fictions) would have been obviated if the thinkers involved had been always careful to mark these distinctions.

Remember that it is the fundamental nature of a term to stand for a concept, and that a concept is a mental representation of a general meaning which is applicable to things. A term is thus a

word or words (verbal existence)

which stands for

a concept (mental existence)

which represents

a general meaning (signification—comprehension)

which is applicable to

things (real existence—extension).

It is thus that *comprehension* and *extension* are the two most fundamental properties of *concepts,* and the basis of the two most fundamental properties of terms, *signification* and *supposition.* The various classifications of concepts and terms that we have studied in this chapter should then be clear. Most of these classifications are summarized in the following table.

CONCEPTS

Comprehension (meaning-essence)
- Considered with a subject (concrete concept)
- Considered apart from a subject (abstract concept)

Extension
- Unrestricted (universal concept)
- Restricted to some (particular concept)
- Restricted to one (singular concept)
- Singulars are individuals (divisive concept)
- Singulars are groups (collective concept)

TERMS

Comprehension (meaning-essence)
- One comprehension (univocal term)
- More than one comprehension
  - partly similar (analogous term)
  - quite dissimilar (equivocal term)

Extension (singulars-existence)
- Stands for singulars or real existents (real supposition) in a proposition
- Does not stand for singulars or real existents in a proposition but for
  - verbal existent (material supposition)
  - or
  - mental existent (logical supposition)

37

Chapter 2

JUDGMENT AND PROPOSITION

Section 1: Judgment

Definition of Judgment. The complete and proper operation of the mind is called *judgment*. Judgment may be defined as:

the act by which the intellect unites by affirmation, or separates by negation.

What is it that the mind unites or separates? In the primary or basic type of judgment, the *categorical* judgment, two *terms*, and thereby two *concepts*, are united or separated. In *hypothetical*, or *compound*, judgments the mind unites or separates two *enunciations*, rather than two concepts or terms. Since, however, hypothetical judgments presuppose the existence of the categorical judgment, it is the latter which is principally designated by the definition, and with which we shall first concern ourselves.

Notice that in categorical judgment, while we unite *terms* and *concepts*, we also and principally unite the *things* for which these terms and concepts stand. When I judge:

"The stove is hot"

I do not affirm that my concept of "stove" is identical with my concept of "hot," nor certainly that the term "stove" is identical with the term "hot," but that the *things* symbolized by these terms and concepts are identical *in existence.* So long as we confine ourselves to simple apprehension, we remain in the realm of mere *meaning* or *essence;* we do not touch the order of *existence.* That is achieved only when we judge, when we think something *is* or *is not* something else. It is the nature of a judgment to refer always to existence—actual or possible, real or ideal. To ignore this existential reference and to think of judgment only as an association or juxtaposition of concepts or terms, is to mistake that nature grievously.

It is the *affirmation or denial* in terms of existence that constitutes the very soul of the judgment, its *form*, as the ancients said. The two concepts and terms united or separated by this act of interior affirmation or denial are only the judgment's body, or *matter*. I may think two terms together, e.g., "hot" and "stove" or "hot stove." I do not, on that account, judge. "Hot stove" is only a complex concept, not a judgment.

Some textbooks in logic define a judgment as the *perception* of the agreement or disagreement of two concepts, and of the things for which the concepts stand. This is inaccurate. To perceive that the stove is hot is a *necessary condition* of the judgment, "The stove is hot," but the perception by itself *is not* the judgment. That takes place only when there is mental affirmation or denial. Do not confuse the *mental* affirmation or denial, which is immanent and unvoiced, with the *verbal* expression of that affirmation or denial which we call the *judicative proposition*.

Enunciative and Judicative Propositions. It is also the fashion in textbooks of logic to speak of judgment as an act of the mind following immediately upon simple apprehension. We have concepts, this position states, and to form judgments we simply unite these concepts by affirmation or negation. We thereupon express this judgment verbally in a proposition. Such an explanation has at least the merit of simplicity. Jacques Maritain, however, seems to have both reason and experience on his side when he argues that the actual procedure of the mind is not so simple.[1] For Maritain, the order that the mind follows is somewhat like this: (A) First we have concepts. (B) These concepts are expressed in terms. (C) Terms, and thereby concepts, are united by us in *enunciative* propositions. (D) Our assent to this union of terms takes place, and this *is* the judgment. (E) We express this assent verbally in a *judicative* proposition.

In other words, according to Maritain, there are two kinds of propositions; one kind which *precedes* the judgment and *upon which*

[1] *Formal Logic*, New York, Sheed and Ward, 1946. P. 84 ff.

the judgment bears; another that *follows* the judgment and *expresses* it. Where the judgment is not immediate, experience certainly bears out this contention. Let us consider the following judgment:

"Every changing being is imperfect."

Do you agree to the truth of this statement? If you consider it for a moment, I think you will. Consider that, if a thing changes, it must be either gaining something or losing something, and if it is subject to gain or loss, it cannot be perfect. You now agree that "Every changing thing is imperfect." In other words, you *now* make this judgment, you affirm mentally, that "Every changing being is imperfect." But *before* you performed this mental act, did you not apprehend and consider (and, therefore, *formulate*) the *statement* or proposition, "Every changing being is imperfect"? Was not your judgment a mental assent to the truth of this proposition which you had *previously* formed?

We can see here what is probably the root meaning of St. Thomas' contention that every judgment, affirmative or negative, is essentially an *assent*. If the enunciative proposition constructed is a *negative* proposition—for example, in the case above, the proposition might have been: "A changing thing is *not* perfect"—our assent to this negatively formulated proposition constitutes a negative judgment. The act of the mind itself, of course, remains a positive act, an assent or affirmation of a negative proposition.

In *immediate* judgments, like "This chalk is white," it is extremely difficult to separate the enunciative proposition which precedes the judgment from the judicative proposition which follows and expresses the judgment. Yet, logically, if every judgment is an assent, there must be a proposition *to which* it is an assent. A court cannot render a decision unless there is a motion before it, and the mind cannot judge unless it judges about something. To say that it judges about *things* is true, but irrelevant, since the things must be *considered together* before the mind can affirm their existential union or separation. It is the function of the enunciative proposition to bring distinct things together for such consideration. Thought is swift and many of its preparatory phases unconscious, so that it is not remarkable that we are often not reflectively and fully conscious of the proposition which precedes the judgment.

Nevertheless, since the judgment *bears on* this proposition, it must exist *before* (logically, if not chronologically) we judge.

In the proposition which precedes the judgment (the *enunciative* proposition), the *words* are exactly the same as in the *judicative* proposition which follows the judgment. But they do not have the same force. Again, we can see this most clearly in the proposition which is not immediate. Before I actually affirm, for example, that "Every hypocrite is a liar," the "is" of the proposition I construct does not have assertoric force. I say to myself, "Every hypocrite is a liar—let's see—is that right?" I put the proposition to myself in a tentative or questioning form: "Every hypocrite is (?) a liar." It is only *after*, after I assent, that the "is" takes on the character of an actual affirmation. "That's right, every hypocrite IS a liar." It is then that we have the proposition in the complete sense—the *judicative* proposition, the expression of a judgment.

Many propositions which we say to ourselves, or which are spoken aloud or written, are not the expressions of judgments, but simply enunciative propositions. The character in a play who says "I am shot" is not really judging that this is so. And if I, in reading the play, form that proposition, I cannot be said to be expressing a judgment. Whenever we read, especially if we are reading fiction or somebody else's opinions, we doubtless form hundreds of propositions which imply no corresponding judgment on our part.

Parts of the Judgment. From what has been said it should be clear that the judgment is a single, and indeed indivisible, action of the mind, bearing upon a complex statement. The matter of the act is complex; the act itself is simple. The constructive labor of grouping concepts and terms into an enunciative proposition—a delicate manifold of conception and tentative statement of which we are ordinarily only partly conscious—is prior and preparatory to the formal act of assent in which the judgment resides. That is why, if I break a judgment down, I do not get parts which together make a whole, because in the strict sense a judgment has no parts. I obtain simply concepts and terms, deprived of that living unity which the act of interior affirmation gives them. This is a subtle point in introspective psychology, but one which the logician must understand. For judgment is the act towards which all other mental acts converge. Simple apprehension is related to judgment as grasping is to holding; in simple apprehension we grasp the meaning of an object, but we do not possess it as it *is* (*in existence*) until we judge; and we reason only in order to come to a *conclusion,* which is a judgment, by means of *premises,* which are also judgments. (The proper name for reasoning, in fact, is *mediate* judgment, i.e., judgment arrived at *by means* of other judgments.) To judge is to *think* in the full and proper sense, so that when we define logic as "the art and science of right thinking," we might just as properly say "the art and science of right judgment."

The two concepts which the judgment unites or separates are called the *subject* and the *predicate.* In the judgment, "Every rational being is capable of free decision," the subject is "every rational being," the predicate is "capable of free decision." The subject is that *to which* the mind applies or denies a determination; the predicate is the determination *which* the mind applies or denies to the subject. The subject is that *about which* I am affirming or denying something; the predicate is *what* I affirm or deny about it.

Section 2: Judicative Propositions

Remembering the distinction between the enunciative and the judicative proposition, we can now turn our attention to the latter, the proposition which is the verbal expression of the judgment. The ancients defined the *proposition* admirably as:

a complete discourse signifying the true or the false.[2]

Today we might prefer to put the same idea in slightly different words and define the proposition as:

a sentence or statement which expresses truth or falsity.

Obviously, not everything which the grammarian calls a *sentence* would be accepted by the logician as a *proposition.* Interrogative sentences or questions like "What time is it?"; imperatives like "Open your books to page 71"; hortatories like "Oh, for a nice long vacation"; vocatives like "Mr. President, distinguished guests, ladies, and gentlemen"—these are not propositions, because, what-

---

[2] Henceforth when "proposition" is used without qualification, it should be taken to mean "judicative proposition."

ever they may *imply* of a propositional nature, they are not and cannot be *in themselves* either true or false.[3] On the other hand, statements like

"The preparation of lectures is a nuisance"

or

"The majority of houses are beautiful"

are propositions, because the first is true and the second is false.

The Parts of the Proposition. In the categorical proposition we distinguish three elements:

the *subject-term,*
the *predicate-term,*
and the *copula*

designated respectively as *S, P,* and *c.* The subject-term (S) is the verbal expression of the subject of the judgment, the predicate-term (P) of the predicate. They are called the *matter,* or *body,* of the categorical proposition. The copula (c) is designated the *form,* or *soul,* of the proposition because it expresses verbally the *affirmation or negation,* which is the essence of the judgment. Strictly, logic recognizes only one copula in categorical propositions, the verb "to be," and it accords privileged status to the *present indicative* (*am, is, are*) of that verb. It has no great objection to the simple past of "to be" (*was, were*), and can usually put up with the simple future (*will be*); but imperfect, conditional, subjunctive, and similar forms of the verb, which cause the verb to do more than *simply unite* or join the subject- and predicate-term, are not true copulas, and are not acceptable as such to logic. This does not mean that these forms cannot be used in logic, but only that in a few important types of logical operation they must be modified in certain ways before the operations in question can be properly performed. We shall consider the nature of these modifications in detail in the next section (starting on p. 46) and when we come to

[3] Imperatives, questions (particularly negative questions like "Haven't I seen you somewhere before?") and the like may *imply* that the speaker has formed or will form a proposition, but until the declarative implication of such sentences is made explicit, there is no possible truth or falsity, and they are not to be classified as propositions. The only "border-line" type of proposition is the *future contingent* statement ("The weather will be clear tomorrow," "Our team will win"). These are explicitly, but *indeterminately,* true or false.

study the operations of *obversion, conversion,* and *contraposition.* In the simple categorical proposition:

"The extremely fat man is ordinarily a ridiculous person"

the copula (c) is "is," the subject-term (S) is "the extremely fat man," the predicate-term (P) is "ordinarily a ridiculous person." Notice that in logic, unlike grammar, the subject (S) *includes* all the modifiers.[4] The same is true of the predicate (P), which is not to be identified either with the grammatical "predicate" or with the grammatical "object," though it is sometimes equivalent to the "predicate adjective," "predicate nominative," or "predicate complement" of grammar. Thus, in the proposition given, the subject is not "man," but "the extremely fat man," because that is the subject *about which* we are judging, the logical subject; and the logical predicate, similarly, is not "person," but "ordinarily a ridiculous person," because that is *what* we are judging about our logical subject. The *S,* in short, includes *all* that we are talking about, and the *P* all that we say of that *S. S* and *P,* then, refer not merely to terms taken in themselves, but to terms taken with all the modifications and shades of meaning which the intellect gives to them in uniting them in a judicative proposition.

Logical Form of Propositions. Frequently categorical propositions are stated whose copula is not the present indicative of the verb "to be," and, as we have indicated, it is not always necessary to tamper with such propositions or put them into correct logical form. A proposition, however, cannot be readily *obverted, converted,* or *contraposed* if its copula is other than "to be," nor can the precise character of the predicate-term be always determined in such cases, since in verbs other than "to be" (*to think, to run, to draw,* for example) the *copulative* and *predicative* functions are merged. Thus in the proposition "Man thinks," "thinks" is both a *predicate*

---

[4] Exception must be made for the *syllogistic* term and the *converted* term, which are considered apart from their *quantifying* modifiers (such as *every, all, some, no*). This is because the syllogistic term occurs in *two* propositions and may have a different quantity in one from what it has in another; and the converted term is separated from its quantifying modifiers (which apply only to the *subject* of a proposition) when it migrates from subject to predicate. Outside the syllogism and the converted proposition, even quantifying modifiers are considered part of the term, and in the syllogism and the converted proposition, all other modifiers are so considered.

and a *copula*. As a *predicate* it relates to a certain action, namely, "thinking," while as a *copula* it unites "man" with this action. This copulative function is merely implicit, however ("buried," we might say), if we do not use the verb "to be" to make it stand out. In other words, when the verb "think" (or any similar verb) is employed in a proposition, it implicitly contains the verb "to be." Now, instead of saying "Man thinks," we can say:

$$\overset{S}{Man} \overset{c}{is} (a) \overset{P}{thinking} (being)$$

or

$$\overset{S}{\text{MAN}} \overset{c}{is} \overset{P}{such\ that\ he\ thinks.}$$

In this way we make the copulative function of the verb distinct from its predicative function without changing the sense of the statement, and this is all that is meant by *putting a proposition in logical form*. For the form *S cP* in which the *P* and *c* are fused, we substitute the form *S c P*, in which the three essential elements in the proposition are clearly distinguished. The proposition "A man approaches" is easier to manipulate logically if stated in the form "A man is approaching," and "Water boils at 212° F" if stated as "Water is such that it boils at 212° F." To put a proposition in logical form, therefore, we have only to substitute the verb *to be* plus a *participial form* (*is approaching*) for any other verb (*approaches*), or if this does not seem to make too good sense we may use the verb *to be* plus a *relative clause* (*such that it boils at 212° F*). The English language is fortunate in its possession of a grammatically correct *present progressive tense* which permits the expression of almost any proposition dealing with a present action or condition in the logical form: *S c P*. What the Latin expresses in one word, "Cogito," and the French in two "Je pense," the English may conveniently express in three, one for each of the logical elements involved, "I am thinking," *S c P*. This form, however, may be used only where the verb relates to a presently ongoing action, and not to a permanent or past condition or property of a subject. In the proposition cited above "Water *boils* at 212° F," it would not do to say "Water *is boiling* at 212° F" as equivalent, for the latter conveys the notion that the *water is now boiling*, which is no part of the meaning of the first statement. For the sake of logical clarity, it is sometimes permissible to use forms which are grammatically somewhat inelegant, but it is seldom necessary for the logician to talk like a character out of Damon Runyon, and one should never change the basic meaning of a proposition in reducing it to logical form. In those instances where the use of the present progressive tense would alter the sense, we may employ instead a *relative clause* (a clause introduced by "such that," "that which," "one who," etc.) after the verb "to be." Thus "Fire burns" becomes "Fire is such that it burns"; "Character counts above everything else" becomes "Character is what (that which) counts above everything else," and so on.

Perhaps the most troublesome propositions to put in logical form are those dealing with a simple past action, like "Tony broke a dish last week." The past progressive (imperfect) form, "Tony was breaking a dish last week" says something quite different from the original, while the customarily accepted equivalent "Tony is one who broke a dish last week" takes the emphasis off the *action*, where the original proposition had it, and transfers it to the *subject,* and is therefore not truly equivalent to the original. Perhaps some barbarous circumlocution like "Tony was a dish-breaker last week" is the nearest we can come to retaining the original meaning while employing the *S c P* form. Fortunately, propositions of this type seldom enter importantly into logical discourse.

Section 3: The Classification of Propositions

Categorical and Hypothetical Propositions. The most important division of propositions is into the *categorical* and the *hypothetical,* or *compound*. This division is based chiefly upon an essential difference in the kind of *copula* which the two types of proposition employ. *Hypothetical,* or *compound,* propositions, which we shall subsequently examine in detail, are propositions with a *non-verb copula;* while the *categorical proposition,* the basic type, with which we are now concerned, may be defined as:

a statement which unites two terms by a verb copula.

(Remember that for logic every verb is reducible to the verb "to be.") Consider now the divisions of these *categorical propositions.*

Division of Categorical Propositions According to Quantity. In the first place, we may divide categorical propositions according to:

the different possible extensions of their subject-terms

and this division is said to be according to *quantity*. (Whenever, then, we speak of the *quantity of a proposition*, what we mean is the *extension of its subject-term*.) The subject of a proposition may be a *singular* term, a *particular* term, a *universal* term, or an *indefinite* term, and the propositions in question are accordingly designated:

Singular. This man is a liar. Paul is trustworthy.
Particular. Some man is selfish. Not all men are cowards.
Universal. Every man is fallible. All men are free. No dog is fish.
Indefinite. Woman is fickle. Men are selfish. Beauty is truth.

As can be seen from the examples, certain syncategorematic words, called *quantifying particles* ("every," "no," "some," "this," "all," and the like) are the principal signs of the extension of the subject-term. Certain of these words are *always* signs of a given quantity or extension, while others under different circumstances stand for *different* kinds of quantity. This is an extremely important point which is often misunderstood by the beginning student. We shall list the most important of these signs of extension, or quantifying particles, and return later to a fuller consideration of their distinguishing functions.

Type of Quantity	*"Always" signs*	*"Sometimes" signs*
Universal	"No"	"Every," "All," "Each," "The"
Particular	"Some," "Certain"	"Every," "Each," "All," "A," "One"
Singular	"This," "That," *Proper name*	"The," "A," "One"

Indefinite propositions are so designated precisely because they *lack* any quantifying particle or sign of extension. They are ordinarily *taken as universal,* but sometimes *falsely* so, and should be carefully distinguished from the explicit universal.

The student should note that the words "All" and "Every" are *not always* signs of universality, and hope that this paradoxical point will be clarified when we discuss the *quality* of propositions.

The difference between *singular* and *particular* propositions should be borne carefully in mind. A *singular* proposition applies to a certain *determinate* individual: *"This* gold is fourteen karat," *"That* man is guilty"; while a *particular* proposition applies to a universal nature taken in some *indeterminate* part of its extension, or (secondarily), to a certain unspecified number of individuals in a class: *"Some* man is brilliant," *"Some* knowledge is picked up by a student in college," *"Certain* hits are home runs." To say "Some a is b" implies that *at least one* "a" is "b," but does not imply that we know which "a" it is; while to say *"This* a is b" denotes identification of the determinate or definite individual "a" which is "b."

Since logical inference depends primarily on an understanding of *natures* or *essences,* rather than on enumerating or cataloguing of individuals, and since the essence as conceived by the mind is *one,* it is preferable to use the *singular* of the verb "to be" *(is)* in both universal and particular propositions. It is better to say: "Every . . . is" or "All . . . is" and "Some . . . is" rather than "All . . . are" and "Some . . . are." When, for example, I predicate "mortal" of "man" taken universally ("Every man is mortal"), my judgment does not express a simple *enumeration.* I did not first determine that Peter is mortal, and then that Paul is mortal, and that Socrates is mortal, and so on through many instances to conclude finally by a kind of *totalization* that "All men are mortal." To the extent that my judgment is of significance to logic, it rather expresses the truth that the *nature* "man" (which, as conceived intellectually, is one), since it is necessarily a *composite* nature, is capable of dissolution or corruption. The form which comes closest to expressing the logical character of that judgment is "All man is mortal" *(Omnis homo est mortalis),* but unfortunately English usage does not always sanction the "All . . . is" form when the subject-term is a concrete noun, so that in most instances we do best to employ the "Every . . . is" form. Thus "All weakness is pitiable" is an acceptable form because the subject-term is abstract, but "Every dog is vertebrate" is to be preferred from the standpoint of English usage to "All dog is vertebrate," though the latter would probably be the proper form in an ideally logical language.

In similar fashion, the proposition "Some man *is* a liar" expresses the fact that the nature "man" is susceptible of the predicate "liar," if not in its universality, at least in a limited degree, contingently if not necessarily. A proposition such as "Some men *are* liars" expresses simply an enumeration based upon experience, and it is of value in demonstration only to the extent that it casts light on the nature "man"; to the extent that it shows the nature "man" can receive the predicate "liar," even if not universally or necessarily. "Some men are liars" is of interest to the logician, in short, only because it indicates that "Some man is a liar."

We must also acknowledge that from the standpoint of usage the forms "All . . . are" and "Some . . . are" are too thoroughly sanctioned to bear rejection. We use them constantly in our everyday speech, in logical discourse, and in factual description. The logician has no objection to the employment of these forms, provided the imperfect quality of their expression of logical relationships is also admitted. The scientist may employ an expression like "The sun rises in the east" in polite conversation or in writing a scientific textbook, but he never for a moment supposes that this expression describes accurately the real relation between the sun and the earth. In like manner, the student of logic may say "All men are mortal" or "Some triangles are isosceles," while recognizing that the plural form is a concession to popular usage rather than a precise indicator of the relation between a nature and its attributes.

Let us review why it is that for a proposition to give rise to a genuine deductive inference, it must tell us something about a certain *nature,* and not merely be the result of "counting heads." When I reason, for example, as follows:

> Every direct concept is abstract,
> But the concept of body is a direct concept,
> Therefore, the concept of body is abstract

I am making a genuine inference because my conclusion, "The concept of body is abstract," marks an *advance in knowledge* over my major premise, "Every direct concept is abstract." It is *very easy* for me to know that conclusion, once I know that premise, but I *might* know that premise without ever knowing the conclusion which it implies, because I never happened to think simultaneously that "The concept of body is a direct concept." In the same way, I might know a potential major premise, "Every triangle has its angles equal to 180 degrees," without recognizing that "This figure inscribed in a semicircle has its angles equal to 180 degrees," simply because I did not think of or realize the potential minor premise, "This figure inscribed in a semicircle is a triangle." It is thus that when the student of Euclidean plane geometry has understood the axioms and postulates of this science, he knows *implicitly* or *potentially* every theorem in his textbook. It requires a good deal of genuine and hard thinking of the deductive type, however, before this implicit and potential knowledge becomes actual and explicit. On the other hand, in an argument of this sort:

> All members of the class are present
> Cooper is a member of the class
> Therefore, Cooper is present

there is *no* inference, because there is no real *advance* in knowledge from major premise to conclusion. Since the major premise is only an *enumerative* universal, the result of "counting heads," I must know the conclusion of the alleged syllogism *before* I know the major premise. I must know that "Cooper is present" before I can say that "All the members of the class are present." It is only because there are universal propositions which are *not enumerative*, self-evident generalizations like "Every event requires a cause," and inductive universals based on *incomplete* induction (where we do not have to have explicit knowledge of each single individual in order to know the general statement) like "Every mammal is warm-blooded," that deductive inference is possible. If all universal propositions were like "All the members of the class are present," or "All countries in North America are democratic," the syllogism would be entirely circular and meaningless, a mere show of proving what was already known before we started the proof.

Division According to Quality. We may also divide categorical propositions according as they are *affirmative* or *negative*, that is, *as the copula unites or separates the subject- and predicate-*

term. This division is said to be according to *quality.* Note that it is the *copula,* and the copula alone, that determines whether a categorical proposition is affirmative or negative. The fact that the *S* or *P* is affirmative or negative has no bearing on the quality of a proposition. "A is non-b" and "Non-a is non-b" are thus affirmative propositions.

The Major Types of Categoricals. Taking our divisions according to quantity and quality together, we may say that there are eight possible types of categorical propositions:

(1) Universal Affirmative   (2) Universal Negative
(3) Particular Affirmative   (4) Particular Negative
(5) Singular Affirmative   (6) Singular Negative
(7) Indefinite Affirmative   (8) Indefinite Negative

Indefinite propositions, as we have already remarked, are ordinarily understood as *universal.* When I say "Fish are vertebrates," I mean or should mean the same as when I say *"Every* fish is vertebrate" or *"All* fish are vertebrates." For this reason, the ancient logicians classified indefinite propositions under universals. From the purely formal standpoint, there is no reason to object to this reduction of the indefinite to the universal. In certain contexts, however, the indefinite proposition may be used to describe a *group tendency*—as in "Murder will out" or "Native Hawaiians have lower IQ's than Japanese Hawaiians"—which is really particular rather than universal; or at times the indefinite form may be the equivalent of "Most of" or "The majority of," or even just "Some of." By reason of the *matter* or *context,* the following propositions cannot be rightfully classified as universal:

Men are selfish   (Most?)
Liberty is destroyed by government regulation   (Some?)
Women are fickle   (Some? A large minority? Most?)
Children are more impressionable than adults   (Most?)
Criminals cannot be trusted   (Some? Most?)

To attempt to pass such propositions off as universal is a crude and not uncommon fallacy, against which the student of logic should be on his guard. While agreeing, then, that from the standpoint of *form* a proposition like "A is b" should be considered equivalent to *"All*

or *every* a is b," and a proposition like "X is not y" should be taken
to denote *"No* x is y," the logician should take some means of noting
the actually indefinite quantity of such propositions, so that he may
be prepared to detect a particular masquerading as a universal should
it occur. Universal affirmative and negative propositions are classified
respectively as *A* and *E* propositions, and traditional logic classifies
indefinite affirmative and negative propositions by the same letters.
While adhering in general to this practice, we shall employ a subscript *i*—thus "A_i" and "E_i"—to distinguish the indefinite affirmative and negative from the properly quantified universal proposition.

The ancient logicians were also much struck by the functional
similarity of *singular* and *universal* propositions. In such logical operations as *conversion, obversion,* and *contraposition,* and in most syllogistic functions as well, the *singular* proposition functions very
differently from the *particular* proposition but almost identically
with the *universal.* It was therefore considered justifiable to classify
singular affirmative and negative propositions by the same letters—
"A" and "E"—used to designate universal propositions. We should
remark, however, the existence of certain important operations—
notably *opposition*—in which singulars behave very differently from
universals. On this account it is suggested that a subscript *s* be employed to distinguish the singular affirmative and negative propositions ("A_s" and "E_s") from the properly universal propositions ("A"
and "E") which they so much resemble. Accordingly, we can accept
the traditional simplification, which reduces the major types of categorical propositions to *four* ("A" and "E" for *universal* affirmative
and negative respectively, "I" and "O" for *particular* affirmative and
negative propositions respectively) while retaining a means of identi-
fying the sometimes distinctive *indefinite* and *singular* propositions.
The ancient division of categorical propositions as thus modified may
be illustrated as follows:

(A) *Universal Affirmative,* or *A,* propositions (*A* from the first
vowel of the Latin *affirmo,* "I affirm"): *All matter is contingent; Every spermatophyte has a flower.*
Also *Indefinite Affirmative* (A_i) and *Singular Affirmative*
(A_s) propositions: *Man is fallible; This insect is poisonous.*
(E) *Universal Negative,* or *E,* propositions (*E* from the first

vowel of the Latin *nego,* "I deny"): *No fish is inverte-brate.*

Also *Indefinite Negative* (E_i) and *Singular Negative* (E_s) propositions: *Beauty is not sensible; Hector is no more.*

(I) *Particular Affirmative,* or *I,* propositions (the second vowel of *affirmo*): *Some animal is carnivorous; Certain misfortunes are unavoidable.*

(O) *Particular Negative,* or *O,* propositions (the second vowel of *nego*): *Some criminal is not blameworthy; Not every politician is honest; Not all runs were earned; Everyone is not prepared; All animals are not four-legged.*

Note, and note carefully, that the proper form of the true *universal negative,* or *E,* proposition is not "Every S is not P," but "No S is P." *There is no exception to this rule.* Note also the many forms of the *particular negative* (O) proposition, of which "Every S is not P" is one example. A proposition like

"Every dog is not vicious"

is often mistaken for a universal negative proposition, but this designation is *never* correct. "All" and "Every" are not (as indicated above and on p. 47) always signs of universality. When the copula is negative, "all" and "every," on the contrary, are always signs of *particularity.* The proposition "Every dog is not vicious" (or what is the same thing, "Not every dog is vicious") does not assert that *every* dog is without viciousness, but rather that some is or are such. To say "Every dog is not vicious" or "Not every dog is vicious" is to say that it is *false* that "Every dog *is* vicious," that is, it is to say that *"Some* dog is not vicious."

Another mistake which we must avoid is that of thinking that "Every dog is not vicious" means the same as "Some dog *is* vicious." The assertion of the *O* proposition, "Some (or every) dog is not vicious" may often *imply* the truth of the corresponding *I* proposition, "Some dog is vicious," but this is not always the case, and in no event does the *O* proposition *state* the same thing as the *I* proposition. In everyday discourse, "some is not" frequently means *"only* some is not," and this, of course, implies that "some is." In itself, however, "some" does not mean "only some," but simply *"at least* some," and this is the supposition which logic attaches to "some." Thus the proposition *"Some* man is rational" is perfectly true, even though the broader proposition *"Every* man is rational" is likewise true. Here again, in ordinary speech when we say "Some men are bald," for example, we mean "only some." This implies that "Some men are not bald," and that it is false that "All men are bald." But this is not necessarily the case, and no such implication is intended in logic. As far as logical necessity is concerned, if it is true that "Every animal is conscious," it is thereby true that "Some (at least some) animal is conscious"; and if it is true that "No fish is mammal," it is thereby true that "Some fish is not mammal."

Since "every" and "all" with a negative copula are signs of *particularity,* and since the "every" or "all" may be written either with the copula or before the subject,[5] it follows that there are four additional forms of the *O* proposition. The proposition "Some S is not P" may also be written:

> "Not every S is P"
> "Every S is not P"
> "Not all S is P"
> "All S is not P"

In *no* case is "Every" or "All" with a negative copula to be taken as a *universal* negative proposition, nor are the "Not all . . ." or "Not every . . ." forms ever to be classified as *E* propositions. In the propositions "Not all men are selfish" and "Not every success is earned," we should note that the "not" which is *written* or *spoken* with the subject, is to be *understood* with the copula, for it is logically part of the copula, not of the subject. A negation in a proposition is always understood as modifying the copula unless it is joined by a hyphen to the *S* or *P* ("The *not-guilty* are innocent") or is part of a relative clause modifying the *S* or *P* ("All *who are not guilty* are innocent"). In these cases, the copula is affirmative, and the propositions cited would be classified as *A$_s$* and *A*.

---

[5] Grammatical usage prefers the forms "Not every . . ." and "Not all . . ." to the "Every . . . is not . . ." and "All . . . is (are) not . . ." forms. Popular speech and writing, however, are as likely to use one form as the other, and may even show some preference for placing the negation with the verb rather than with the subject. We should therefore familiarize ourselves with all four forms.

Thus, too, in the *E* proposition, "No S *is* P," the *apparently affirmative* copula is *really negative*. While the "No" is *written* with the subject, its negative quality affects the *copula*. With regard to the subject the "No" is to be understood only as a sign of *universality*. (Recall that "no" is the only word which is *always* a sign of universality, p. 47.) The quantified universal negative proposition has, therefore, only *one* form: *No S is P.*

The definite article "the," which is sometimes the sign of the common concrete singular proposition, as in

> "The farmer is in his hayfield"
> "The day's at the morn"

may also be the sign of the *abstract* singular, which is universal in the sense of *unrestricted,* but singular by reason of the manner in which the mind conceives the nature in question. The *mathematical singular* is a typical instance of the abstract singular:

> "The area of a square is the product of two sides"
> "The square root of sixteen is four"
> "The hypotenuse is the side opposite the right angle."

Nonmathematical truths may also lend themselves to this type of abstract singular statement, as in the following examples:

> "The clock is an instrument for telling time"
> "The opera is an Italian institution"
> "The race is not to the swift"
> "The horse is a quadruped."

These propositions should be classified as *A* if affirmative, *E* if negative. If we wish to use a subscript "s" for these propositions, it is permissible to do so, but in that case we should probably employ a subscript "a" (for "abstract") after the "s," to distinguish these from the concrete singular. In this system, the proposition

> "The clock is not a recent invention"

would be classified as E_{sa}. Since these propositions, however, nearly always function as universals, the simple designation *A* or *E* is ordinarily sufficient identification for the abstract singular.

In many *indefinite* propositions whose subject is an abstract term, also, the universal nature is taken not according to the diverse being it may have in things, but according to the *unity which it has in the mind*. As Maritain notes,[6] these indefinite propositions too are essentially similar to the *abstract singular* proposition. The following may serve as examples:

> "Beauty is truth"
> "Justice is the virtue which renders to each his due"
> "Color is a quality of material substance"

Affirmative and negative propositions of this type would be classified as *A* and *E* respectively, and if we employ a system of subscripts to distinguish them from the ordinary A and E possibilities, we may use an "a" (for "abstract") after the "i" (for "indefinite") to render their classification still more precise. Thus:

> "Virtue is its own reward" (A_{ia})
> and
> "Truth is not easy to attain" (E_{ia}).

We should also at this time note that certain words and phrases which are customarily written or spoken with the *predicate* may affect the quantity (*subject*) or quality (*copula*) of a proposition. Such expressions generally do not affect the quantity or extension of the subject-term *in itself*, but in relation to certain contingencies of *time*, *place*, or *circumstance*. Let us designate these expressions as *circumstantial quantifiers*, and exemplify their division as follows:

Universal Negative Circumstance (*E*)	*Never, nowhere, under no circumstances,* etc. *Men are never happy, Honesty is nowhere valued,* etc.
Universal Affirmative Circumstance (*A*) (copula affirmative)	*Always, everywhere, in every instance,* etc. *Men are always striving for status, Selfishness is condemned everywhere,* etc.

[6] *Op. cit.*, p. 116 ff.

Particular Negative Circumstance (*O*)	*Not always, not everywhere, sometimes not,* etc. *People are not always willing to sacrifice for an ideal, He is sometimes not a very understanding teacher,* etc.
Particular Affirmative Circumstance (*I*)	*Sometimes, occasionally, once, somewhere,* etc. *Aggression is sometimes necessary, Integrity was once a public virtue, This is allowable under certain conditions,* etc.

Since the circumstantial quantity and quality of a proposition have to be considered when the proposition is employed in logical argument or discourse, these propositions should be classified as *A, E, I, O* according to the character of this circumstantial quantity and quality. Once again, we may employ a subscript ("c" for *circumstantial*) to distinguish these propositions from the ordinary A, E, I, or O proposition.

"Men are always striving for status" (A_c).
"Children don't always do what they're told" (O_c).
"You're not likely to get this straight ever" (E_c).
"Under certain conditions air is a liquid" (I_c).

One last note on particular propositions. Ordinary usage makes frequent employment of words which indicate degrees within particularity, e.g., "few," "the majority," "most," "very little," and the like. The degree of particularity expressed by such words is important in the logic of probability, in the social sciences, and in practical life. It is not, however, of much interest to the logic of pure demonstration, or formal deductive logic, because these degrees of particularity, no matter how high, never achieve universality. *"Most* men are selfish" says more than *"Some* man is selfish," but it is still a particular proposition, and from such propositions alone (i.e., without their being united with a genuinely universal proposition) *nothing* can be inferred deductively. So far as the formal laws of deductive demonstration are concerned, "Most men are selfish" can just as well be rendered "Some man is selfish." The one apparent exception to this rule, which occurs in the third figure of the syllogism, we shall show later to be *merely* apparent.

Modal Propositions. The *modal proposition* is a species of *categorical* proposition, since it has a verb copula. It is different from the ordinary categorical or *assertoric* proposition, in that while the *assertoric* or *simple categorical* proposition simply *asserts* (or denies) the predicate of the subject (is *simply attributive:* S *is* P), the modal proposition not only asserts (or denies) the predicate of the subject, but also states the *manner* or *mode* in which the predicate is identified with the subject or denied to the subject. It states not simply *that* P belongs to S, but *how* P belongs to S, or does not belong to it. For instance:

"S *must be* P"

or

"S *cannot be* P."

The English language is singularly rich in modes (or *moods*) affecting the verb "to be." "May be," "might be," "would be," "could be," "should be," and their negations, are examples over and above those usually considered by the traditional logic. Some of these, as we shall see, are important in the understanding of the hypothetical proposition. With respect to the categorical proposition, however, we can be content with the ancients to distinguish *four* principal modes, as indicated in the table which appears on the opposite page.

Note that the *contingent* and *impossible* modes are *always negative,* being equivalent to "is *not* necessarily" and "is *not* possibly," respectively, and that they are the exact opposites of the always affirmative *necessary* ("*is* necessarily") and *possible* ("*is* possibly") modes. Notice too that by the use of a second negative particle we can transform the *necessary* into the *impossible,* the *contingent* into the *possible,* and vice versa. "Must be" is equivalent to "cannot be *not,*" "cannot be" to "must be *not,*" "need not be" to "can be *not,*" and so on. In these cases the second "not" is to be construed with the *predicate* rather than with the *copula,* so that the modes themselves are not equivalent, and always retain their original affirmative or negative quality. The abbreviations, "N" for *necessary,* "Imp" for

Mode	Expression	Equivalent	Example
Necessity (N)	"must be"	"is necessarily" "has to be" "cannot be not"	"Justice *must be* rendered to our fellows"
Contingency (C)	"need not be"	"is not necessarily" "does not have to be" "can be not"	"Honesty *need not be* difficult"
Impossibility (Imp)	"cannot be"	"is not possibly" "is not able to be" "must be not"	"Happiness *cannot be* purchased"
Possibility (P)	"can be"	"is possibly" "is able to be" "need not be not"	"Truth *can be* attained by the intellect"

impossible, etc., may be employed if one wishes to have a set of symbols (analogous to A, E, I, and O) for classifying modal propositions.

The examples of modal propositions so far cited have an abstract indefinite subject-term. Where a modal proposition has a sign of quantity ("every," "some," "no") joined to its subject-term, it is said to possess *dictum* as well as mode. *Dictum,* then, is simply the *quantity of a modal proposition.* Combining dictum and mode, we have eight possible types of modal propositions.

> *Universal Necessity* (UN):
> "Every man must be respected."

> *Particular Necessity* (PN):
> "Some animal must be intelligent."

> *Universal Contingency* (UC):
> "No flatterer need be tolerated."

Particular Contingency (PC):
>"Some courage need not be praiseworthy.'
>"Not all courage need be praiseworthy."
>"All courage need not be praiseworthy."
>"Not every excuse need be accepted."
>"Every excuse need not be accepted."

Universal Impossibility (UI):
>"No psychopath can be trusted."

Particular Impossibility (PI):
>"Some anger cannot be justified."
>"Not all anger can be justified."
>"All anger cannot be justified."
>"Not every criminal can be trusted."
>"Every criminal cannot be trusted."

In classifying quantified modal propositions, it is the custom to specify first the *dictum* (e.g., universal), and then the *mode* (e.g., possible). Here again, the abbreviations "UN," "PC," "UI," and so on may be used as symbolic equivalents. Where a modal proposition is *unquantified* (has no *dictum*), no quantity is specified, and the proposition is classified simply as *necessary* (N), *impossible* (*Imp*), etc.

Notice that there is only one form for the universal contingent and universal impossible modes ("No . . . need be . . ." and "No . . . can be . . ."), and that these propositions are precisely analogous to the E proposition ("No S is P"). They are, in fact, species of universal negative propositions, since the impossible and contingent modes are *always negative*. By the same token, the particular contingent and particular impossible modes are precisely analogous to the O proposition (particular negative), and each will have, therefore, *five* equivalent forms:

>"Some can (need) not"
>"Not all can (need)"
>"Not every can (need)"
>"All can (need) not"
>"Every can (need) not"

Remember that, when the copula is negative, "every" and "all" are *signs of particularity*. "Every criminal cannot be trusted" means the same as "*Some* criminal cannot be trusted." "Every flatterer need not be tolerated" means the same as "*Some* flatterer need not be tolerated." Lastly, do not make the mistake of thinking that "No S *can* be P" is a form of *possible* modal, for the "no" negates the copula, and the modal sign is not "can be" but "cannot be." "No . . . can be," like the popular "no can do" indicates *impossibility*, not possibility.

In summary, the modal proposition is a species of categorical proposition, since the copula is the verb "to be." It is the verb "to be" *affected by some mode*, however, indicating the *manner* in which S and P are related. Modes that affect parts of the proposition other than the copula do not receive separate treatment in logic, nor are the propositions in question called *modal propositions*. Thus:

"He is the sort of fellow that must be coaxed"

is an *assertoric*, rather than a modal, proposition and classified A_s.

Hypothetical or Compound Propositions. We come now to the *hypothetical* or *compound* proposition, which exhibits an essential difference from the categorical proposition. We have seen that both the assertoric categorical and the modal proposition have a *verb copula*. The copula in hypothetical propositions is always something *other than the verb*—most often a *conjunction*—and what this copula unites is not two terms, but *two enunciations*. The proposition

"If this being is man, this being is free"

is an example of one type of hypothetical or compound proposition, the *conditional*. The copula here is not "is" but "if"; and what this copula unites is not the two terms "man" and "free," but the two enunciations "this being is man" and "this being is free." It should be evident to the careful reader that propositions of this type presuppose at least the implicit formation of categorical propositions. In the proposition "If this being is man, this being is free," the categorical proposition presupposed would seem to be "Every man is free." Though the hypothetical or compound proposition presupposes the categorical, it is in no sense *reducible to* the latter, and must be considered by the formal logician as a specifically distinct mode of utterance. An exhaustive classification of hypothetical or compound propositions would go beyond the purposes of our inquiry. We shall attempt to distinguish only the more important types.

Division of Hypothetical or Compound Propositions. The first and most important division is that which includes the

truly hypothetical or sequential

proposition on the one hand, and the

merely compound or copulative

proposition on the other. Under each of these major divisions of the hypothetical or compound proposition we can distinguish several significant subdivisions. The principal form of the *sequential* proposition is the *conditional,* an example of which we have already cited, and the other two types of sequential proposition, viz., the *disjunctive* and the *conjunctive,* are, under certain conditions, reducible to the conditional form. The *copulative* proposition, which is not sequential because it does not necessarily assert any *sequence* between the enunciations it joins, can be divided into

the openly copulative

on the one hand, and

the hiddenly copulative or exponible

on the other, and each of these in turn can be analyzed into certain subtypes. Let us outline these major divisions of the hypothetical or compound proposition, noting the principal verbal signs which enable us to identify them:

    (I) *Sequential* or truly hypothetical propositions
        (A) Conditional ("if," "unless," "whenever")
        (B) Disjunctive ("either . . . or," "or")
        (C) Conjunctive ("not . . . both")
    (II) *Copulative* or merely compound propositions
        (A) *Openly* copulative or compound propositions
            (a) Pure Copulative ("and")
            (b) Remotive ("neither . . . nor")
            (c) Adversative ("but," "although," "nevertheless")

(B) *Hiddenly* copulative, or *exponible,* propositions

  (a) Exceptive ("except," "but" (prepositional), "save")

  (b) Exclusive ("only," "alone")

  (c) Reduplicative ("as," "inasmuch as," "insofar as")

  (d) Causal ("because," "since," "by reason of," "on account of")

We may now consider each of these major types in some detail.

The Conditional Proposition. The *conditional* proposition is the purest example of the hypothetical proposition, and the term "hypothetical" is often (though not quite correctly) used as synonymous with "conditional." It is important not only because the *disjunctive* and *conjunctive* forms can have their precise significance tested by being reduced to it, but because it forms the basis of the *conditional inference,* perhaps the commonest form of deduction employed in scientific and practical thinking. A typical conditional proposition, like

"If a is b, a is c"
or
"If a being is intelligent, that being is free"

does not assert that either of its separate parts, or enunciations, is true, but only that *if* the first part (called the *antecedent* or *protasis* —"a being is intelligent") is true, the second enunciation (called the *consequent* or *apodosis*—"that being is free") is also, *consequently and necessarily,* true. It is the distinctive nature of the conditional proposition to assert *nothing but the necessity of a certain sequence between two enunciations.* When we say: "If this figure is a triangle, its angles total 180 degrees" we are saying in effect:

"*If* this figure is a triangle, *it follows necessarily that* its angles total 180 degrees"

without implying that this figure *is* a triangle, or that its angles *actually* total 180 degrees. It may happen, then, that *both* the antecedent and consequent of a conditional proposition are *false,* while the conditional proposition itself is perfectly *true*. Consider the example:

"If you are dead, you are not now studying logic."

It is false that "you are dead," and it is equally false that "you are not now studying logic"; it is nevertheless true that *"if* you are dead, you are not now studying logic," and this *follows necessarily,* for if you were dead you *could not be* studying logic. The "if" copula which is the ordinary distinguishing mark of the conditional proposition, indicates only a *necessary sequence* between the two enunciations it joins. That is why the kind of proposition of which the conditional is the prototype is called *sequential.* The consequent of a conditional proposition is always, at least implicitly, in a necessary mode. I say "If a is b, a is c," but I mean *"If* a is b, *then* a *must be* c."* If the consequent really *follows from* the antecedent, irrespective of whether or not either by itself is true, the conditional proposition is true. If, on the other hand, the consequent *does not follow from* the antecedent, even though both antecedent and consequent are true, the conditional proposition is *false.* Consider the following proposition:

"If I am a human being, I am less than six feet tall."

It is true that "I am a human being" and also that "I am less than six feet tall," but my being less than six feet tall does not follow necessarily from the fact that I am a human being. The asserted necessary sequence, therefore, does not obtain, and the conditional proposition in question is *simply false.*

The antecedent or consequent of a conditional proposition may be affirmative or negative, and if the antecedent is negative we frequently say "unless" instead of "if . . . not." Thus, the following proposition

"Unless he is careful, he will have a breakdown"

is identical in meaning with

"If he is *not* careful, he will have a breakdown."

"Whenever" and "wherever" are often equivalent to "if" plus some circumstance of time or place specifying the sequence between antecedent and consequent. Thus:

> "Whenever I tell a joke, my students look uncomfortable"
> and
> "Wherever politicians rule, wise men suffer"

are essentially conditional propositions. "Where" and "when" may have the same function as "wherever" and "whenever" in such propositions, and the particle indicating the antecedent of the condition may be part of the second clause, as in

> "Ill fares the land to hastening ills a prey
> *Where* wealth accumulates and men decay."

Differing from the simple conditional copula ("if"), these circumstantial conditional copulas seem to imply that the enunciations they join are at least *possible*, though they do not of course imply that these enunciations are actually true. We can think:

> "*If* a triangle has four sides, its angles total 270 degrees"

but it would not quite make sense to say:

> "*Whenever* a triangle has four sides, its angles total 270 degrees"

because that would seem to imply that a triangle *might* have four sides. The pure conditional does not imply even the possibility, let alone the actual truth of its enunciations, but lest the person addressed should think it does, we are told by the grammarians that we should use the subjunctive and conditional moods to designate contrary-to-fact conditions even with an "if" copula. Thus we say:

> "If a triangle *were* four-sided, it *would* be quadrangular"

rather than:

> "If a triangle *is* four-sided, it *is* quadrangular."

But this is a matter of *grammatical* nicety, and the second example is above exception *logically*.

The consequent in *every* conditional proposition is implicitly in the necessary mode, as we have indicated, but if, for any reason, we wish to stress this necessary sequence we can employ the *explicit* necessary or (for negative consequents) impossible mode, as in:

"If logic is a science, it *must* demonstrate its principles"

or

"If a man is intelligent, he cannot lack responsibility."

These propositions reinforce and make clearer the necessity of the sequence, but are in no way essentially different from:

"If logic is a science, it demonstrates its principles"

and

"If man is intelligent, he does not lack responsibility."

Propositions where "if" has the sense of "although," are not conditional but *copulative* propositions. "*If* wealth is power, it is not happiness" asserts no sequence, and is equivalent to "*Although* wealth is power, it is not happiness" or "Wealth is power, *but* it is not happiness," a copulative proposition of the *adversative* type. (A principal use of adversative propositions beginning with an "if" is to *contradict* conditional propositions, so that, far from being equivalent to conditional propositions, they are exactly opposed to them.) If what appears to be the consequent of a conditional proposition is an *imperative,* or a *question,* then the sentence is not a proposition at all, because it is neither true nor false. Thus:

"If you're looking for credit, go somewhere else."
"If you can't pass the fingernail test, why not try washing your hands?"

The Disjunctive Proposition. Another important type of sequential proposition is the *disjunctive.* The disjunctive proposition customarily takes the form:

"A is either b or c"
"A proposition is either true or false."

The two enunciations are: "a is b" ("a proposition is true") and "a is c" ("a proposition is false"), and the copula joining the two enunciations is "either . . . or," or sometimes just "or." A disjunctive proposition does not assert that *both* its members or enunciations are true, but, unlike the conditional, it does state that *one or the other must be so.* (Like the conditional, the disjunctive is at least implicitly in the necessary mode: its meaning is "one or the other *must be* so.") In "Either we have price controls or inflation," the implication (which forms the basis for the *disjunctive syllogism*) is that if we *do not have* price controls, we *must have* inflation; and if we *do not have* inflation, we *must have* price controls. For a disjunctive proposition to be true, therefore, *at least one member of the disjunction must be true.* If both enunciations *can be* false, then the disjunctive proposition itself is false.

> "A colored surface is either black or white"

is a false proposition, since a colored surface may be neither.

Considering disjunctive propositions from the standpoint of their *content* or *matter*, we may distinguish two types,

> the *perfect* and the *imperfect.*

In the *perfect disjunctive*, the members of the disjunction are, in effect, *contradictory* of each other, like "a is b" and "a is not b," or "a is intelligent" and "a is unintelligent." Now when two enunciations are diametrically opposite, not only must one or the other be true (as the disjunctive form asserts), but both *cannot be true.* By reason of the disjunctive *form*

> "It must be one or the other"

but by reason of the contradictory *content*

> "It cannot be both."

For example, in:

> "A living being is either mortal or immortal"

we have a *perfect disjunctive,* for we can say not only that the being *must be either* mortal or immortal, but that it *cannot be both* mortal and immortal. On the other hand, in a proposition like:

> "A man with acute appendicitis either undergoes an operation
>   or dies"

the case is considerably different. The proposition may be presumed to be true, and the disjunction, either "an operation" or "death" may be taken as valid. But in this instance, though it must, by reason of the disjunctive form, be "one or the other," this does not permit us to think that "it cannot be both." By reason of the matter or content, it *"may be both"*: the man may undergo the operation and still die. Therefore, this is an example of an *imperfect disjunctive*. The two enunciations or members are so related that one must be true, and hence they can be united by an "either . . . or" copula, but both *may* be true. Since at least one must be true, if you *deny* one, you must affirm the other; but since both may be true, you can affirm one without being forced to deny the other.

From the standpoint of *form*, all that the disjunctive proposition says is that "it must be one or the other." Unless, therefore, we know that the two members are contradictory or mutually exclusive, we have no right to assume that the proposition is a perfect disjunctive, that "it cannot be both." "A is either b or c" would thus be taken to be an *imperfect disjunctive*, while "A is either b or non-b" would be a *formally perfect disjunctive*.

Relatively (rather than *absolutely*) *necessary* connections lend themselves to imperfect disjunctive statements. If there is a relatively necessary connection between "studying" (A) and "passing" (B), then we can unite the first member, "studying" (A), with the *opposite* of the second member, "failing" (non-B) in an imperfect disjunctive statement:

> "Either you study or you fail."

Similarly, by reason of the connection between "trying" and "success," "eating" and "not growing thin," "paying your taxes" and "staying out of jail," we can form imperfect disjunctives like:

> "Either you try or you don't succeed."
> "Either you eat or you grow thin."
> "Either you pay your taxes or you go to jail."

But since more than study is required to insure passing, more than eating to insure your not growing thin, and since other conditions than not paying your taxes may put you in jail, we cannot think of the members of these disjunctions as mutually exclusive. We can study and fail, pay our taxes and go to jail, eat and grow thin.

In *necessary matter*, however, we can form a rather awkward species of imperfect disjunctive from any true A proposition (Every S is P), the P of which is a *generic* (not a *specific*) characteristic of the S. For example, "Every man is mortal" forms the basis of the imperfect disjunctive:

"A being is either mortal or non-man."

Here "mortal" and "non-man" are the opposed terms of the disjunction. Since a being "must be one or the other," if you *deny* mortal, you must affirm "non-man"; if you *deny* "non-man" (which you do by *affirming* "man"), you must affirm "mortal"; but a being (e.g., a *pig*) can be *both* "non-man" and "mortal," so that if you *affirm* "non-man" you are *not* justified in *denying* "mortal," and if you *affirm* "mortal" you are *not* justified in *denying* "non-man." From this disjunctive, 1 can rightly say:

"If a being is *not* mortal, it *is* non-man"
and
"If a being is *not* non-man (if it is man), it *is* mortal"

but I cannot say:

"If a being *is* mortal, it is *not* non-man (it is man)"
or
"If a being *is* non-man, it is *not* mortal."

Similarly, the A proposition "All silver is gray" yields the imperfect disjunctive "A metal is either gray or not silver." As an exercise, the student may form imperfect disjunctives from the following A propositions:

"Every scientific principle is proved."
"Every horse is animal."
"Every judgment is an act of the mind."

The A proposition whose predicate is *specific* of the subject— i.e., belongs exclusively to it—can form the basis of a *perfect* disjunctive. For example, "Every man is rational" yields the perfect disjunctive:

"A being is either rational or not-man."

Here the being must be either "rational" or "not-man," and it *cannot be both* "rational" and "not-man." In like manner, we can form perfect disjunctives from propositions like the following:

> "Every triangle is three-sided."
> "Every animal is sentient."
> "Every organism is a living body."

The simplest way to form perfect disjunctives, however, is to secure terms which, when applied to a subject, are *contradictory*, or equivalent to contradictory, of each other, for then we can be sure that one or the other must be true of the subject, and that both cannot be true—for instance, "mortal" and "immortal" in regard to "living being," any predicate (P) and its exact contradictory (non-P) in regard to any subject (S), "open" and "shut" in regard to "window" and the like.[7] The following would thus be considered to be perfect disjunctives, though only the last of the propositions cited could be designated as *formally perfect:*

> "A living being is either mortal or immortal."
> "A window is either open or shut."
> "A is either b or non-b."

The distinction between the perfect and the imperfect disjunctive is most easily understood when we *reduce* the disjunctive to the *conditional* form. A *perfect* disjunctive can be reduced to *four* conditional propositions, since to deny one member is to affirm the other ("one must be true"), and to affirm one member is to deny the other ("both cannot be true"). Thus "A window is either open or shut" is reduced to the conditional form as follows:

> "If a window is not open, it is shut."
> "If a window is not shut, it is open."
> "If a window is open, it is not shut."
> "If a window is shut, it is not open."

---

[7] "Open" and "shut" *in themselves* can be considered *contraries*, but when applied in a proposition to a "window" or a "door" are *equivalent to contradictories:* "shut" is equivalent to "not open," and "open" to "not shut." The same may be said of "mortal" and "immortal" in regard to "living being." Non-living things are neither mortal nor immortal, but living things must be one or the other, and obviously cannot be both.

The *imperfect* disjunctive, on the other hand, can be properly reduced to only *two* conditional propositions, both of whose *antecedents deny* one member of the disjunction, and both of whose *consequents affirm* the other member. "Either you study or you fail" becomes:

"If you *do not* study, you fail"

and

"If you *do not* fail, you study."

Since one member or the other must be true, to deny one is to affirm the other; but since *both may be true,* to affirm one member is not to justify denying the other. The two other conditional propositions that might seem to be derivable from the original proposition can thus be *false,* despite the truth of the original disjunctive:

"If you study, you do not fail"

and

"If you fail, you do not study."

Remember that the distinction between perfect and imperfect disjunctive propositions is made on the side of *matter*. Most disjunctive propositions are probably perfect, and the perfect form seems a *more natural* mode of disjunctive utterance. *Formally,* nevertheless, we must consider the disjunctive proposition as *imperfect,* unless the two members are formally contradictory, as in:

"A is either b or non-b."

If the members are not formally contradictory, we must know by reason of their content or matter that they are mutually exclusive (contradictory or equivalent) before classifying the proposition as a perfect disjunctive.

The Conjunctive Proposition. The *conjunctive proposition* is exactly complementary to the disjunctive. The disjunctive states:

"It must be one or the other."

The conjunctive states:

"It cannot be both."

The conjunctive is often mistaken for the ordinary *impossible modal* proposition, but what it asserts is not a simple impossibility, but rather the *simultaneous impossibility of two enunciations*, like "having your cake" and "eating your cake," or "serving God" and "serving Mammon." The negative necessity of two members not being simultaneously true is conveyed by means of the impossible mode. (In the *conditional* and *disjunctive*, the necessity of the sequence is *implicit*. In the conjunctive, it is made *explicit* by the impossible mode.) Thus:

> "You *cannot* eat your cake and have it."
> "*No* man *can* serve both God and Mammon." [8]
> "You *cannot* be both soldier and sailor."

Any disjunctive can be transformed into a conjunctive by negating its members and uniting by the "cannot be both" copula. Thus:

> "Either you study or fail"

can be stated conjunctively as:

> "You cannot not-study and not-fail"

while the *conjunctive* can be expressed *disjunctively* in the same way.

> "You cannot serve God and Mammon"

becomes:

> "Either you don't serve God or you don't serve Mammon."

Formally, the conjunctive asserts that "it cannot be both," but if the members are contradictory or equivalent, then *materially* it implies that "it must be one or the other." From the standpoint of *content* or *matter*, we can also distinguish *perfect* from *imperfect* conjunctives.

> "Man cannot be both mortal and immortal"

---

[8] Here the conjunction is quantified by the "No," and the proposition would be classified as a *universal conjunctive*.

is a *perfect* conjunctive, since man must be one or the other.

"You cannot be soldier and sailor"

is, on the other hand, an *imperfect* conjunctive, for though you cannot be both, *you may be neither* soldier nor sailor. As with the disjunctive, this distinction of perfect and imperfect conjunctive propositions becomes clearest when we reduce to the conditional form. The ordinary conjunctive (which is imperfect) can be reduced to only *two* conditional propositions. "You cannot be both soldier and sailor" becomes:

"If you *are* a soldier, you are not a sailor"
and
"If you *are* a sailor, you are not a soldier."

In both cases, the *antecedent* of the conditional *must affirm* one member, while the consequent denies the other. Though "You cannot be both soldier and sailor," it is *false* to say:

"If you *are not* a soldier, you are a sailor"
or
"If you *are not* a sailor, you are a soldier."

You may, happily, be neither.

If the two members are equivalently contradictory, the conjunctive is *perfect,* and may, like the perfect disjunctive, be reduced to *four* conditional propositions. "A window cannot be both open and shut" becomes:

"If a window is open, it is not shut."
"If a window is shut, it is not open."
"If a window is not open, it is shut."
"If a window is not shut, it is open."

Since the properties of the disjunctive and conjunctive are precisely complementary, they are easily confused. The differences are summarized in the table on p. 74.

Remember generally that the distinction between *perfect* and *imperfect* with respect to both conjunctive and disjunctive propositions is made on the side of *matter* or content, rather than on that of *form.* Formally, the *disjunctive* simply states "one or the other," the

Proposition	Formal Statement	Material Implication	Conditional Reduction
Disjunctive	One or the other	*Perfect:* not both *Imperfect:* can be both	Four forms Two forms: antecedent must deny
Conjunctive	Not both	*Perfect:* one or the other *Imperfect:* can be neither	Four forms Two forms: antecedent must affirm

conjunctive "not both," so that *formally* each may be reduced to only *two* conditional propositions. The one exception is where the disjunction or conjunction is *formally perfect*, as in:

> "A is either b or non-b."
> "X cannot be both y and non-y."

In this instance only, *on formal grounds,* we may reduce either proposition to *four* conditional propositions.

Copulative Propositions. The propositions we have so far been considering under the heading "hypothetical" are all *sequential,* i.e., they assert some *connection* or sequence between the two enunciations or members, and they never assert the truth of all their members. The *conditional* asserts that there is a necessary sequence between two enunciations without asserting that *either* enunciation is true; the *disjunctive* asserts that there is a necessary connection between its members such that *one* must be true; and the disjunctive a necessary connection such that *one* must be *false*. The *copulative proposition*, with which we are now concerned *does not necessarily assert any sequence,* and, most characteristically:

> *it asserts that all of its members are true.*

When we say:

> "Integrity is rare and selfishness is rampant"

we are asserting *two* things to be true. If *either* of these things is false, the original proposition is false. This holds for any type of copulative proposition: if *one* of its members is false, *the whole proposition is false*. If it is false that "integrity is rare" *or* that "dishonesty is rampant," our original proposition is *simply false*.

The basic type of copulative proposition is the *pure copulative*. Here the copula is "and," and the proposition may take any of the following forms:

> "A is b *and* a is c" ("A is b *and* c").
> "A is c *and* b is c" ("A and b are c").
> "A is b *and* c is d."

When, as in the first example, the subject of both enunciations is the same, it is not usual to repeat the subject in the second enunciation. We say:

> "Spinoza was a lens grinder and a mathematician"

rather than:

> "Spinoza was a lens grinder and Spinoza was a mathematician."

Likewise, when the predicate is the same in both enunciations, as in the second example, it is not usually repeated. We say:

> "The eye and ear are organs of sense"

rather than:

> "The eye is an organ of sense and the ear is an organ of sense."

In the third example the subjects and predicates of the two enunciations are different, and in these cases there can be no doubt of the compound character of the proposition, as in:

> "Spinoza was a lens grinder and Leibniz a diplomat."

Where the subject or predicate is not explicitly repeated, the proposition may be classed with the *exponible*, or *hiddenly copulative*, propositions, but since in these cases the compound character of the proposition is revealed by the "and," it would seem simpler to classify them with the *pure copulatives*. By reason of the content or *matter*, certain propositions which look like pure copulatives must be classified as *categorical*. These may take the forms:

"A and b are c" ("Robert and John are friends").
"A is b and c" ("This couple is brother and sister").
"A and b are c and d" ("John and Mary are husband and wife").

When we advert to the matter of these propositions, we see that "Robert and John are friends" does not mean "Robert is a friend and John is a friend," and that "John and Mary are husband and wife" does not mean "John is a husband and John is a wife and Mary is a husband and Mary is a wife." The intended sense is that the *single relationship* "being friends" or "being husband and wife" applies to the two *taken together*. "Robert and John" are two *physical* subjects, but one *logical* subject, as are "John and Mary." These, then, are *categorical* propositions (of the form *S is P*) in which the predicate expresses a *relationship between* two beings as subject. In such cases the "and" is not a copula, but a sign that the subject is a *collective* rather than a *divisive* term. It is the relational character of the predicate, however, which enables us to distinguish this kind of proposition from the pure copulative, so that on purely formal grounds we cannot make this distinction.

"A and b are c"

may be a *copulative* and may be a *categorical* proposition, depending on the sense of "c." Consider the following:

"The eye and ear are sense organs."
"The eye and ear are interdependent."
"Wealth and health are requirements of the good life."
"Wealth and health often do not go together."

A *remotive proposition* is a copulative of the "neither . . . nor" form:

"Neither wealth nor health produces happiness."

Such a proposition is the exact equivalent of the *pure copulative*:

"Wealth *does not* produce happiness *and* health *does not* produce happiness" since "neither . . . nor" means simply "not . . . and not." As with other copulatives, if *either* of the members of a remotive proposition is false, the proposition as a whole is false.

Adversative propositions are copulatives with a "but," "nevertheless," "yet," "although," or some similar copula. The second member of an adversative proposition customarily places some *qualification* or *limitation* on the first member, and is frequently negative in form or sense, as in:

> "He is clever but imprudent"
>
> or
>
> "Though science can teach us to build weapons it cannot teach us to control them."

The adversative copula ("but," "though," etc.) seems to indicate that there is some connection or sequence between the first member and the *opposite* of the second member. Where no such possible connection is ordinarily presumed, the adversative proposition does not quite make sense. Thus:

> "She is intelligent but a very good student"

has a faint ring of dementia about it, while

> "She is intelligent but *not* a very good student"

sounds eminently sensible. Yet the connection between "being intelligent" and "being a good student," or between "being clever" and "not being imprudent," or between "building weapons" and "controlling weapons" is very tenuous and *in no sense a necessary connection*. All that the adversative proposition requires is the sort of connection between one of its members and the opposite of the other that might be *presumed or imagined* to hold by some people, without any real or necessary basis. Sometimes, in fact, this connection may be *fantastic,* in which case we may suspect sarcasm:

> "He has a disabling hang nail, but I think he'll live."

We cannot, therefore, be logically sure from the adversative form that there is any real connection between one member and the opposite of the other. There *may* be a necessary connection, and then again the connection may be so faint as to amount to no more than an imaginative nuance. We can be certain of only one thing, that the adversative proposition asserts that *all of its members are true*. We therefore treat it as though it were a *pure copulative proposition*, as though "but" meant the same as "and." There is more to "but" than there is to "and," but from the *form* of the adversative proposition we cannot be sure what this something more is, so we are forced to pass over it in formal logic.

In speaking of openly copulative propositions we have generally used examples in which there were just *two* enunciations. There is, however, no limit to the number of enunciations in a single copulative proposition. However many members a proposition may have, as long as they are connected by a copula, written or understood, it is just one proposition. An "and" or a "nor" may be replaced by a comma in ordinary usage without this affecting the singleness of the proposition. Thus:

"Edward is tall, dark, handsome, rich, and feeble-minded"

or

"This novel is neither original, plausible, nor interesting."

The members of a sequential proposition (conditional, disjunctive, or conjunctive) may be copulative, in which case the *members* come under the rules of the copulative proposition, while the *proposition as a whole* follows the rules of the particular sequential form. Consider the following examples:

"You cannot be inattentive in class or lax in doing your assignments and expect to get much from your courses or [9] make the Dean's list."
"Either you give up daydreaming and do your work or you'll be looking for another job."

> For if it see the rud'st or gentlest sight
> The most sweet favor or deformed'st creature
> The mountain or the sea, the day or night,
> The crow or dove, it shapes them to your feature.

[9] As is sometimes the case in dependent clauses, "or" here has the sense of "and." The second member is thus *copulative*, rather than *disjunctive*. The sentence after the examples which begins "Statements . . ." also contains an "or" which means "and."

Statements of this sort are highly complex logically, though by no means unusual in everyday speech or literary exposition. They represent no exceptions to the laws of logic, and can be completely analyzed by combining the elementary principles we have so far considered, just as the most difficult problems in mathematics can be solved by appropriate combinations of the fundamental operations of addition, subtraction, multiplication, and division.

Exponible, or Hiddenly Copulative, Propositions. *Exponible propositions,* often have the appearance of simple categoricals, but they are always copulative and frequently of a highly compound nature. We shall consider the four most important types of exponible propositions.

The *exceptive proposition* is one of the commonest forms of the exponible. Its sign is "except," the prepositional "but," or some equivalent, as in:

> "None *but* the brave deserve the fair"
> or
> "Every metal *except* mercury is a solid."

The first proposition is a *negative* exceptive, and it is the equivalent of:

> "The brave deserve the fair *and* no others do."

It is really therefore a *copulative* proposition, containing *two* enunciations. The second example, an *affirmative* exceptive, can be said to contain *three* enunciations:

(A) "Mercury is a metal and mercury is not a solid and every other metal is a solid."

Or in many cases we may say that the first enunciation is covered by the word "other" in the third enunciation, and that the affirmative exceptive can be reduced to a pure copulative with *two* enunciations:

(B) "Mercury is not a solid and every other metal is a solid."

Since this proposition could not be true unless mercury *were* a metal, it may be considered equivalent to (A) above. In any possibly doubt-

ful case, however, all three enunciations should be made explicit.
The falsity of:

> "Every metal except water is a solid"

is seen most clearly when the first enunciation ("Water is a metal")
is explicitly stated.

The *exclusive proposition,* whose sign is "alone" or "only," is very
closely allied to the exceptive.

> "Man alone is rational"

says:

> "Man is rational *and* no other being is rational"
>   or
> "Man is rational *and* no non-man is rational."

In like manner, "Only a saint is unselfish" says "A saint is unselfish
and no other man is unselfish." Notice the resemblance between the
exclusive proposition, and the *negative exceptive.*

> "*Only* the brave deserve the fair"

says exactly the same thing as:

> "*None but* the brave deserve the fair"

namely, "The brave deserve the fair and no others deserve the fair."
Notice, too, that in the exclusive or negative exceptive, the subject
of the first enunciation is not necessarily taken universally. Thus:

> "Only females are mothers"

in pure copulative form should read:

> "*Some* females are mothers and no non-females are mothers"

and should not be taken to imply that "*All* females are mothers."
Here is an instance where an *indefinite* term is really *particular,*
and failure to note this fact may lead to fallacies in reasoning. Whenever an exponible proposition enters into argument which we are
forming or judging we should fully explicate it, by reducing it to
the pure copulative form. In so doing we should be careful not to

omit the "and," for this is the copula which links two or more enunciations into *one* proposition.

Reduplicative and *causal propositions* are very similar. Both are exponible; both contain at least three enunciations, the third of which regularly asserts a *connection* or *sequence* between the first two. *Materially,* they thus resemble the *sequential proposition,* but *formally* they are *copulative propositions* because they assert that *all* their members are true. The *reduplicative* has a deceptively uncomplex appearance. The apparently simple statement:

> "Man *as* rational is free"

says *three* things:

> (A) Man is rational and
> (B) man is free, and
> (C) man's being rational is what makes him free.

Similarly, "The coward as a man is not to be despised" says "The coward is a man and the coward is not to be despised and it is from the fact that the coward is a man that he is not to be despised." Notice that the "as" in exponible propositions of the reduplicative type may have a *limiting* or *restrictive* function. For example, when I say "The Communist *as a man* is not to be hated" I do not assert that "The Communist *as an enemy of the democratic way of life* is not to be hated." The enunciations contained in a reduplicative proposition are thus more closely intertwined than in any other type of copulative, so that the sense of an enunciation *outside* the proposition may be considerably different from what it is within the proposition. As may be suspected from the examples cited, the reduplicative proposition plays an important role in moral philosophy and in metaphysics, where very subtle distinctions often mark the difference between profound truth and profound error. The proposition in which Aristotle couches his famous definition of motion:

> "Motion is the actualization of that which is in potency *insofar as it is in potency*"

has often been misunderstood and its profound philosophical implications lost because insufficient attention was paid to its *reduplicative* form. We cannot, in an elementary exposition of this sort, do justice to all the nuances which the reduplicative proposition may convey, but the student who will pursue courses in philosophy should mark this form as singularly important, and, having learned its elementary significance, should treat it with gingerly respect.

The compound character of *causal propositions* is usually less difficult to detect.

> "*Because* he is human, he is worthy of respect"

says in effect:

    (A) He is human and
    (B) he is worthy of respect and
    (C) it is from the fact that he is human that he is worthy of respect.

The causal proposition is thus like a conditional proposition which asserts the truth of its *members* as well as the truth of its *sequence*. Syncategorematic words like "since," "hence," "thus," "so," "for" may also signify causal propositions. Each of the following may, like any other causal proposition, thus be reduced to the pure copulative form:

> "*Since* Friday is a holiday, there is to be no school."
> "Friday is a holiday, *so* there's no school."
> "He is an introvert and *hence* inclined toward pessimism."
> "He is an introvert and *thus* inclined toward pessimism."
> "He is inclined toward pessimism, *for* he is an introvert."

In the pure copulative form, the first of these examples would read:

    (A) Friday is a holiday and
    (B) there is to be no school Friday and
    (C) it is by reason of the holiday that there is to be no school Friday.

If we always made fully explicit the parts of causal (and similar exponible) propositions which we employ, our speech would take on a very childlike simplicity. The advantage of the exponible proposition is precisely that it permits us to convey complex thought in a relatively simple statement, and there is no reason for the logician to object to this economy of expression. Once we are certain of the full implication of these hiddenly compound propositions, it is ordinarily unnecessary to explicate their content.

The important point for the student of logic to remember is that since exponible propositions are really *copulative,* they affirm the truth of *all* their members. If, therefore, any *one* enunciation contained in an exponible proposition is false, the proposition *as a whole* is false. Thus "Man alone learns" is false, because while it is true that "Man learns," it is false that "No other being (non-man) learns." "Man as intelligent is subject to the law of gravity" is false, because though it is true that "Man is intelligent," and true that "Man is subject to the law of gravity," it is false that "Man's being intelligent is what makes him subject to the law of gravity." "Man *as a material substance* is subject to the law of gravity" would be an acceptable proposition.

Section 4: The Opposition of Categorical Propositions

The Opposition of Assertoric Propositions. Considering the arrangement of simple categorical, or assertoric, propositions according to *quantity* and *quality* into A, E, I, and O propositions, the logicians have devoted considerable attention to the properties arising out of the *opposition of propositions.* To *oppose* propositions is to:

affirm and deny the same predicate of the same subject

and the full import of a proposition is nowhere better revealed than by considering it in relation to its opposite or opposites.

With respect to A, E, I, and O propositions there are three principal types of opposition:

(1) *contradiction*
(2) *contrariety*
(3) *subcontrariety*

and one type of inferior-superior relationship—*subalternation*—which, for reasons of convenience, is usually treated under opposition, though the propositions in question are not truly opposite. Let us define each of the propositional pairs involved in these relationships.

Contradictories are opposites which differ in both *quality and quan-*

tity. One is the pure and simple negation of the other. There is contradiction between

"Every man is happy"

and

"Some man is not happy" ("*Not* every man is happy")[10]

and between

"No man is happy"

and

"Some man is happy."

Contraries do not differ in quantity, for both are *universal.* One contrary does not simply deny the other, it denies what a *less extended* proposition than the first would affirm. There is contrariety between

"Every man is happy"

and

"No man is happy."

"No man is happy" does not merely deny that "*Every* man is happy," it denies that "*Any* man is happy." Contraries are thus *more extremely* (but *less perfectly*) opposed than contradictories.

Subcontraries are two *particular* opposites. Like contraries, they differ in quality but not quantity. Unlike contraries, however, they are *less extremely* (as well as *less perfectly*) opposed than contradictories, since both are particular. Between

"Some man is happy"

and

"Some man is not happy" ("Not every man is happy")

there is the opposition of subcontrariety.

[10] Hereby, in all probability, the origin of the misleading "Not every (all) . . ." or "Every (all) . . . not" forms. If we contradict the A proposition "Every man is happy," we say in effect "It is false that *every* man is happy— *not every* man is happy or *every* man is not happy," and this negation of the A proposition, though it retains the word "every" from the A proposition, really amounts to the O proposition "*Some* man is *not* happy." Likewise "*Not all* a is b" or "*All* a is *not* b" is the contradictory of "All is b," and is therefore identical with "*Some* a is not b." The simple negation or contradiction of a universal proposition is always a particular proposition, and since there are five ways of negating the universal affirmative (A) proposition, there are five forms of the particular negative (O) proposition.

Subalterns are not really opposites, since they do not differ in quality. They are two propositions with the same subject, predicate, and copula, one of which is universal and the other of which is particular. The universal is called the *subalternant* or *superaltern,* and the particular proposition the *subaltern.* There is a relation of subalternation between

"Every man is happy"
and
"Some man is happy"

and between

"No man is happy"
and
"Some man is not happy."

The famous *square of opposition* is a chart of these relationships:

A   E
Every man is happy.   CONTRARIES   No man is happy.

```
              C                               S
                O                           E
S                 N                     I                 S
U                   T                 R                   U
B                     R             O                     B
A                       A         T                       A
L                         D   C                           L
T                           I                             T
E                         D   C                           E
R                       A         T                       R
N                     R             O                     N
S                   T                 R                   S
                  N                     I
              O                           E
I        C        SUBCONTRARIES        S        O
```

Some man is happy.   Some man is not happy.
(5 forms)

Thus A and O are *contradictories,* as are E and I. A and E are *contraries,* I and O *subcontraries.* I is the *subaltern* of A, and O is the *subaltern* of E. Notice that the subalternant or superaltern is in no way denied by its subaltern. (Remember that from the standpoint of formal logic, "some" does not mean "*only* some," but "*at least* some.") The subaltern only affirms (or denies) the same predicate of the same subject as its superaltern, but that subject is taken in a less extended supposition than in the superaltern. If it is true that "No man is happy," it is certainly true that "Some man (at least) is not happy." The superaltern and subaltern are not, however, identical, since the subaltern may be *true* (e.g., "Some man is not bald"), while the corresponding superaltern ("No man is bald") is false. (Remember also that the O proposition may be written in any of five different ways, all of which are exactly equivalent.)

The square should help us to understand the *laws of opposition*.

FIRST LAW: *Contradictories cannot be at the same time true, nor at the same time false.* If one is true, the other must be false. If one is false, the other must be true. If one is doubtful, the other is doubtful. If it is true that "Some man is happy," it is false that "No man is happy." If it is false that "Every man is happy," it is true that "Every (some) man is not happy." If one of these propositions is doubtful, its contradictory cannot be true or false, because then the original proposition would be false or true, not doubtful.

SECOND LAW: *Contraries cannot be at the same time true, but they can be at the same time false.* If one is known to be *true*, the other must be false; but if one is known to be *false*, the other may or may not be true. If it is true that "No man is impeccable," it is surely false that "Every man is impeccable," but given as false that "Every man is bald," we have no right to assume that "No man is bald" is true. One contrary here is as false as the other. We have already noted that contraries have universality in common, and we now see that they may have falsity in common. It is only contradictories that can have *nothing* in common, neither quantity nor quality, neither truth nor falsity. To oppose a false proposition by its contrary is to run the risk of falling into the opposite error, while to *contradict a false proposition is automatically to assert the truth*. Contradiction is thus the most complete, and the only *perfect*, kind of opposition.

THIRD LAW: *Subcontraries may be at the same time true, but they cannot be at the same time false.* From the square of opposition we can see that the subcontraries (I and O) are the contradictories respectively of the contraries (E and A). Since both contraries cannot be *true*, their contradictories, the subcontraries, cannot both be *false*. Of two subcontraries, one *must* be true, and the other *may* be true. "Some man is bald" and "Some man is not bald" are both true, "Some man is mortal" is true, while "Some (every) man is not mortal" is false. Since both subcontraries may be true, subcontrariety is the weakest form of opposition. In those cases, indeed, where both subcontraries are true, it is difficult to think of them as opposites at all.

FOURTH LAW: Since they are not opposites, *subalterns may both be true or both be false*. If the particular is *false*, the universal is false. If the universal is *true*, the particular is *true*. Otherwise their status is doubtful or indeterminate: if the particular is true, the universal may or may not be true; if the universal is false, the particular may or may not be false.

From the laws of the square, given any one opposite as true or false, we can immediately ascertain the status of the related propositions in the square as *true, false,* or *doubtful*. ("Doubtful" or, better, "indeterminate" simply means that from the formal relationships of the square alone we cannot say that a given proposition is either necessarily true or necessarily false.) If, for example, we know that A is true, we know that its contradictory O and its contrary E are false; and since E is false, its contradictory I (the subaltern of A) must be true. If we know, on the other hand, that A is false, we know only that its contradictory O is true; its contrary E, and its subaltern I (the contradictory of E) may or may not be true, and must be labelled *doubtful* or *indeterminate*. See the table on p. 88.

Singular propositions have no contraries. There is only one opposite to "John is man" (A_s), and that is "John is not man" (E_s). In this respect, then, singular propositions are very different from universals. This ordinarily holds for abstract singulars as well. A proposition like "The triangle is a polygon" is usually opposed only by its contradictory, "The triangle is not polygon."

Indefinite propositions, too, in general are without contraries. An abstract indefinite like "Liberty is our most precious heritage" is opposed properly only by contradiction: "Liberty is not our most precious heritage." In this case the A_i proposition is opposed by the contradictory E_i. In those instances where an indefinite proposition

	True	*False*	*Indeterminate*
If A true	I	E, O	(Doubtful)
If A false	O		E, I
If E true	O	A, I	
If E false	I		A, O
If I true		E	A, O
If I false	E, O	A	
If O true		A	E, I
If O false	A, I	E	

is passing for a concrete universal, we may make the universal quantity explicit and then contradict by a particular. If someone says

"Mammals are live-bearing"

we can contradict by saying: "It isn't true that *all* mammals are live-bearing. *Some* mammals are not live-bearing." This would seem to hold when the indefinite proposition is really an abbreviated universal, and where the indefinite term is not taken as *one* (according to the unity which it has in the mind, as in the abstract indefinite). In such cases we *interpret* the proposition *as universal,* and may contradict by a particular. Where the indefinite proposition is not interpreted as a universal but *left indefinite,* we contradict by another indefinite. The indefinite proposition *as indefinite,* we might say, is opposed only by another indefinite proposition, while the indefinite, interpreted *as universal,* may be contradicted by a particular. Thus:

"Gold is lighter than silver" (A_i)

would be contradicted by

"Gold is not lighter than silver" (E_i)

while

"Gold is yellow" (A_i)

may be interpreted to mean "All gold is yellow," (A) and may be contradicted by

"Some gold is not yellow" (O)

The *circumstantially quantified* proposition, to which we referred above (p. 56), is in effect either particular or universal, as well as either affirmative or negative. Propositions of this type, therefore, can be arranged in a square of opposition, illustrating all the types of opposition we have considered.

CONTRARIES

A_c

Men are *always* unhappy.

Integrity is *everywhere* despised.

Homicide is evil *under all conditions.*

E_c

Men are *never* unhappy.

Integrity is *nowhere* despised.

Homicide is evil *under no conditions.*

CONTRADICTORIES

SERIOT... *(diagram letters crossing)*

Men are *sometimes* unhappy.

Integrity is *somewhere* despised.

Homicide is evil *under certain conditions.*

I_c

Men are *not always* unhappy.

Integrity is *not everywhere* despised.

Homicide is not evil *under certain conditions.*

O_c

SUBCONTRARIES

Notice that the particular negative circumstance (O_c) may be written in a variety of ways. Thus "Men are not always unhappy" is the same as "Men are not unhappy sometimes" or "Sometimes men are not unhappy." "Integrity is not everywhere despised" is equivalent to "Integrity is not despised somewhere" or "Somewhere integrity is not despised." Notice also that "certain" is generally equivalent to "some." *Circumstantial* quantification does not preclude *ordinary* quantification, and double quantification is fairly common in everyday discourse. Thus:

> *"Some* men are *never* satisfied"
> *"No* man is *always* polite."

In such cases ordinary quantification takes precedence over circumstantial quantification in determining the character of the proposition, and the circumstantial modifier is considered simply as part of the predicate. When the proposition is contradicted, the circumstantial modifier usually remains unchanged. Consider the following examples:

Original	*Contradictory*
Some men are never satisfied	No men are never satisfied
No man is always polite	Some man is always polite
Some goods are everywhere prized	No goods are everywhere prized
Everyone is always complaining	Not everyone is always complaining (Someone is not always complaining)
Every man is sometimes selfish	Not every man is sometimes selfish (Some man is not sometimes selfish)

Only in the last example might it be deemed advisable to alter the circumstantial modifier, and here only for the sake of avoiding ambiguity or amphiboly. "Every man is sometimes selfish" is correctly contradicted by

$$\overset{\text{S}}{\text{Some man}} / \overset{\text{c}}{\text{is not}} / \overset{\text{P}}{\text{sometimes selfish}}$$

but since the "sometimes" might be construed apart from the predicate as the proposition is ordinarily written or spoken, it might be clearer to say "Some man is not *ever* selfish," or by obversion, "Some man is *never* selfish." In most cases, however, no such ambiguity is likely to arise, and we can disregard the circumstantial quantifier in contradicting a doubly quantified proposition.

Opposition of Modal Propositions. Modal propositions may be arranged in a square of opposition, analogous to that of the simple or assertoric categorical. The *necessary* and *possible* modes are always *affirmative,* and since "must be" is broader than "can be," the necessary and possible would be the analogues of the *A* and *I* propositions respectively. In like manner, the always *negative* *impossible* and *contingent* modes would be analogous respectively to the *E* and *O* propositions.

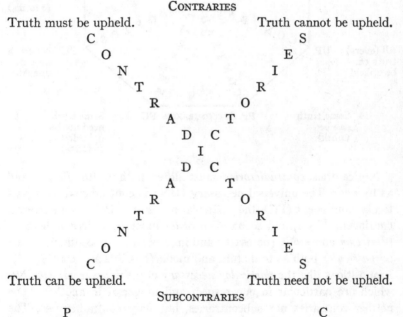

N   Imp

CONTRARIES

Truth must be upheld.   Truth cannot be upheld.

Truth can be upheld.   Truth need not be upheld.

SUBCONTRARIES

P   C

The rules of the square hold for modal as for assertoric propositions. Thus if N is true, P is true, and Imp and C are false. If P is false, Imp is true, N is false, and C is true, and so on, exactly as with the A, E, I, and O forms.

We have already noted (above, p. 59) that when the subject-term of a modal proposition is quantified, the proposition has *dictum* as well as mode, and that there are *eight* possible forms. These can be arranged in an *octagon of opposition,* exhibiting four contradictories, two contraries, and two subcontraries.

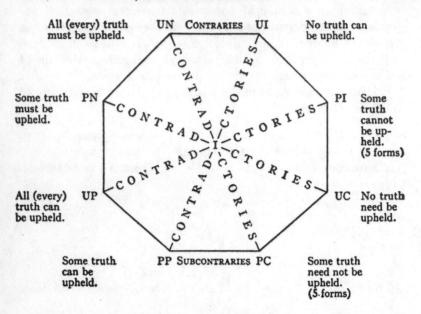

All (every) truth must be upheld.   UN CONTRARIES UI   No truth can be upheld.

Some truth must be upheld.   PN   PI   Some truth cannot be upheld. (5 forms)

All (every) truth can be upheld.   UP   UC   No truth need be upheld.

Some truth can be upheld.   PP SUBCONTRARIES PC   Some truth need not be upheld. (5 forms)

Notice that *contradictories* must differ both as to *dictum* and as to *mode.* The universal necessary (UN) is contradicted by a particular contingent (PC), the particular necessary (PN) by a universal contingent (UC), and so on. *Contraries* must be *universal* both as to *dictum* and *mode* (necessary and impossible); subcontraries must be *particular* both as to dictum and mode (possible and contingent). Propositions like the *particular necessary* and the *universal possible,* which are particular in one respect and universal in another, have neither contraries nor subcontraries, but only contradictories. The particular impossible and particular contingent forms, since they are both particular and negative, can, like the O proposition, be written in any of five equivalent ways. Do not make the mistake of classifying "Not every a need be b" or "All x cannot be y" as *universal* propositions, since these are instances of the *particular* contingent and the *particular* impossible forms respectively. The universal impossible (UI) and the universal contingent (UC) propositions each have only *one* acceptable form:

> No a can be b (UI) and no a need be b (UC).

Section 5: The Opposition of Hypothetical or Compound Propositions

Perhaps the most useful way to make clear the precise import of a compound proposition is to determine its *contradictory*. For many hypothetical propositions we can also determine *contraries,* but because contrariety is of secondary importance, we shall, to avoid unnecessary complication, concentrate on the contradictories of the various types of hypothetical propositions we have named.

Contradiction of Conditional Propositions. The conditional proposition, you will remember, asserts simply that if one thing is so, another follows necessarily from it.

> "If a is b, a is c"

means

> "If a is b, *it follows necessarily that* a is c."

All that is asserted is the *necessity of a certain sequence.* To contradict a conditional, therefore, we need only

> *conditionally reaffirm the antecedent,*[11] *and deny that the consequent follows from it.*

We contradict "If a is b, a is c" by saying:

> "If a is b, *it does not follow necessarily* that a is c"

or briefly and idiomatically:

> "If a is b, a *may not be* c."

The modal form "may not be" has the effect of denying the *necessity of the sequence,* which is all that the original proposition asserted. We have already remarked that the consequent of every conditional

---

[11] Do not make the mistake of *denying the antecedent* in contradicting a conditional, for the proposition does not assert that its antecedent is so, but only that *if* it is so, the consequent necessarily follows from it. To destroy the original proposition, then, you must deny that the consequent follows *when the antecedent is so.*

proposition is implicitly in the necessary mode, and it is this which requires the "may not be" or even "need not be" in the second part of the contradictory.[12] If we take the conditional proposition:

"If Paul is rich, he is happy"

we can oppose that proposition by asserting:

"If Paul is rich, he *is not* happy"

using the assertoric form in denying the consequent. But the latter statement does more than simply deny that "If Paul is rich, he is happy"; it seems to assert that "If Paul is rich, *it follows necessarily that he is not happy*," which is more the *contrary* than the *contradictory* of the original proposition. As a matter of fact, we can arrange a square of opposition about the ordinary conditional proposition as follows:

If Paul is rich, he is (or will be) happy.

If Paul is rich, he is not (or will not be) happy.

CONTRARIES

```
        C                           S
         O                         E
S         N                     I         S
U          T                   R          U
B           R                 O           B
A            A               T            A
L             D   C         I             L
T              I                          T
E             D   C                        E
R            A               T            R
N           R                 O           N
S          T                   R          S
          N                     I
         O                         E
        C                           S
```

SUBCONTRARIES

If Paul is rich, he may be happy.

If Paul is rich, he may not be happy.

[12] Logically, "may not be" seems to be only a slightly weaker form of "need not be," as "may be" is of "can be." This slightly weakened form seems ideally suited for denying the *implicit* necessity of the sequence.

Or, if we follow the grammarians' recommendations with regard to "contrary to fact" conditions, we can use the conditional mood "would" in the consequent of the original, and the subjunctive "might not" in the consequent of the contradictory. Our square would then take the form:

If Paul were rich, he would be happy.   If Paul were rich, he would not be happy.

CONTRARIES

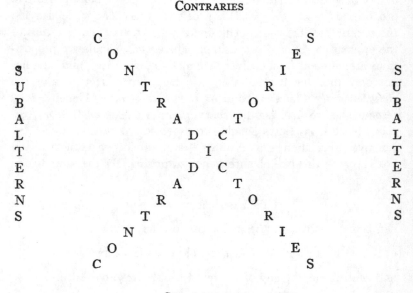

SUBCONTRARIES

If Paul were rich, he might be happy.   If Paul were rich, he might not be happy.

It is also possible to contradict a conditional proposition by means of a quasi-copulative proposition, which employs a possible (or equivalent) mode in its first enunciation, and a contingent (or equivalent) mode in the other. Thus:

"If Paul is rich, he is happy"

can be contradicted by:

> "Paul can be rich and he may not be happy"
> or
> "Paul may be rich and he may not be happy"
> or
> "Paul can be rich and he need not be happy"
> or
> "Paul might be rich and not happy"

or any of several variations of the same form. These quasi-copulative propositions assert the *possibility* of the antecedent while denying the *necessity* of the consequent, thereby destroying the assertion of the original conditional proposition. These quasi-copulative propositions are different from ordinary copulatives, since the "and" implies not only that the two members are true, but that they are true *simultaneously* ("and" = "and *at the same time*"). Thereby, they resemble, as we shall see, the *contradictories* of *conjunctive propositions*. Since it is always possible to express a conditional by a conjunctive proposition—for example "Paul cannot be both rich and not happy"—this resemblance is not surprising. By the same token, the conditional

> "If Paul is rich, he is happy"

can be expressed as a *disjunctive* proposition:

> "Either Paul is not rich or he is happy"

and contradicted by any of the quasi-copulatives above or by:

> "Paul may be neither not rich nor happy."

The common sequential nature of the conditional, disjunctive, and conjunctive propositions makes it possible to express any one in the form of the other, and therefore to contradict any one by the contradictory of the equivalent other.

The simplest way, however, to contradict the conditional form is as originally indicated:

Reaffirm the antecedent conditionally and deny the necessity of the consequent.

Consider the following examples of original conditional propositions and their contradictories:

Original	*Contradictory*
If a metal is gold, it is yellow.	If a metal is gold, it may not be yellow.
If man is rational, he must be free.	If man is rational, he need not be free.[13]
If all remain, all must suffer.	If all remain, some need not suffer.
If all fight, some will die.	If all fight, none may die.
If man is naturally free, he need not be a slave.	If man is naturally free, he may have to be a slave.
If a man has ambition, he can succeed.	If a man has ambition, he may not be able to succeed.[14]

[13] In this and the succeeding proposition, the necessity of the sequence is made *explicit* (and perhaps reinforced slightly) by the use of the necessary modal form "must." It would, therefore, seem best to contradict the original by the explicitly contingent "need not" in the consequent of the contradictory.

[14] In the last two examples, a complication is introduced by a *contingent* or *possible* mode in the consequent of the original. When we say "If man is naturally free, *he need not be* a political slave" the meaning is:

> "If man is naturally free, *it follows necessarily* that he *need not be* a political slave,"

and this in turn is the same as "If man is naturally free, it follows *necessarily* that he is not necessarily a political slave." This can be contradicted by "If man is naturally free, it does *not* follow necessarily that he need not be a political slave" or "If man is naturally free, it does not follow necessarily that he is not necessarily a political slave." Though acceptable, these forms are cumbersome and neither idiomatic nor very clear. In compact English they can be rendered "If man is naturally free, *he may necessarily be* a political slave" or "If man is naturally free, *he may have to be* a political slave." Similarly, "If a man has ambition, he *can* succeed" could be rendered "If a man has ambition, it follows *necessarily* that he *possibly succeeds*" and contradicted: "If a man has ambition, it does *not* follow necessarily that he possibly succeeds," but it is much simpler to contradict by saying "If a man has ambition, *he may not possibly* succeed" or even more idiomatically "If a man has ambition, *he may not be able* to succeed," as indicated above. Recall from the discussion of the modal proposition (above, p. 59) that "is necessarily" and "has to be" are equivalent, as are "is possibly" and "is able to be," "is not possibly" and "is not able to be." Usage seems to prefer "is (not) able to be" to "is (not) possibly" and "has to be" to "is necessarily." This preference has governed the choice of forms in the examples of contradictories given.

Though the contradictory of a conditional apparently retains the conditional form, if we attend carefully we can see that its sense is rather *adversative* (copulative) than truly conditional. Relative to the original proposition, the "if" of the contradictory has the sense of "although" or "though." The contradictory is not *asserting* that a consequent follows from an antecedent—which is the function of the true conditional—but *denying* it. A true conditional may have a negative consequent, but it still *asserts* that this consequent follows. The contradictory of a conditional *must deny* this consequent whether affirmative or negative. As should be almost self-evident, the contradictory of a conditional is not identical in logical structure with its original, but precisely opposite. The adversative sense of the contradictories given above can be verified by substituting "though it be" for "if it is" in each of them. You will observe that thereby the sense of the contradictory is not changed. If we substitute "though . . . be" for "if . . . is" in the original propositions, however, we alter the sense completely. The conditional and its contradictory in the square of opposition may appear to have the same logical structure, but granted only that the original is truly conditional, this cannot really be so. The contradictory of a conditional is what may be called a *quasi-adversative* [15] rather than a conditional proposition.

Contradiction of Disjunctive Propositions. The *disjunctive proposition* asserts that one or the other of its members *must be true*. (Like the conditional, the disjunctive is implicitly in the necessary mode.) To contradict "It must be one or the other" we simply assert that "it need be neither," or preferably (since the necessity is implicit) "it may be neither." The simplest contradictory of a *disjunctive* ("either . . . or") is thus a *remotive* ("neither . . . nor").

---

[15] The difference between the contradictory of a conditional and the ordinary adversative proposition is that in the former (the quasi-adversative) the first enunciation is not affirmed to be *actually* so. To withhold actual affirmation, we use a *subjunctive* in the first enunciation. To contradict "If man is irrational, man is not free" by an adversative, we say "Though man *be* irrational, he may be free," which does not imply the truth of the enunciation "Man *is* irrational." The second enunciation in the quasi-adversative is always, of course, the negation of the necessity of the sequence which the original conditional asserted. This calls for a *contingent* (or equivalent) form. The ordinary adversative "Though man *is* irrational, man *is* free" asserts the actual truth of both enunciations: "Man is irrational" and "Man is free."

For example:

> "An action is either good or bad"

is contradicted by:

> "An action *may be neither* good nor bad"

in which the "may be neither" negates the "has to be either" of the original disjunction. Since the remotive "neither . . . nor" is exactly equivalent to the *pure copulative* "not . . . and not," we can also contradict a disjunctive by a pure copulative:

> "An action *may not* be good *and may not* be bad."

In either case, we use the subjunctive mode ("may not be" or "may neither be") to negate the implicit necessity of the disjunction. The assertoric form "is not" or "is neither" in the opposing of a disjunctive proposition would yield a *contrary* rather than a contradictory of the original. (In a disjunctive square of opposition about "A is either b or c," the contrary would be "A *is* neither b nor c" ["A is not b and a is not c"]; the contradictory "A *may be* neither b nor c" ["A may not be b and a may not be c"], and so on.) Neglecting contrariety, which is ordinarily unimportant with disjunctive propositions, let us consider some examples of contradiction.

Original	*Contradictory*
We shall have either discipline or disorder.	We may have neither discipline nor disorder (We may not have discipline and we may not have disorder).
A man with acute appendicitis either undergoes an operation or he dies.	A man with acute appendicitis may neither undergo an operation nor die (A man with acute appendicitis may not undergo an operation and he may not die).
Either you study or you fail.	You may neither study nor fail (You may not study and you may not fail).
Our team must either win or lose.	Our team need neither win nor lose (Our team need not win and need not lose).

Original	*Contradictory*
Either some must lead or all must perish.	Neither need some lead nor need all perish (None need lead and some need not perish).
Either a or b can be c.	Neither a nor b may be able to be c (A may not be able to be c and b may not be able to be c).
Either a man must work or he need not expect to live.	Neither need a man work nor need he not expect to live (A man need not work and he may necessarily expect to live *or* A man need not work and he may have to expect to live).

Notice that in contradicting by the "neither . . . nor" form, we do not change either the quantity or quality of the original enunciation. The "neither" and the "nor" *simply negate the enunciation as a whole*. If we were to make any other change in the quantity or quality of the enunciation we would undo this negation.[16] In negating both members of the disjunctive proposition, as in negating the consequent of the conditional, we must take account of the implicit necessity of the sequence. *In these cases only,* we contradict "is" by "may not be," "need not be" by "may have to be" or "may necessarily be," and "can be" by "may not be able to be." In all other cases, we contradict "is" by "is not," "need not be" by "must be," and "can be" by "cannot be." The *disjunctive proposition* and the *consequent of the conditional proposition* are thus special cases, where the ordinary rules of contradiction are complicated by the presence of the implicitly necessary mode. The special rules for these cases should not be applied to the categorical or copulative propositions, where no implicitly necessary sequence exists.

Contradiction of Conjunctive Propositions. In the last of the sequential propositions, the *conjunctive,* the necessity of a negative sequence is made *explicit* by the impossible mode ("cannot be"). Its contradictory will therefore take the explicit *possible* mode ("can

---

[16] In contradicting "Either . . *must*" we conform to grammatical usage by saying "Neither . . . *need,*" but even this change of "must" to "need" is not *logically* necessary. "Neither . . . must" and "Neither . . . need" have a logically *identical* import.

be"). The conjunctive asserts the *simultaneous impossibility* of two alternatives. Its contradictory is a quasi-copulative proposition which asserts their *simultaneous possibility.*

Original	*Contradictory*
You cannot eat your cake and have it.	You can eat your cake and have it.
No man can serve both God and Mammon.	Some man can serve both God and Mammon.
All cannot be both charitable and prudent.	All can be both charitable and prudent.

Contradiction of Copulative Propositions. The *copulative,* or non-sequential type of compound proposition, is distinguished from other compound or hypothetical propositions in that it asserts that *all* of its members are true. An openly copulative proposition like:

"Art is long and life is short"

asserts the truth of "Art is long" and the truth of "Life is short." If *either* of these two enunciations is false, the copulative proposition is false. The contradictory of a copulative, therefore, should be of the "either . . . or" form. That is to say, the contradictory of a copulative must be in the form of a *disjunctive,* just as the contradictory of a disjunctive is, as we have seen, always a copulative. Since all other types of copulative propositions—the remotive, adversative, and the various exponibles—can be reduced to the pure copulative, all will be contradicted in essentially the same fashion. To contradict:

"A is b and c is d"

we say *"Either* a is not b *or* c is not d." If we oppose a copulative by *another copulative,* for example:

"Gold is yellow and silver is gray"
by
"Gold is not yellow and silver is not gray"

we express *contrariety,* rather than contradiction. Both propositions given *might be false,* and therefore cannot be contradictories.

The disjunctive which contradicts a copulative proposition is not truly *sequential*, or implicitly necessary. It simply states that one or the other of the original copulative's members *is* false, with no hint of "must be," unless the original copulative was explicitly in the contingent mode itself. The true disjunctive, on the other hand, asserts "one or the other" not merely as a matter of *fact*, but as a matter of *necessity*. The contradictory of a copulative is thus a *quasi-disjunctive*, as the contradictory of any sequential proposition is a *quasi-copulative*. We may now exemplify the contradiction of openly copulative propositions.

Original	*Contradictory*
Peter and Paul were poor.	Either Peter or Paul was not poor.
Beauty passes but love remains.	Either beauty does not pass or love does not remain.
Neither justice nor truth need triumph.	Either justice or truth must triumph.
Vestibular sensation is unconscious, distinct from hearing, and mediated by the inner ear.	Either vestibular sensation is not unconscious, or not distinct from hearing, or not mediated by the inner ear.
Personality and temperament are hereditary and chemically determined.	Either personality is not hereditary or not chemically determined or temperament is not hereditary or not chemically determined.
Joe and Dom are athletic and stupid.	Either Joe is not athletic or not stupid or Dom is not athletic or not stupid.
Philip and Susan are brother and sister.	Philip and Susan are not brother and sister (Original not copulative).

Contradiction of Hiddenly Copulative or Exponible Propositions. The exponible proposition will be contradicted like any other copulative proposition, but we must first make clear its copulative nature. To contradict an exponible proposition, first reduce to the pure copulative form, then contradict each of its enunciations, and finally connect all the contradicted enunciations with an "either

. . . or" copula. The *exceptive* proposition:

> "Every love except mother love is selfish"

says:

> "Mother love is not selfish and every other love is selfish."

Its contradictory, then, is:

> "Either mother love is selfish or some other love is not selfish."

The *reduplicative proposition:*

> "Man as rational is responsible"

says, when explicated into the pure copulative form:

> "Man is rational and man is responsible and it is man's being rational that makes him responsible"

and is contradicted by:

> "Either man is not rational or man is not responsible or it is not man's being rational that makes him responsible."

In the examples given below, the intermediate step of explicating or "exposing" the original proposition will not be given. The student, however, should write out all the enunciations implicit in the original. (See above, p. 79 ff.)

Original	*Contradictory*
The U. S. alone is a democracy.	Either the U. S. is not a democracy or some other nation is a democracy.
Only females are mothers.	Either no females are mothers or some non-females are mothers.
Every a except b is c.	Either b is c or some other a is not c.
Man as animal is selfish.	Either man is not animal or man is not selfish or it is not man's being animal that makes him selfish.
Galileo, because he was proud, defied the College of Cardinals.	Either Galileo was not proud or he did not defy the College of Cardinals, or it was not his being proud that made him defy the College of Cardinals.

Original	*Contradictory*
None except fools is in favor of war.	Either no fools are in favor of war or some others are in favor of war.
He is an introvert and hence inclined toward pessimism.	Either he is not an introvert or he is not inclined toward pessimism or it is not his being an introvert that makes him inclined toward pessimism.

SECTION 6: THE DISTRIBUTION OF THE PREDICATE-TERM

The law regarding the *distribution* or *extension* of the predicate-term is one of the most important and most persistently misunderstood principles in logic. Upon it hinges the very important operation of *conversion*, and much of the theory of the categorical syllogism.

The problem of the distribution of the predicate-term, with respect to both affirmative and negative propositions, is this: What is the supposition, or *status in regard to extension*, of the predicate in these propositions? Is it *taken universally* (distributed), or *taken particularly* (undistributed)? Does it stand for *all* the singulars, or subjects, to which the term applies, or only for *some?* We may formulate the law in the following form:

IN AFFIRMATIVE PROPOSITIONS THE PREDICATE IS *ALWAYS* TAKEN PARTICULARLY, AND IN NEGA–TIVE PROPOSITIONS THE PREDICATE IS *ALWAYS* TAKEN UNIVERSALLY.

The only possible exception to this rule is in those rare and, logically speaking, unnatural instances where the predicate-term is a *singular*, and therefore *cannot* be either particular or universal, distributed or undistributed.

The Extension of the Predicate-Term in Affirmative Propositions. If we consider an A proposition like

"Every man is animal"

there is little difficulty in seeing that the extension of the term "animal" is limited in this proposition. We do not assert the identity of "every man" with "*every* animal," but of "every man" with *some indeterminate part of the extension of "animal."* The predicate-term is thus *taken particularly,* or *undistributed.*

The Swiss mathematician, Euler, thought that the relation of subject- to predicate-term in this type of proposition could be represented by circles, with the term of lesser extension symbolized by a smaller circle enclosed within a larger circle (representing the term of greater extension). Since the smaller circle is coincident with only part of the area of the larger circle, this may be taken to illustrate the undistributed character of the predicate-term.

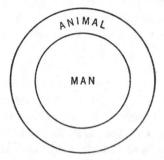

Such schemas are permissible, as imperfect illustrations of the *material* relations between terms of different extensions, but they in no sense explain, or even well illustrate, the *formal* relations involved. Even from the standpoint of matter, "man" is not contained in "animal" the way a little circle is contained in a larger one. The relationship between the two concepts is not *spatial* at all, and "quantitative" only in an analogous sense of that term. Even materially, the connection between "man" and "animal" is a relation of *meanings,* of universal natures which stand to each other as *species* to *genus.* As far as the *formal* relations between subject- and predicate-term in a proposition are concerned, Euler's circles tell us very little indeed, and are almost certain to lead to misunderstanding unless employed very critically and in the light of formal principles previously established.

The *formal reason why* the predicate of an affirmative proposition is always taken particularly is derived from the rule that every affirmative proposition places its P in the comprehension of its S, and its S in the extension of its P. From the very fact that the proposition places the S in the extension of the P, we know that from the standpoint of *form,* the proposition takes the P to be of *greater* extension than the S; yet by the fact that the same proposition, again viewed from the standpoint of form, *identifies* the S and P—S *is* P— we know that *it must limit the greater extension of P* in order to make this identification.

By the same token, in an affirmative categorical proposition the *comprehension* of the subject-term is also limited. When we say "S is P" we are saying from the standpoint of *extension* "S is identical with *part of P*"; and from the standpoint of *comprehension* "P is *one of the characteristics of S,*" so that the extension of P and the comprehension of S are similarly limited. In the proposition

"This man is tall"

the identification which the "is" connotes limits the comprehension of "this man" to "tall," though the comprehension of "this man" *in itself* (outside this proposition) includes many notes besides that of "tall." In the same way, the identification of "this man" and "tall" in the proposition limits the extension of "tall" to "this man," though apart from this proposition, "tall" includes many things besides "this man" in its extension. In every affirmative proposition, therefore, the comprehension of the subject and the extension of the predicate are limited, and this means that the predicate of an affirmative proposition is always taken particularly or undistributed with respect to extension.

Even when, by reason of the matter of the proposition, it happens that the predicate- and subject-term are of *exactly the same* extension —when the P is the definition of the S, or a property which belongs to nothing besides the S—the predicate is still, by reason of the *form* of the affirmative proposition, *taken particularly.* Consider the terms "man" and "rational animal." Since the latter is the definition of the former, the two terms are materially perfectly coincident as to extension. Nothing besides "man" is "rational animal," and nothing besides "rational animal" is "man." Yet in the proposition:

"Every man is rational animal"

the predicate-term is still *taken particularly.* The formal sense of the proposition is not that "Every man is *every* rational animal," for in that case I could say that since "Peter is man," "Peter is *every* rational animal," which is nonsense. Euler's circles may be used to illustrate the material relationship between the terms "man" and "rational animal," but by that very fact they *fail* to represent the undistributed character of the predicate-term in the proposition "Every man is rational animal." Euler's circles have helped to spread the notion that in such propositions the predicate-term is distributed, because the two circles representing "man" and "rational animal" coincide:

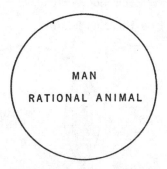

and this notion is simply false. If one must use circles to illustrate the relationship here, then the circle for "rational animal" might be drawn larger than the circle for "man," and indicated by a broken line to denote a nonexistent class (the "rational animals" outside the class of "men"). Thus:

In this way, the formally undistributed nature of the predicate-term will at least not be necessarily misinterpreted.

It is important to realize that the universal affirmative, or **A**, proposition is not universal in all respects. Only the subject-term is distributed; the predicate-term is taken particularly. Because it is the subject-term which determines the quantity of a proposition, the A proposition is said to be *universal as a whole,* but this does not mean *universal in all respects.*

On the other hand, the particular affirmative, or I, proposition is particular in *all* respects, since neither the subject nor the predicate is distributed. An ordinary I proposition, like

"Some dog is vicious"

would be symbolized by Euler as follows:

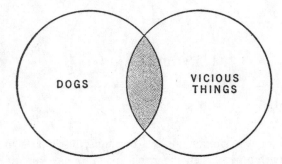

with the shaded portion representing the *partial coincidence* of the two classes, the material identity of *"some* dogs" and *"some* vicious things." But Euler's circles again fail to represent accurately the extension of the predicate-term in an I proposition like:

"Some men are carpenters"
or (more accurately)
"Some man is carpenter"

for they convey the material relationship according to which the *entire* class of "carpenters" ("carpenters" *taken universally*) is included within the class of "men." From Euler's diagram of the proposition "Some men are carpenters" (see the opposite page) the predicate-term would appear to be distributed, while in reality it is, as in every I proposition, *taken particularly.* It is incorrect to say "Some men are *all* carpenters," since, when this proposition is stated in acceptable form, "Some man is every carpenter," it implies that *each* man who is a carpenter is *every* carpenter. It is always improper, moreover, to place any quantifying particle (like "some," or "all") before the predicate of an affirmative proposition. The affirmative copula is the only indication needed to show that the predicate-term is taken particularly

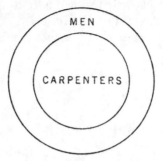

One can roughly illustrate the extension of the predicate-term in this kind of I proposition by employing the broken line to indicate the *null class,* or class without members, like the class "carpenters-who-are-not-men."

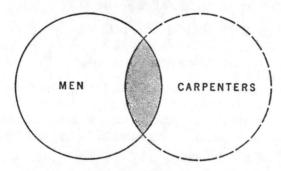

In this way it is seen that the formal character of the predicate-term is no different in this proposition from what it is in any other I proposition.

The Extension of the Predicate-Term in Negative Propositions. In a negative proposition like:

"No man is fish"

the P is excluded from the comprehension of the S, and the S is excluded from the extension of the P. Now if I exclude "man" from the extension of "fish," I must exclude "man" from the *whole extension* of "fish," and therefore I must be *taking "fish" in its whole extension, or distributively*. From the standpoint of extension, "No man is fish" indicates that "man" is not to be identified with *any* of the subjects or singulars that come under the extension of "fish," i.e., "man" is excluded from the *extension of "fish" taken universally*. Euler's circles would represent this proposition as follows:

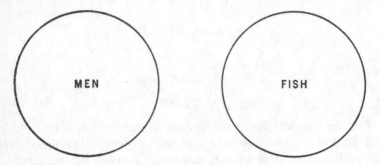

The same rule holds for the particular negative, or O, proposition: the predicate-term is distributed. When I judge:

"Some men are not bald"

or

"Some man is not bald"

I must think that the "some men" who are "not bald" are excluded from the *whole extension* of "bald things," just as "baldness" is excluded from the entire comprehension of those subjects who are not bald. If we represent the extension of "man" and "bald thing" by two intersecting circles:

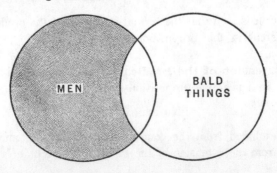

the shaded portion of the circle on the left represents the "some men" who are not bald, and this "some men" or "some man" will be altogether outside of the *whole extension* of "bald thing." Taking "bald thing" in its *full universality,* I must think that "some **man**" is outside it, else I could not judge "Some man is not bald."

In an O proposition like

"Some men are not carpenters"

the material relationship between S and P is out of the ordinary, but the same rule applies: the P is always distributed. Euler's circles customarily illustrate this type of proposition as follows:

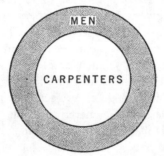

with the shaded portion of the outer circle denoting the "men who are not carpenters" and who are, therefore, excluded from the extension of "carpenter" taken universally. Since the formal rule is in no way different, it would seem preferable to employ the same diagram as for any other ʊ proposition, only once again symbolizing the "null class" by a broken line:

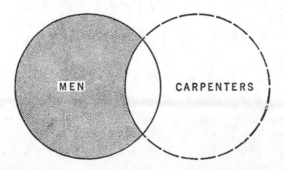

We can thus see that the O proposition, though particular *as a whole* (by reason of its undistributed subject-term), is not particular *in all respects*. In all logical operations concerned with categorical propositions it becomes important to know the distribution or extension of each term in each of the four major kinds of proposition. Let us therefore note carefully what terms are distributed in each:

A propositions   One term distributed, the S.
E   "   Both terms distributed, S and P.
I   "   No term distributed, neither S nor P.
O   "   One term distributed, the P.

Singular and *indefinite* propositions which are *negative*, distribute their predicates; *singular* and *indefinite affirmatives* leave their predicates undistributed. In this respect, the A_s, E_s, A_i, and E_i are no different from the ordinarily quantified A and E propositions. We know that the *subject* of a singular proposition is traditionally taken as equivalent to a universal, and this practice may be justified by the consideration that a singular subject in a proposition takes its predicate *as a whole,* and not merely in some part of itself. Thus, when I say "John is man" or "John is thin," it is *all John* that is "man," and *all John* that is "thin," not "some of John" that is "man" or "thin." When, however, a singular term becomes the *predicate* of any proposition, we have a unique situation, for the understanding of which special effort is required.

The laws regarding the distribution of the predicate-term, as we have seen, follow from the principle that in affirmative propositions the P is placed in the comprehension of the S, and, reciprocally, the S in the extension of the P; and that in negative propositions the P is excluded from the comprehension of the S, the S from the extension of the P.

Now when a singular term is the predicate of a negative proposition, as in:

"The mayor is not John"

we may argue that something like the original principle holds: "the mayor" is excluded from "John" *taken as a whole,* so that the singular term, "John," may be understood as though it were a universal. *"As though it were,"* we say, for in truth a singular is *not* a universal term, but happens to function more or less like one in this and many other instances. In the strict sense, of course, a singular term, like "this man," does not have the potentiality of applying to one *or* many in a proposition, as an ordinary term like "man" does, but is always restricted to this one determinate individual. A singular term, therefore, *does not have extension* in the sense in which a non-singular term does, so that the laws of extension can be applied to it only in a manner of speaking, *secundum quid*.

When a singular term is made the predicate of an *affirmative* proposition, the inapplicability of the ordinary laws of comprehension and extension is obvious. When we say "S is P," we regularly mean that "P is in the comprehension of S" or "P is a characteristic of S"; but this does not hold where P is a singular term. In the proposition:

"The culprit is Edgar"

the intended sense is certainly *not* "Edgar is in the comprehension of the culprit" or "Edgar is a characteristic of the culprit." A singular term stands for a *subject,* and a subject is not a characteristic or part of the comprehension of *anything*. Since in this type of proposition we do not place the P in the comprehension of the S, we cannot be said to place the S in the extension of the P. The rule regarding the restricted or undistributed character of the predicate-term in affirmative propositions, therefore, does not apply where the predicate is a singular term. A singular term is always singular, whether it functions as a subject or a predicate, and therefore neither distributed nor undistributed, taken universally nor taken particularly. What this amounts to is not so much an exception to the laws regarding the extension of the predicate-term as an admission that a *singular term is never truly a predicate,* and that therefore the laws respecting the distribution of the predicate *do not apply* to it. Where a term is such that it *can be* taken universally *or* taken particularly, and that term is the predicate of a proposition, there is no exception to the law:

*If the copula is affirmative the predicate-term is undistributed;
if the copula is negative, the predicate-term is distributed.*

Section 7: Conversion, Obversion, Contraposition

Most textbooks of logic treat of *conversion, obversion,* and *contraposition* as types of *immediate inference*. Since in the classical definition of the term the word "inference" means a *"mediate* judgment," i.e., "a judgment arrived at *by means of* other judgments," the expression *"immediate* inference" would mean "immediate mediate judgment," a terminological monstrosity of the first water. We shall reserve the term "inference" for the third act of the mind, and treat the operations of *conversion, obversion,* and *contraposition* not as "immediate inferences," but simply as:

different ways of rendering the same fundamental truth that an original proposition expressed.

As a result of these operations, the fundamental truth of the original proposition is given a *different* (and sometimes *diminished*) emphasis, but they do not assert any *new* truth, or truth not inherent in the original proposition itself. It is possible to perform analogous operations upon conditional and other hypothetical propositions, but conversion and the like are properly applied only to *categorical propositions*. It is to these that we shall restrict our consideration.

Conversion.   The first and most important of these operations is *conversion*. To convert a proposition is:

to re-express the truth of a proposition by interchanging subject and predicate, taking account of the distribution of both terms.

Considering the distribution of both subject- and predicate-term, we convert:

> *"Every* man is animal"

into:

> *"Some* animal is man"

and

> "No man is fish"

into

> "No fish is man."

The two propositions cited illustrate the two types of conversion, *simple* and *accidental*. *Simple conversion* takes place when the *quantity* of the original proposition is *unchanged*. This can take place only where the quantity of the original S and P is the same, i.e., in E and I propositions. E, as we have seen, converts to E ("No bird is mammal" to "No mammal is bird"), and I converts to I:

> "Some triangle is isosceles"

converts to:

> "Some isosceles (figure) is triangle."

Accidental conversion is the conversion applicable to A, where S and P have a different distribution, so that it is necessary, in converting, to *change the quantity* of the proposition. In the proposition:

> "Every fish is vertebrate"

the term "vertebrate" is *undistributed,* or taken particularly, because it is the predicate of an affirmative proposition. When that predicate becomes the subject of the new proposition (the converse), its undistributed, or particular, character must be made manifest. We therefore quantify it by the sign of particularity, "some," and state our converse as:

> "*Some* vertebrate is fish."

Since the term "fish," which was universal in the original proposition, is taken particularly in the converse, the assertion of the original proposition has been somewhat diminished in converting. The accidental converse is thus not the *exact,* but the diminished, equivalent of the convertend. It is the exact equivalent of the *subaltern* of the original A, and is, in fact, identical with the *simple converse of the subaltern*. "Some b is a" is the accidental converse of the A proposition "All a is b," and the *simple* converse of its subaltern "Some a is b."

It is the grossest sort of logical error ever to attempt simple conversion of an A proposition: to go, for example, from:

> "Every religious paranoiac is convinced of a divine mission"

to:

> "Everyone convinced of a divine mission is a religious paranoiac"

but such crudity is not unknown in everyday thinking, and would seem to play a significant role in the formation of social prejudices and the specious wisdom of folklore. What is sometimes called the *simple converse* of an A proposition is not a converse at all, but the *reciprocal* of the original proposition. The reciprocal of "Every man is animal" is "Every animal is man." This latter proposition uses universally a term which the original takes particularly, and on that account cannot be said to express the same fundamental truth as the original. If occasionally the reciprocal of a true A proposition is itself true—as when the P of the original is the definition or a specific property of the S—this is only by reason of the *matter,* or content, of the proposition. *Formally,* the reciprocal of a true A proposition is *doubtful.* It may be true, but in most cases it is false, and it is *never* correct to state it as the converse of the original.

Recall that it is always incorrect to place a sign of particularity or universality before the predicate-term. It is incorrect to say "Some animal is *every* man" or "Some isosceles figure is *some* triangle" or "No man is *any* fish." The affirmative or negative copula is sufficient indication that the predicate is taken particularly or taken universally.

In summary, *simple conversion* applies to E and I propositions—remember the two vowels in *"sImplE."* A propositions convert *accidentally,* or *per accidens*—remember the first vowel of *"Accidental."*

An O proposition *cannot be converted.* "Some man is not carpenter" does not convert into "Some carpenter is not man." The reason is not far to seek, for in an O proposition the S is *undistributed,* or taken particularly. If we transpose S and P, we make the undistributed S of the original the P of a negative proposition, and thereby *distributed,* or taken universally. Thus:

"Some a is not b"

would become:

"Some b is not a"

and the term "a," which in the original proposition was taken *particularly,* would now be taken *universally,* and the new proposition could not express the *same* truth as the original. Hence, even if the new proposition is true, it cannot be the converse of the original.

Suppose we attempt to convert the O proposition:

"Some matter is not visible"
Into
"Some visible thing is not matter."

We may note that while the original proposition is *true* (air, for example, is matter, and yet not visible), the alleged converse is *false* (if a thing is visible, it is certainly material, all ghost stories aside). We may, on the other hand, be troubled by the fact that the proposed converse of an O proposition seems to be true. Thus, if we transpose S and P in the O proposition:

"Some man is not healthy"

we get what seems to be an equally true proposition:

"Some healthy being is not man"

but we can nevertheless be sure that these two propositions do not express the *same truth*. To exclude "man" *taken particularly* from the extension of "healthy" taken universally is certainly not the same thing as to exclude "healthy" taken particularly from the extension of "man" *taken universally*. It is possible in conversion for a term to pass *from universal to particular* status—this happens in accidental conversion—but it is never permissible for a term in conversion to pass from *particular to universal*, and for this reason the O proposition cannot be said to have a converse. (You may remember the inconvertibility of the O proposition by recalling that the vowel "O" does not occur either in "simple" or "accidental.")

The ancient logicians also spoke of the *accidental conversion* of E propositions. Thus "No fish is mammal" would convert *simply* to:

(E) "No mammal is fish"

and *accidentally* to the subaltern of (E):

(I) "Some mammal is not fish."

Since there is no objection to taking a term *less broadly* in a converse than it was taken in the convertend, the accidental conversion of E propositions must be regarded as a legitimate operation. It is seldom necessary, however, so that if we remember that the subaltern of a true proposition is also necessarily true, we can for the most part forget about accidental conversion of any but A propositions.

Where a proposition uses a verb copula other than the assertoric "to be," it is necessary to express the proposition in *logical form* (*S is P, S is not P*—*cf.* above, p. 44 ff.), before attempting to convert. The converse of "Each man kills the thing he loves" is *not* "Some thing that he loves best kills man." Before converting a proposition of this type, we must, even at the expense of metric and grammatical nicety, substitute for the original copula some form of the verb "to be": "Every (each) man is such that he kills the thing he loves." And this less poetic but logically more tractable form converts to "Someone who is such that he kills the thing he loves is man." (Be careful *not* to place any quantifying particle before the predicate-term. Do not say "Someone who is such that he kills the thing he loves is *every* man.") Similarly, the converse of:

> "Every dog has fleas"

is not:

> "Some fleas have dog"

but rather:

> "Some animal which has fleas is dog"

for the first proposition should be stated in logical form:

> "Every dog is an animal which has fleas"

before we attempt to convert. In converting, we should note that the S of the convertend becomes the P of the converse, so that if our original S is, as above, "dog," "dog" must be our new P. That part of the verb which does more than simply unite, i.e., which is over and above the verb "to be," is part of the original P, and in converting must be carried over to the new S. In the proposition "Every dog has fleas," "having" is part of the predicate-term ("Every dog is *having fleas*), and must, therefore, form part of the subject-term in the converse: "Something *having* fleas is dog" or "Some animal which *has* fleas is dog." Do *not* give as the converse:

> "Some fleas *are had by* dog"

for in thus changing from active to passive *voice*, we alter the original S and P completely, and by transposing part of one and part of the other make a complete hash of the original sense. In converting or otherwise manipulating propositions, changes in voice are to be avoided like the plague.

Singular propositions convert like universals. The converse of:

(A$_s$) "Percy is impudent"

is:

(I) "Some impudent person is Percy."

The converse of:

(E$_s$) "The mayor is not a baboon"

is

(E) "No baboon is the Mayor."

The converse of a singular proposition represents an *unnatural* mode of utterance, because its predicate-term is a singular, and, as we have seen, a singular is not properly in the comprehension of anything, as the propositional form would seem to imply. A singular does not naturally belong to a subject; rather, predicates belong to it. Propositions like "Some impudent person is Percy" (I) and "No baboon is the Mayor" (E) are thus very different from the ordinary I and E propositions, since their predicates are neither taken particularly nor taken universally, but are simply *singular*. Singular propositions, i.e., propositions whose *subject-term* is a singular, on the other hand, have nothing unnatural about them and behave, on the whole, much like universal propositions. They, too, must often be placed in logical form before being converted. Do not convert "I smell a rat" into "Some rat smells me." The latter proposition may be of some historical interest, but is scarcely the equivalent of the former.

The student has probably noticed that where the predicate of a proposition to be converted is an adjective—what the logician calls a "connotative term"—as in "Harry is *tall*" or "Some crow is *white*" or "No circle is *rectilinear*," then some absolute term, standing for a possible *subject* (such as "person," "being," "thing," "animal," "figure") is to be understood along with the predicate-term when converting. Thus, "Harry is tall" is to be understood as "Harry is a tall (being or person)," so that the converse may be stated "Some tall (being or person) is Harry." So, to the proposition "Some crow is white," we give the converse "Some white (bird) is crow" or

"Some white (being) is crow." Some examples may serve as models for this and other rules of conversion which we have discussed.

Convertend	*Converse*
No dog has intelligence.	No being having intelligence is dog.
Every dog has his day.	Some being which has his day is dog.
Some fish is oviparous.	Some oviparous animal is fish.
Curiosity killed the cat.	Something which killed the cat is curiosity.
Every triangle has three sides.	Some figure which has three sides is triangle.
Every man is rational.	Some rational animal is man.
No insult is unintentional.	No unintentional act is an insult.
Some fish is not edible.	*None*
This man is not ambitious.	No ambitious person is this man.
He has inhibitions.	Someone who has inhibitions is he.

Remember that the predicate (unless it is a singular term) is always taken particularly in affirmative propositions and taken universally in negative propositions. It is for this reason that the A proposition has *no simple converse,* and the O proposition *no converse at all.* What looks like the converse of an O or the simple converse of an A proposition may itself be a true proposition, but it is never a converse, and it is always *formally incorrect* to state it as the converse. Transposing S and P without changing quantity or quality in an A or O proposition yields the *formally doubtful reciprocal.* To the rule regarding the accidental conversion of A, and the inconvertibility of O, there are *no* exceptions.

Obversion.　To *obvert* is:

> to state negatively what an original proposition stated affirmatively, or to state affirmatively what an original proposition stated negatively.

In obverting we change the *quality* of a proposition without changing its sense. There is never any change in quantity in obversion, as there is in accidental conversion, so that the obverse is always the exact equivalent of the original. To obvert a proposition we simply *negative its copula and its predicate*. The O proposition:

$$\overset{\text{S}}{\text{Some man}}/\overset{\text{c}}{\text{is not}}/\overset{\text{P}}{\text{honest}}$$

will obvert to:

$$\overset{\text{S}}{\text{Some man}}/\overset{\text{c}}{\text{is}}/\overset{\text{P}}{\text{non-honest}}$$

or

$$\overset{\text{S}}{\text{Some man}}/\overset{\text{c}}{\text{is}}/\overset{\text{P}}{\text{dishonest.}}$$

The I proposition:

"Some man/is/intelligent"

obverts to:

"Some man/is not/ unintelligent."

Notice that in obversion *we do not disturb the subject-term of* the original proposition, the obvertend, and that the quantity of the proposition remains unchanged. If we separate subject-term, copula, and predicate-term, as in the examples given, we can be certain of negating the proper parts, namely, copula and predicate.

In obverting universal propositions (A and E), we must make sure that the obverse is also universal. If we take the A proposition:

"Every acid is corrosive"

we observe that "corrosive" is *affirmed universally* of "acid." To obvert, we must *deny universally* the opposite of "corrosive" ("noncorrosive") of the same subject "acid." Now to deny "noncorrosive" universally of "acid," we must say:

"*No* acid is noncorrosive"

and *not* "Every acid is not noncorrosive," for the latter is a *particular* negative (O), rather than a universal negative (E) proposition. (Recall that when the copula is negative "every" and "all" are signs not of universality but of particularity.) In the same way, an E proposition obverts to an A:

"No fish is mammal"

obverts to:

"Every fish is non-mammal."

Remember that in an E proposition, though the "No" is *written* with the subject, its negative quality is to be understood as applying only to the *copula.* "No" marks the subject-term as *universal,* not as negative.

Before obverting, too, we must be sure a proposition is in logical form. Do not obvert "Haste makes waste" into "Haste does not make non-waste," but first put in logical form:

"Haste/is/such that it makes waste"

and then obvert to:

"Haste/is *not*/such that it does not make waste."

Consider the following examples:

Obvertend	*Obverse*
Every dog is unintelligent.	No dog is intelligent.
No man is impeccable.	Every man is peccable.
Every criminal is not un-trustworthy.	Some criminal is trustworthy.
Some man is tall.	Some man is not non-tall.
No man hates himself.	Every man is such that he does not hate himself.
Every a is b.	No a is non-b.
Everyone has his price.	No one is such that he does not have his price.
Some who do not study are not unintelligent.	Some who do not study are intelligent.
All who are not wretched are insensible of life's misery.	None who are not wretched are sensible of life's misery.
Walter feels sick.	Walter is not such that he does not feel sick (Walter is not feeling well).
Ignorance is not willed.	Ignorance is unwilled.

There is no *accidental* obversion, and no type of categorical proposition which cannot be obverted. A obverts to E, E to A, I to O, and O to I. The order of transference may be symbolized by the vowels of the following mnemonic, and the syllable "ob" may serve to remind the student that it applies to *obversion: ErAs ArE ObvIOus.*

Partial Contraposition. The operation of *partial contraposition* combines obversion and conversion. To obtain the partial contrapositive of a given proposition:

Obvert the original and then convert the obverse.

"Every fish is vertebrate" obverts to "No fish is invertebrate," which converts to "No invertebrate is fish." The partial contrapositive of I cannot be obtained, because I obverts to O, which is inconvertible. Contraposition provides a method of manipulating O propositions, for when we obvert the O to an I proposition, we can then apply simple conversion. A few examples should suffice to make clear this operation:

Contraponend:	Every dog is unintelligent.
Obverse:	No dog is intelligent.
Partial Contrapositive:	No intelligent being is dog.
Contraponend:	No fish is mammal.
Obverse:	Every fish is non-mammal.
Partial Contrapositive:	Some non-mammal is fish.
Contraponend:	Some man is tall.
Obverse:	Some man is not non-tall.
Partial Contrapositive:	*None*
Contraponend:	Some criminal is not depraved.
Obverse:	Some criminal is non-depraved.
Partial Contrapositive:	Some non-depraved person is criminal.
Contraponend:	All anger is not wrong.
Obverse:	Some anger is non-wrong.
Partial Contrapositive:	Some non-wrong thing is anger.
Contraponend:	Every man fears the unknown.
Obverse:	No man is such that he does not fear the unknown.
Partial Contrapositive:	No being such that he does not fear the unknown is man.

Contraponend:	No man has wings.
Obverse:	Every man is such that he does not have wings.
Partial Contrapositive:	Some being which does not have wings is man.
Contraponend:	Some who do not study are not unintelligent.
Obverse:	Some who do not study are intelligent.
Partial Contrapositive:	Some intelligent persons are those who do not study.

In partial contraposition, the quantity of E is reduced, since E obverts to A, which converts to I. The partial contrapositive of a given E proposition and of its subaltern O are the same. Thus the partial contrapositive of "No a is b" and of "Some a is not b" is "Some non-b is a." A *converts accidentally,* and O cannot be converted; E *contraposes accidentally,* and I cannot be contraposed, since, in contraposing, E and I obvert to A and O respectively. (Students who dislike grades of zero in examinations may be said to "hAtE EllIpsOIds," and may remember the order of transference in partial contraposition by the order of the vowels in that phrase.)

Full Contraposition. In the operation of *full contraposition* we go one step further, and *obvert the partial contrapositive:*

Contraponend:	Every animal is mortal.
Obverse:	No animal is non-mortal.
Partial Contrapositive:	No non-mortal is animal.
Full Contrapositive:	Every non-mortal is non-animal.
Contraponend:	No lion is herbivorous.
Obverse:	Every lion is non-herbivorous.
Partial Contrapositive:	Some non-herbivorous animal is lion.
Full Contrapositive:	Some non-herbivorous animal is not non-lion.
Contraponend:	Some lion is not herbivorous.
Obverse:	Some lion is non-herbivorous.
Partial Contrapositive:	Some non-herbivorous animal is lion.
Full Contrapositive:	Some non-herbivorous animal is not non-lion.

For obvious reasons, the I proposition cannot be fully contraposed, and, as indicated in the second and third examples above, the full contrapositive of an E proposition and of its corresponding subaltern O are identical.

In the case of A and O propositions, the operation of full contraposition may be performed *at one stroke.* Simply:

reverse subject and predicate, attach negative particles to each, leaving the quantity and quality of the proposition undisturbed.

Thus:

Contraponend	*Full Contrapositive*
Every animal is mortal.	Every non-mortal is non-animal.
Some truth is not useful.	Some non-useful thing is not non-truth.
Every circle is round.	Every non-round figure is non-circle.
Some men do not lack prudence.	Some who are not lacking in prudence are not non-men.
Every event demands a cause.	Everything which does not demand a cause is a non-event.

In giving the full contrapositive of A and O propositions, remember to leave the copula and the sign of quantity unchanged. (In O propositions, for the sake of avoiding ambiguity, use "some" rather than "all" or "every" to denote particularity.) Also be sure to *reverse* subject and predicate. This is especially important with the A proposition, for if we attach negative particles to the S and P of an A proposition, without interchanging S and P, we obtain not the full contrapositive, but the *formally doubtful inverse,* of the original proposition. Thus the *inverse* of:

"Every man is animal"

is

"Every non-man is non-animal"

and this proposition, unlike the full contrapositive, does not express the same truth as the original proposition. The inverse of a true proposition *may be* true (e.g., "Every animal is sentient" and "Every non-animal is non-sentient"), but it is more often false ("Every man is animal" and "Every non-man is non-animal"). In no case, however, is the inverse of an A proposition the *exact equivalent* of the original, while the full contrapositive of an A proposition always is. The inverse of an A proposition, like the reciprocal, is *formally doubtful* when the original proposition is true, while the full contrapositive is necessarily true. The inverse is, in fact, simply the *reciprocal of the full contrapositive.* Reciprocation and inversion, then, are *formally unprofitable* operations, since they yield a *doubtful* product when applied to a *true* A proposition. Similarly unprofitable operations may be applied to the O proposition:

"Some a is not b" (true) → "Some b is not a," "Some non-a is not non-b" (doubtful)

but it is usual to reserve the terms "reciprocal" and "inverse" for the characteristic derivatives of *A* propositions which we have just described.

Eduction of Propositional Relations. By combining the theory of *opposition* with the principles governing *conversion, obversion, contraposition, reciprocation,* and *inversion,* we can draw up some interesting exercises in the logic of propositional relations. The operations of *opposition, conversion, contraposition,* etc. are generically known as *eduction.* Given an original A proposition ("Every x is y") as true, for example, we can determine by eduction the *truth, falsity,* or *formally doubtful* character of all the possible combinations of "x" and "non-x," "y" and "non-y" as S and P, in all of the four types of categorical proposition, A, E, I, and O. Let us suppose as true the A proposition:

"Every a is b."

We can thereupon see immediately that the following propositions are also necessarily *true:*

Subaltern:	Some a is b.
Converse:	Some b is a.
Obverse:	No a is non-b.
Partial Contrapositive:	No non-b is a.
Full Contrapositive:	Every non-b is non-a.

Given as true that "Every a is b," we can also by the same token see that the following propositions are necessarily *false:*

Contrary:	No a is b.
Contradictory:	Some a is not b.

Lastly, from the truth of "Every a is b," we can be sure neither of the truth nor falsity of the following propositions, and must classify them as *formally doubtful,* or *indeterminate:*

    Reciprocal: Every b is a.
    Inverse: Every non-a is non-b.

There remain 22 other possible combinations of "a" and "non-a," "b" and "non-b" in the A, E, I, O forms, whose truth, falsity, or doubtfulness is not so manifest. Given as true that "Every a is b," what shall we say of the following:

        No b is a.
        No non-b is non-a.
        Some a is non-b.
        Some non-a is not non-b?

Are they true, false, or doubtful, and how can we determine this with certainty? If we draw up a square of opposition about the original proposition, "Every a is b," and about its *full contrapositive,* "Every non-b is non-a," we can usually determine rather simply the status of any of the 22 additional eductions of the original proposition. Thus:

Every a is b (True).   CONTRARIES   No a is b (False).

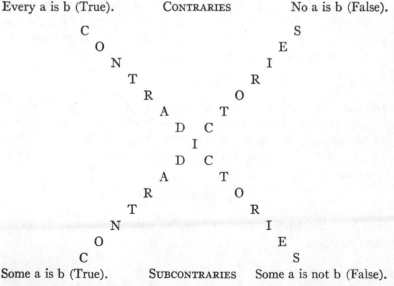

Some a is b (True).   SUBCONTRARIES   Some a is not b (False).

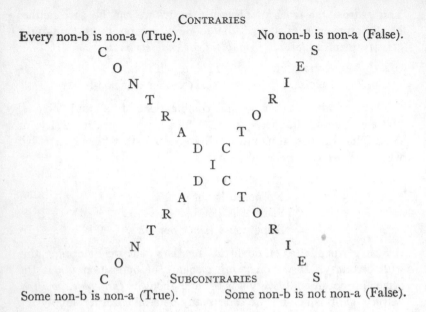

Contraries

Every non-b is non-a (True).   No non-b is non-a (False).

Subcontraries

Some non-b is non-a (True).   Some non-b is not non-a (False).

Given, then, a proposition like "No b is a" or "Some non-a is not b," we need only manipulate this proposition by *obversion* and *simple conversion* until it has the same S and P either as the original or its full contrapositive. By then adverting to the two squares of opposition we have drawn up, we can immediately tell whether this proposition is *true* or *false*. For example, the proposition:

"No b is a"

will have the same S and P as the original if we *convert it simply*. "No b is a" converts to "No a is b," and "No a is b" is the *contrary* of the original, and therefore false. "No b is a," then, is also false because it is the *simple converse of the contrary of the original proposition*. The proposition:

"No non-a is non-b"

will have the same S and P as the *full contrapositive* if we simply convert it to:

"No non-b is non-a."

This proposition, in turn, is seen as the *contrary of the full contra-positive,* and false. Therefore,

"No non-a is non-b"

would be classified as "false: simple converse of contrary of full contrapositive of original." Let us consider one more example:

"Some non-a is not b."

Obverse:	Some non-a is non-b.
Simple Converse:	Some non-b is non-a.

From our square of opposition, this last proposition is seen as: "true, subaltern of full contrapositive of original," so our first proposition would be classified as "true: obverse of simple converse of subaltern of full contrapositive of original." Notice that it is *not* necessary to remember the operations performed to render the given proposition comparable with the original. Simply mark each operation as performed, and then *read them back in the same order.* Thus, given to judge:

"Every non-a is b"

we mark each operation performed as follows:

Every non-a is b

Obverse:	No non-a is non-b
Simple Converse:	No non-b is non-a (*Contrary of full contrapositive, false*)

and read back the designations: *obverse of simple converse of contrary of full contrapositive, false.* This then constitutes a complete and accurate statement of the eductive relation of "Every non-a is b" to the original "Every a is b," given as true.

If the status of a given proposition cannot be determined by comparison with the original or its full contrapositive, then it *must be a derivative of the reciprocal or the inverse,* and, therefore, *doubtful.* Of the 31 possible variations on the A form, "Every a is b," there are, in addition to the reciprocal and the inverse, six others (see p. 130) which are always formally doubtful.

Obverse of Reciprocal:	No b is non-a.
Obverse of Inverse:	No non-a is b.
Contradictory of Reciprocal:	Some b is not a.
Contradictory of Inverse:	Some non-a is not non-b.
Obverse of Contradictory of Reciprocal:	Some b is non-a.
Obverse of Contradictory of Inverse:	Some non-a is b.

Together with the reciprocal ("Every b is a") and the inverse ("Every non-a is non-b"), these are the eight forms which are formally doubtful, given an original A proposition as true. In general, one should not compare a given proposition with the *reciprocal* or *inverse* of the original proposition, unless it cannot be compared with the original itself or with its full contrapositive. Thus, given as true that "Every a is b," the proposition "No b is a" must be false, and this latter proposition is the *contrary of the reciprocal.* It is not false, however, *because* it is the contrary of the reciprocal, but because it is the *simple converse* of the *contrary* of the original. In the same way, "Some b is a" is true, not because it is the subaltern of the reciprocal, but because it is the accidental converse of the original, and "Some non-a is non-b" is true by reason of its relation to the full contrapositive, rather than by reason of its being the subaltern of the inverse. To label a proposition as "formally doubtful" implies that there is no way of demonstrating that it is necessarily true or necessarily false, and we cannot know this until we have compared the proposition in question with the original or its full contrapositive.

One of the chief values of performing these exercises in eduction is that it will provide a convenient review of most of the functional properties of categorical propositions which we have studied in this chapter. Even Euler's circles may be employed, if not to demonstrate the necessity of the relationships involved in eduction, at least to check results. Thus the proposition "Every a is b" may symbolize a material relationship like "Every man is animal" (*generic predicate*), or one like "Every man is rational animal" (*specific predicate*), and these two possible types of reference may be illustrated by the two sets of circles on the opposite page.

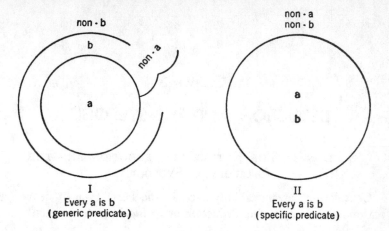

I
Every a is b
(generic predicate)

II
Every a is b
(specific predicate)

"Every a is b" may stand for a material relationship where "a" and "b" are perfectly coincident, and thereby also "non-a" and "non-b." This is symbolized in II above. Or "a" may be included within "b" so as to be partially coincident with it, so that thereby "non-a" is partially coincident with "b," and partially coincident with "non-b," as illustrated in I. Since the predicate of a true A proposition must be either generically true of the subject, or specifically true of it, these two sets of circles illustrate all the possible meanings of a given A proposition. A given eduction may then be judged as true, false, or doubtful as follows:

> *True,* if true in both I and II;
> *False,* if not true in either I or II;
> *Doubtful,* if true in one and not true in the other.

Euler's circles, of course, do not enable us to state *why* a given eduction is true, false, or doubtful, and can therefore be properly used only to verify conclusions arrived at by other methods. The student who can successfully complete the exercises in this section by applying what he has learned concerning *opposition, conversion, obversion,* and the like, has a good grasp of the logic of categorical propositions, and is ready to begin the analysis of categorical deductive inference, which is our next topic.

Chapter 3

DEDUCTION AND THE SYLLOGISM

Considering categorical inference as the basic type of deductive reasoning, we may define deduction or *deductive inference* as:

> *an act of the mind in which, from the relation of two terms to a third term, we infer* (i.e., understand and affirm) *their relation to each other.*

The relation in question is always one of *identity* or *non-identity*, and the inference, correspondingly, either affirmative or negative.

In deduction, two judgments (which between them have a common term) are so related that a third judgment necessarily follows from them. The three terms involved, and the three judgments which bind those terms together, are expressed in three propositions. When these propositions are arranged in suitable order we have a *categorical syllogism.*

> Every contingent being requires a cause,
> But every material thing is contingent,
> Therefore, every material thing requires a cause.

Matter of Deductive Reasoning. The two propositions which are supposed to imply the third are together called the *antecedent* or *premises,* while the single proposition which they are said to imply is called the *consequent* or *conclusion.* Recalling that these three propositions contain only three terms, we may say that the *matter* of the act of deductive reasoning and of its verbal expression, the syllogism, is the same:

> *three terms arranged in three propositions.*

132

The act of the mind *bears on* and *assents to* these three propositions —they are, so to speak, the field of the mind's movement—while the syllogism *expresses verbally* this mental act of *moving assent* (or *assenting movement*) in the same three propositions. (Recall the distinction between the *enunciative* and the *judicative* proposition, above, p. 39 ff.) The three *terms* are called the *remote matter,* while the three *propositions* are called the *proximate matter.* In reasoning, the mind first constructs two enunciative propositions to which it assents, and in its *second* assent it sees that the assent to a *third* proposition is demanded. In the same moment, it constructs this third proposition, and moves on to assent to it. This final act is the act of *mediate judgment* (judgment arrived at *by means of* other judgments) or reasoning.

Form of Deductive Reasoning.   The *form* or *specifying principle* of deductive reasoning is:

> *the connection between the antecedent and the consequent.*

It is this connection which the mind, in affirming the antecedent, sees, and which *compels* the movement whereby it affirms the consequent also. This connection which makes us *advance* from truths previously known to truths previously unknown is called:

> the *sequence* or *consequence.*

Do not confuse the *sequence* or *consequence*—which is the vital connection between antecedent and consequent—with the *consequent* itself.

The form, or specifying principle, of the *syllogism* is the *arrangement* of the propositions so as to make evident the sequence. The three propositions must be so arranged that the connection between premises and conclusion stands out. In the syllogism:

> No immediate judgment is an inference
> But conversion is an immediate judgment
> Therefore, conversion is not an inference

it is the words "but" and "therefore" which come closest to conveying the mind's apprehension of the sequence. I say "but" because I am thinking my second proposition (the *minor premise*) in vital relation to my first proposition (the *major premise*); and because that vital union of the two premises *produces* a new truth, or *causes* a new truth to be evident to me, I say "therefore," and state my conclusion. It is the intangible movement of the mind in perceiving a sequence, and the necessity thereby of affirming a consequent, that the words "but" and "therefore" indicate. It is only when thinking a second proposition *under* a first, and perceiving that this second proposition, when thought under the first, *implies necessarily* the truth of a third proposition, that we may be said to reason deductively.

To summarize what we have said concerning the *matter* and *form* of deduction and the syllogism, we may propose the following scheme:

Act	*Matter*	*Form*
Mental:	Remote:	The sequence
Deduction	Three terms	
	Proximate:	
	Three propositions	
Verbal:	Remote:	Proper arrangement of
Syllogism	Three terms	terms and propositions
	Proximate:	
	Three propositions	

From this point on, we shall speak almost exclusively of the *syllogism*, but it is well to remember that we are interested in the verbal expression of reasoning and the terms and propositions which are part of it only to the extent that they reveal a *vital and immanent act of thinking*. When, for example, we point to a fallacy in the use of a certain term in a syllogism, it is not because we are preoccupied with the language as such and for itself, but because, since words are the counters of thought, the misuse of a term indicates a shoddy piece of reasoning. From what we have said of the *form* of the syllogism, it should be evident that the business of the terms and propositions in a syllogism is to make clear a *valid inference*. Now a valid inference is revealed when the propositions are set forth so that we see:

the antecedent cannot be true without making the consequent also true.

The fallacious use of a term indicates invariably an *invalid sequence,* that is to say, *no* sequence. The antecedent does not truly imply the consequent, *it only seems to.* The fallacious syllogism stands for a *pseudo-sequence,* for something that passes for an act of reasoning but really is not. Terms are of interest to the logician, in short, only insofar as they are the *signs* of thinking—or of its absence.

Terms of the Syllogism.   In reasoning we naturally begin with premises and arrive at a conclusion, but in analyzing reasoning we reverse the process, and begin with the conclusion, for it is in the conclusion that we should first seek to identify the *terms* of the syllogism. The *predicate of the conclusion* is called the major term, signified by the letter "P." The *subject of the* conclusion is called the *minor term,* designated by the letter "S." The predicate of the conclusion is called the "major" term because a predicate is ordinarily of *greater* extension than its subject (which, being of *lesser* extension, is called the "minor"). The third term, which occurs only in the premises and is the *medium of comparison* between the major and minor terms, is called the "middle term," or simply the "middle." It is customarily designated by the letter "M."

The *major premise* is the premise which contains the major term. It should be written first, but it is not the fact that it is written first that earns for it the title of "major premise." It is called the *major* premise because it unites the middle term with the "greater" term, i.e., the term which is to be the *predicate of the conclusion.* Similarly, the *minor premise* contains the minor term, and it states the relation of this "lesser" term (the subject of the conclusion-to-be) to the middle term.

The first step in the analysis of a categorical syllogism is to identify these three terms, and to label each with the appropriate letter. The syllogism:

> Every man is mortal
> John is man
> Therefore, John is mortal.

should serve as a valuable example, since it is the only thing which many students remember from their logic course. If we designate each of its terms in the fashion demanded by the preceding definitions, the syllogism will be decked out as follows:

$$\overset{M}{\text{Every man}} \text{ is } \overset{P}{\text{mortal}}$$

$$\overset{S}{\text{John}} \text{ is } \overset{M}{\text{man}}$$

$$\text{Therefore, } \overset{S}{\text{John}} \text{ is } \overset{P}{\text{mortal}}$$

Principles of the Syllogism. Every categorical syllogism states the identity or non-identity of two terms (S and P), because of their identity or non-identity with a third term (M). This process, which is analogous to, and indeed the matrix of, the mathematical substitution of equals for equals, is grounded upon four self-evident logical axioms, immediate derivatives of the metaphysical principles of identity and contradiction:

1. *The Principle of Reciprocal Identity:* Two terms identical with a third term are identical with each other. (Notice that we say "identical" rather than "equal," since "equal" applies only to *quantities*, with which mathematics deals.)

2. *The Principle of Reciprocal Non-Identity:* Two terms, one of which is identical with a third term and the other of which is non-identical with that third term, are non-identical with each other. (Notice that if two terms are *both non-identical* with a third term, we can say nothing of their identity or non-identity with each other.)

3. *The Dictum de Omni:* What is affirmed universally of a certain term,[1] is affirmed of every term that comes under that term. (Thus, if "risible" is affirmed universally of "man," it can be affirmed of everything that comes under "man": Peter, John, Michael, *et al.*)

4. *The Dictum de Nullo:* What is denied universally of a certain term is denied of every term that comes under that term. (If "quadruped" is denied universally of "bird," it is denied of "robin," "bluebird," "ostrich," "teal," and of each and every thing that comes under "bird.")

---

[1] Recall that a *term* stands for a *concept*, and a concept for a *nature*. What is true of the *nature* "man," universally and as such, will certainly be true of everything which has that nature.

It is, as we shall see, because the *Dictum de Omni* and the *Dictum de Nullo* are verifiable directly only in syllogisms of the *first figure,* that the first figure is said to be the most evident and perfect. In the first figure the major term, P, is affirmed or denied universally of the middle term, M; and the minor term, S, is stated to come under the middle. It is perfectly evident, then, in terms of these principles that P is to be affirmed or denied of S, according as P was affirmed universally or denied universally of M.

Section 2: The Rules of the Categorical Syllogism

We call *categorical* a syllogism whose premises and conclusion are all categorical propositions. For the categorical syllogism the logicians have formulated *eight* rules, but these may be considered most conveniently under the following *three* general headings:

A. *Terminological Rules.* These follow immediately from the definition of the categorical syllogism as the verbal expression of an inference concerning the identity or non-identity of two terms by reason of their relation to a third term.

B. *Rules Respecting the Quantity of Terms.* These also follow from the definition of the categorical syllogism, but not so immediately. They may be said to follow from the definition, considering the *quantitative properties* of the terms involved.

C. *Rules Regarding Quality.* These rules govern the affirmative or negative character of the propositions involved in the syllogism, particularly the conclusion. They follow immediately from the Principles of Reciprocal Identity and Reciprocal Non-Identity.

RULE 1 (*Terminological*): *There must be three and only three terms.* By definition, as we have seen, the categorical syllogism asserts the identity or non-identity of two terms on the basis of their relation to a third term. This calls for three and only three terms. A third term serves as a medium of comparison between two other terms. A fourth term would be not only superfluous (a "fifth wheel," we might say), but actually destructive of this comparison. If I take the four terms "cow," "cloven-footed," "ruminant," "multi-stomached," I may construct a syllogism out of any three of them, and I may construct two syllogisms out of the four; but I cannot use all four in one syllogism and still make sense. I may say:

> Every ruminant is cloven-footed
> Every cow is ruminant
> ∴. Every cow is cloven-footed

> or

> Every multi-stomached animal is cloven-footed
> Every ruminant is multi-stomached
> ∴. Every ruminant is cloven-footed

but if I say:

> Every ruminant is cloven-footed
> Every cow is multi-stomached

I can obviously draw *no* conclusion. When an argument has more than three terms, we call it a *logical quadruped*. Since such an argument has in effect *two* middle terms, it *lacks* any basis of comparison for its minor and major terms, so that it is impossible to draw a legitimate conclusion.

Formal violations of the rule against more than three terms are rare and easy to detect, but if we reflect that the *subtlest change in meaning* of any term used in a syllogism makes that syllogism a logical quadruped, we shall realize that certain *material* violations of this first and most important rule of the syllogism are neither infrequent nor easily detectable. Take the following example:

> Psychology is a science.
> Every good salesman uses psychology.
> ∴. Every good salesman uses science.

It just happens that the "psychology" which has some claim to be regarded as a science is not the "psychology" that salesmen employ to make their clients buy things they do not really need, so that this syllogism is really a logical quadruped. That arguments of this sort are common enough is no news to anyone who reads the daily papers. At the top of the next page is an excerpt from a nationally syndicated "psychology" column of a few days ago.

Are dictators good psychologists? Yes, they have to be. First they must find out what people want and then fool them into thinking they are getting it. When the people begin to get wise, the dictators fool them again with the notion that somebody is going to attack them and destroy their "liberties"!

One wonders whether the conception of a psychologist as "one adept at fooling other people" prevailed when the author of this "double-talk" received his degree in the subject.

A change in the *supposition* of a term can produce a logical quadruped, just as can a change in meaning. To some it might seem hard to see why this syllogism is valid:

> Man is animal
> Peter is man
> ∴ Peter is animal

while this syllogism is invalid:

> Man is the most perfect animal
> Peter is man
> ∴ Peter is the most perfect animal

In the first syllogism "man" has *real supposition throughout,* but in the second syllogism "man" has *logical supposition* in the major premise and *real supposition* in the minor, so that in this syllogism "man" is in effect *two* terms and not one. "Man" *taken as a whole* (as a universal unity, existing as such only in the mind) is the most perfect animal, but it is false, and indeed self-contradictory, to say that each individual man is the most perfect animal. The middle term in the major premise is in *logical* supposition, and has no necessary community with the same term (in *real* supposition) in the minor premise, so that no conclusion follows.

Here again, very obvious shifts in the supposition of a term are unlikely to escape detection, but even profound thinkers have been deceived by arguments involving very subtle changes in supposition. The "ontological argument," which purported to prove the actual existence of God from the concept of "perfect being," was accepted as valid by dozens of eminent thinkers between the 11th and 18th centuries, though St. Thomas in the 13th century (and many thinkers in later centuries) have pointed to a shift in supposition (*logical* to *real*) from major premise to conclusion of this argument:

> The perfect being *exists necessarily*
> God is perfect being
> ∴ God *exists necessarily*.

Similarly today, physicists are wont to talk about "space-time co-ordinates" and "multidimensional spaces" as though these were *real* entities instead of mathematical constructs (having only *logical* supposition), while chemists, psychoanalysts, and statisticians are also prone to confuse *their logical modes of viewing the real* with the characteristics of the real in itself. In many instances, the unmasking of these fallacies requires a technical knowledge of the material involved, quite beyond the beginning student. We can all, however, become more sensitive to the likelihood of this kind of fallacy and demand that the use of terms in real supposition be justified by evidence-producing statements in which these terms are also used in real supposition. In our own nontechnical reasonings, we can also make sure that we do not use terms *equivocally* (by defining our terms carefully and adhering to these definitions); and we can avoid employing arguments in which there is any possibility of a shift in supposition. With these precautions, the toll which the fallacy of the logical quadruped takes of our thinking should be reduced.

Rule 2 (*Terminological*): *The middle term must not occur in the conclusion.* This also follows simply from the definition of the categorical syllogism. Since the middle term is the *means,* or *medium,* of comparison between minor and major terms (by definition, the S and P of the conclusion), it has no place in the conclusion. If ⁋ affirm:

> Every mammal is warm-blooded
> Every bat is mammal

I cannot conclude anything concerning "mammal," but only concerning "bat" or "warm-blooded": "Every bat is warm-blooded" or (reversing my premises) "Some warm-blooded animal is bat." An argument such as the following:

> Every man is animal
> Every man is material
> ∴ Every man is a material animal

is not really a syllogism, because there is no *advance* in knowledge from premises to conclusion. The conclusion is simply a *summation* of what the premises had already stated, marking no movement of the mind to truth previously unknown, and indicating *no inference.*

RULE 3 (*Quantitative*): *No term may have a greater distribution or extension in the conclusion than it had in the premises.* Obviously, if we have not judged concerning the whole extension of a term in the premises, we have no right to conclude anything concerning the whole extension of that term in the conclusion. From a comparison concerning only a *part* of something we cannot legitimately infer anything respecting the *whole* of that thing. In the following example, the fallacy is quite patent:

> Every bird has wings
> *Some* animal is bird
> ∴ *Every* animal has wings.

It is seldom that the *distribution fallacy* is as palpable as this, but in any case, if we mark each term in the syllogism as *particular,* "p," or universal, "u," we shall be able to determine at a glance whether any term which is taken particularly in the premises is taken universally in the conclusion. In this case, having marked the distribution of each term:

> Mu   Pp
> Every bird has wings
> Sp   Mp
> Some animal is bird
> Su   Pp
> ∴ Every animal has wings

we see that the *minor term* ("animal") is broader in the conclusion than in the minor premise. The syllogism is then declared *"invalid, illicit minor."* A somewhat more plausible instance of an illicit minor term would be:

> Mu   Pp
> Every man is animal
> Mu   Sp
> Every man is organism
> Su   Pp
> ∴ Every organism is animal.

In this case the minor term ("organism") is *taken particularly* in the premise, because it is there the *predicate of an affirmative proposition*. It is therefore quite illegitimate to take it universally in the conclusion.

When the *predicate of the conclusion* has a greater extension than it had in the major premise, we have the fallacy of the *illicit major term*. The *illicit major* is often a more subtle fallacy than the illicit minor, as the following example should show:

$$\text{Every Nazi is a racist} \quad \overset{\text{Mu}}{} \quad \overset{\text{Pp}}{}$$

Mu   Pp
Every Nazi is a racist

Su   Mu
No loyal American is a Nazi

Su   Pu
∴ No loyal American is a racist.

In the antecedent the major term is the predicate of an affirmative proposition and, as such, is taken *particularly,* but in the conclusion the major term is the predicate of a negative proposition and, therefore, is taken *universally.* In this example, the fallacy is further hidden by the fact that the two premises and the conclusion of the syllogism are undoubtedly *true.* But the argument is formally *invalid* no matter how true the conclusion, and how true the premises; the conclusion *does not follow* from these premises. There is *no sequence.* Consideration of the following example may verify the fact that this *form* is intrinsically invalid:

Mu   Pp
Every dog is animal

Su   Mu
No pig is dog

Su   Pu
∴ No pig is animal

although the premises are true, the conclusion is certainly false, and a false conclusion can never *logically* be inferred from true premises. Wherever the premises are true and the conclusion false, we can be sure of a *formally invalid* syllogism.

In the illicit minor or major, the *excess* of extension which the subject or predicate of the conclusion has over its distribution in the premises constitutes, in effect, a fourth term. (Where the premise says "some" and the conclusion "all," the difference between the "some" and the "all" is like an extra term which destroys the community necessary for comparison.) Thus the rule that no term may have a greater extension in the conclusion than it had in the premises follows from the very definition of the syllogism, *considering the quantity of the terms involved,* and is, in fact, a particular instance of the rule requiring three and only three terms.

RULE 4 (*Quantitative*): *The middle term must be taken universally* (distributed) *at least once.* The violation of this rule is called the fallacy of the *undistributed middle.* Consider the following argument:

$$\overset{\text{Pu}}{\text{Every pig}} \text{ is } \overset{\text{Mp}}{\text{animal}}$$
$$\overset{\text{Su}}{\text{Every man}} \text{ is } \overset{\text{Mp}}{\text{animal}}$$
$$\therefore \overset{\text{Su}}{\text{Every man}} \text{ is } \overset{\text{Pp}}{\text{pig.}}$$

No term is broader in the conclusion than in the premises, there are apparently only three terms; yet the true premises and the false conclusion indicate a patently invalid syllogism. What is the source of the fallacy?

It is in the fact that the middle term, as twice the predicate of an affirmative proposition, *is twice taken particularly,* and there is therefore no common term of comparison between the major and minor terms. "Every pig" is identified with *some* part of the extension of "animal," and "every man" is identified with *some* part of the extension of "animal," but there is no guarantee that the two parts coincide, or are the *same.* There is therefore no necessarily common medium of comparison upon which to base the identity of minor and major. Since the two parts of the extension of the middle term may be *different,* here again we have, in effect, *four terms.* The "undistributed middle," like the "illicit minor" and the "illicit major," is a kind of "logical quadruped."

By reason of the *matter* or *content* of the syllogism, it may happen that the two parts of an undistributed middle do coincide. But this is only accidentally so, and in no case does it warrant a conclusion. For example, in:

> Every rectangle is a polygon
> Every square is a polygon
> ∴ Every square is a rectangle

the premises and conclusion happen to be true, but the true proposition "Every square is a rectangle" does not follow from the fact that both "square" and "rectangle" are "polygon." Hence the syllogism is incorrect, or formally invalid.

Notice that it is not necessary for the middle term to be *twice* distributed, and it is rare that it is. Once is enough. If P, for example, applies to the *whole* extension of M, it will apply to any S which comes under *part* of that extension. Thus if "mortal" applies to *"every* animal," and "man" applies to *"Some* animal," then "mortal" applies to "man." So much is evident from the *Dictum de Omni*. The following syllogism is consequently perfectly valid:

$$\text{Every animal is mortal}^{\text{Mu}}$$

$$\text{Every man is animal}^{\text{Mp}}$$

∴ Every man is mortal.

From the standpoint of quantity, we might say that since "animal" is included in "mortal," and "man" in "animal," "man" must be included in "mortal." The quantitative relationships involved may be illustrated by Euler's circles:

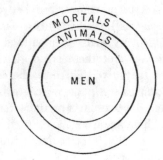

We should remember, however, that reasoning is not a process of putting little circles in bigger circles, but an intangible intellectual movement of inference from a universal nature to the things coming under that nature. The universality of the middle term which every good syllogism demands is not a universality of enumeration nor a universality of physical inclusion. It is therefore only very imperfectly represented by spatial diagrams. The "every animal" in the syllogism above does not represent an actual count; it stands for the nature "animal," which as such receives the predicate "mortal"; and we can reason therefore that anything which shares that nature may receive the predicate which applies to that nature as such and in its universality.

Since it is impossible adequately to represent "meanings" in diagrams, it is not remarkable that many who have considered syllogisms exclusively from the standpoint of quantitative inclusion have concluded that the syllogism is "meaningless." In the ideal syllogism in BARBARA (of which the example just given is an instance), it is because the major term pertains to the *meaning* of the middle, and the middle to the *meaning* of the minor, that we can know that the major pertains to the *meaning* of the minor; just as truly as it is because the middle "comes under" the major, and the minor "comes under" the middle, that we know the minor "comes under" the major. If we recall that an affirmative categorical proposition not only puts its subject in the extension of its predicate, but *more primarily* puts its predicate in the comprehension (meaning) of its subject, we shall be less likely to fall prey to the simplifications and superficialities which are entailed in the consideration of categorical syllogisms exclusively from the viewpoint of extension. The viewpoint of extension is legitimate, but it is only a partial viewpoint. Equally important, for the proper understanding of the process of deductive reasoning, is the viewpoint of comprehension.

RULE 5 (*Qualitative*): *Two negative premises yield no conclusion.* If both major and minor terms are non-identical with the middle we know nothing about their identity or non-identity with each other. Two terms, both different from a third, *may* be the same as each other, but they may not. Therefore, no inference is possible from two negative propositions.

RULE 6 (*Qualitative*): *Two affirmative premises yield an affirmative conclusion.* This is simply an immediate application of the principle of reciprocal identity. If two terms are identical with a third, they must be identical with each other.

RULE 7 (*Qualitative*): *If one premise is negative, the conclusion must be negative.* This is evident from the principle of reciprocal non-identity. If one term (say the minor) is identical with a third term (the middle), and another term (the major) is non-identical with that same third term, then the two terms (major and minor) are non-identical with each other.

RULE 8 (*Quantitative*): *If one premise is particular, the conclusion is particular; if both premises are particular, there is no conclusion.* This is not an independent rule, but a corollary of Rules 3 and 4, respecting the quantity of the three terms employed in the syllogism. Its chief interest lies in the fact that to prove this rule from Rules 3 and 4, we must make use of the method of *complete induction*,[2] a technique which we have not otherwise exemplified in this course.

To demonstrate the first part of this rule, that if one premise is particular, the conclusion is particular, we consider all the possible combinations of categorical premises of which one is particular. These amount to three:

a) A and I   b) E and I   c) A and O

(The combination of E and O is impossible, since two negative premises yield no conclusion.) To show that the conclusion in each of these cases must be particular we have only to show that the *minor term* (the subject of the conclusion) is taken particularly, since a particular proposition is, by definition, one whose subject is a particular term.

Let us consider the first possibility, the syllogism with A and I for premises: Can the minor term (and thereby the conclusion) be universal? No, for with one premise an I proposition and one premise an A, we have *all together* only *one* universal term, the subject of A; and if this one universal term were the minor term, the middle term would be *twice undistributed*, and the syllogism would be invalid. If a syllogism with A and I for premises is to be valid, its one universal term must be the middle; its minor term must be taken particularly, and its conclusion must be particular.

In the second instance, with E and I for premises, on the other hand, we have *two* distributed terms (since both the S and P of an E proposition are taken universally). We know that one of these distributed terms must be the *middle*. Can the other distributed

---

[2] In *complete induction*, we divide a given nature into all its possible subtypes, and show that a given characteristic is true of each of these subtypes. It follows that the characteristic in question is true of the nature as such.

term be the *minor?* No, for since one of the premises in the EI sequence is negative, the conclusion must be negative; and if the conclusion is negative, the *major term* (the predicate of the conclusion) must be distributed. Of the two universal terms in the combination of E and I, therefore, one must be the *middle,* and the other must be the *major.* The minor term cannot be universal, so the conclusion must be particular.

Exactly the same holds for our third possibility, in which we have a combination of A and O for premises. Of the *two* distributed terms in this combination, one must be the middle, and the other (since one premise is negative and the conclusion, therefore, negative) must be the major. The minor term, and thus the conclusion, must be particular.

We have shown, then, that in every possible case where one premise is particular, the conclusion must also be particular if the syllogism is to be valid. If one premise is particular and the conclusion universal, you may be sure of an illicit major or minor, or an undistributed middle. In such cases, it is preferable to specify the exact fallacy, e.g., "illicit major," "undistributed middle," or "illicit minor," rather than to say "This is a violation of Rule 8," for this rule is itself neither specific nor primary.

The second part of Rule 8, that *no* conclusion follows if *both* premises are particular, is also proved by complete induction. The possible combinations are *two:*

> a) I and I   and   b) I and O

(Two O propositions as premises, being negatives, would yield no conclusion.)

In an I and I combination (or, as we usually say, an I I *sequence*), *no* term is distributed, so we are certain to have the fallacy of the undistributed middle.

In an I O or O I sequence, *one* term is distributed, the predicate of O. But a syllogism whose conclusion is *negative*—as the conclusion of I O or O I must be—has to have at least *two* distributed terms: one for the middle, and one for the predicate of the negative conclusion, the major. Any combination of I and O for premises, therefore, would have to have *either* an "illicit major" or an "undistributed middle."

Of the rules, the *quantitative* (3 and 4) are most likely to be *formally* violated, so that the *illicit minor,* the *illicit major,* and the *undistributed middle* are the commonest formal fallacies. Of these, the *illicit major* is ordinarily the most plausible. (Wherever the conclusion is *negative,* check to make sure that the major term is distributed in the premise.) The rule requiring three terms is certainly the most fundamental, since the *quantitative* rules are reducible to it, and the commonest of all fallacies—equivocation—is simply a material violation of it. The best way to master the rules, once the principles involved are understood, is so to familiarize yourself with examples of their violations that you can recognize them at sight. Again, the advisability of *overlearning fundamentals* should be stressed, for it is only when the more obvious examples have been mastered that we can understand more complex and important material. Careful attention to the *sense* of the syllogism, as a whole, usually reveals a logical quadruped or a violation of the qualitative rules, if such is present; careful marking of each term in the syllogism as "universal" or "particular" exposes any violation of the quantitative rules.

SECTION 3: ABBREVIATED CATEGORICAL SYLLOGISMS

In ordinary speech and argument, we do not for the most part express our deductions in formal fashion. Instead of arguing:

> Every human being is possessed of connatural rights
> The Communist is a human being
> ∴. The Communist is possessed of connatural rights

we should be more likely to say something like this:

> "You can't deny the Communist his natural rights. After all, he's a human being."

The three terms required for a syllogistic argument are present in this latter statement, and the movement of the mind is substantially identical with that indicated by the previous formal statement, but the argument has been *compressed,* as well as colloquialized. Such abbreviated syllogisms are usually referred to as *enthymemes,* and the usual method of abbreviation is to omit one of the premises. If the *major premise* is omitted, the enthymeme is said to be of the *first order.* This is the case of the example cited, where the major premise: "Every human being has natural rights" (or some equivalent) is understood, though unexpressed.

A statement like:

> "Since no great thing is easy, truth is not easy"

represents an enthymeme of the *second order,* since it is equivalent to the syllogism:

> No great thing is easy
> Truth is a great thing
> ∴ Truth is not easy

minus the *minor premise.*

Both of the enthymemes we have cited are *causal propositions,* the most common form for expressing enthymemes. The causal proposition, we recall, may employ as copula "hence" or "so" or "thus," as well as "because" or "since," so that these forms too may be used to express enthymemes of the first or second order, as in:

> "The Communist is a human being; *so* he must have natural rights"

and

> "No great thing is easy; *hence* truth isn't easy."

The essential *equivalence* of the various forms of *causal* propositions should be evident from the examples given. A "since" or "because" or "for" preceding a *premise* has exactly the same denotation as a "so" or "hence" preceding a *conclusion,* namely, that both statements are true, and one follows necessarily from the other (cf. above, p. 82). Whether I say:

> "Injustice is harmful to the individual, *for* everything that harms society is harmful to the individual"

or:

> "Everything that harms society is harmful to the individual; *hence* injustice must be harmful to the individual"

the argument in either case is a second order enthymeme, or abbreviated statement of the following categorical syllogism:

Everything that harms society is harmful to the individual
Injustice harms society (*omitted premise*)
∴ Injustice is harmful to the individual.

It is quite possible for an enthymeme to be the vehicle of a fallacious or invalid argument, and one may sense the invalidity of a given enthymeme almost immediately. It is nevertheless best to express a given enthymeme in formal syllogistic fashion, before making any attempt to determine the precise nature of the fallacy. Probably the most common type of enthymeme is the *first order* (major premise omitted), *where the omitted premise is an A proposition;* and this commonest type is the most difficult in which to specify any fallacy that may occur in its construction.

When we wish to express in proper syllogistic form an enthymeme to be adjudged valid or invalid, our first step is to determine the conclusion; for this enables us to identify two of our three syllogistic terms, and also to tell whether the premise given is the major or minor. In the enthymeme:

"Astrology is a profound philosophical system, since it is difficult to understand"

the conclusion is:

$$\overset{S}{\text{"Astrology is a profound}} \overset{P}{\text{philosophical system."}}$$

Knowing thereby that "astrology" is the minor term (S), we know that the premise given:

$$\overset{S}{\text{"It (astrology) is difficult}} \overset{M}{\text{to understand"}}$$

is the minor premise, and that the middle term (M) is "difficult to understand." Since the minor and conclusion are indefinite affirmative propositions (A_i), the missing major must be an A proposition, combining the two terms "profound philosophical system" (P) and "difficult to understand" (M). Now this major premise may take either of two possible forms:

1. "Every profound philosophical system is difficult to understand" (Every P is M)

or

2. "Everything difficult to understand is a profound philosophical system" (Every M is P).

Our enthymeme, therefore, might be the abbreviation of either of two syllogisms:

a) Every profound philosophical system is difficult to understand

Astrology is difficult to understand

∴ Astrology is a profound philosophical system

or

b) Everything difficult to understand is a profound philosophical system

Astrology is difficult to understand

∴ Astrology is a profound philosophical system.

If we take form 1. of the major premise, we begin with a very probably *true* statement; but form 1. for the major yields syllogism a) above, which is a patent instance of an undistributed middle. If, on the other hand, we accept syllogism b) above because it exhibits no formal fallacy, we commit ourselves to form 2. of the major: "Everything difficult to understand is a profound philosophical system," which is an obviously *false* premise. In neither case, then, does our enthymeme bear examination. A true A proposition for major premise yields an undistributed middle, and a formally correct syllogism can be framed only by virtue of a palpably false major premise.

Perhaps the simplest rule for the student to follow in dealing with these enthymemes whose missing premise is an A proposition is to select as major *whichever form of this A proposition seems to be true.* If the syllogism thereby constructed is formally valid, the original enthymeme is valid; if the syllogism is formally invalid, the original enthymeme is invalid.

Let us consider another example of a first order enthymeme, whose missing major is an A proposition:

"Since every triangle is a polygon, every triangle is a plane."

The missing major may take the form:

1. "Every polygon is a plane"

or

2. "Every plane is a polygon."

Of these, the first is a true statement, and using that as our major premise, we obtain a valid syllogism:

Every polygon is a plane
Every triangle is a polygon
∴ Every triangle is a plane.

In the case of an *invalid* enthymeme of this type, we have seen that the precisely opposite situation prevails: only a false major will yield a formally valid syllogism. Thus in the invalid enthymeme:

"Every square is a rectangle, for every square is a polygon"

a true major premise, yields an undistributed middle:

Every rectangle is a polygon
Every square is a polygon
∴ Every square is a rectangle

and a false major must be adopted to avoid this fallacy:

Every polygon is a rectangle
Every square is a polygon
∴ Every square is a rectangle.

It is really impossible to say in these cases whether the invalidity of the enthymeme is due to a false major premise—and this would be an instance of *material*, rather than *formal* invalidity—or to the formal fallacy of the undistributed middle. In other words, the enthymeme may stand for either of the two possible syllogisms; one materially, the other formally, invalid. In any case, the enthymeme is no good. We have suggested that the formal logician does best in these cases to suppose that the missing premise is *true*, and that the error or fallacy is formal in character; though he can with equal justice reason that the argument is *formally valid*, and vitiated only by the assumption of a *false* major premise.

The necessity to combine material with formal considerations in anaÍyzing enthymemes holds only where the two possible forms of the missing premise are significantly different. This would be chiefly where the missing premise is an A proposition, but also possible where it is an O.[3] (Thus "Every M is P" is by no means the equivalent of its *reciprocal* "Every P is M"; and "Some S is not M" is a far cry from "Some M is not S.") Where the missing premise is an I or E proposition, however, reversing subject and predicate makes no significant change, since both I and E can be converted simply.

Consider the following enthymeme of the second order:

"Because every Communist is pro-labor, no good American is pro-labor."

In syllogistic form, this reveals an illicit major term:

> Every Communist is pro-labor
> No good American is a Communist
> ∴ No good American is pro-labor

and since the missing premise is an E proposition, transposing its subject and predicate does not change the fallacy. We might therefore argue that an enthymeme of this sort, which has only *one* syllogistic equivalent, can be adjudged valid or invalid on purely formal grounds. Though such a position is not logically impregnable,[4] it can be used as a working rule to detect invalidity in most instances.

---

[3] Enthymemes where the missing premise is an O proposition are too rare and complicated to merit more than mention in this course.

[4] Even in these cases, it can be argued that an enthymeme can never be invalidated on purely formal grounds. We can argue that the missing minor above is not simply "No good American is a Communist," but something like "No good American is anything that a Communist is" or "No good American is 'pro' *anything* that every Communist is 'pro'." This double quantification undoubtedly yields a *false* proposition, but a formally valid syllogism, for instance:

> Every Communist is pro-labor
> No good American is anything that a Communist is
> ∴ No good American is pro-labor

or:

> Every Communist is pro-labor
> No good American is "pro" anything that every Communist is "pro"
> ∴ No good American is pro-labor

Enthymemes where the missing premise is an I proposition can be rather simply handled. Thus:

"Since every platypus is egg-laying, some mammal is egg-laying" is expressed syllogistically:

Every platypus is egg-laying
Some mammal is platypus (*or* Some platypus is mammal)
∴ Some mammal is egg-laying.

Now this syllogism is valid, and no significant change is made by reversing the subject and predicate of the I proposition which is the minor premise. The original enthymeme, then, is also valid.

The great difficulty with certain invalid enthymemes of the first and second order is in *specifying* rather than in detecting their falla‧ cious character. And this is, after all, a rather academic difficulty. In addition, we should also note that in actual argument we can always demand that the framer of an enthymeme make explicit his suppressed premise, so that the problem of how to put the enthymeme in proper syllogistic form is his rather than ours. We have then only to judge the argument as a syllogism, the rules for which are unequivocal.

The enthymeme, nevertheless, is a most important form, for it is the most common method of expressing the categorical syllogism. For the student who wishes to make *use* of logic, practice in constructing and analyzing enthymemes, reducing them to various syllogistic forms, and exercises in determining their validity or invalidity are indispensable.

The so-called *enthymemes of the third order* (those in which the *conclusion* is the omitted member) are neither important nor common. They have an occasional use in the rhetorical device of *innuendo* or in logical exercises, in which the premises having been

––––––––––––––––

The form:

M is P
No S is anything that M is
∴ No S is P

though not included in traditional lists of valid syllogistic forms, seems to follow logically and necessarily, however absurd materially the minor premise may be.

stated, the reader or listener is left to draw the obvious (or not-so-obvious) conclusion for himself. Thus:

"Cowardice is always contemptible, and this was clearly a case of cowardice"

is an enthymeme of the third order, expressing innuendo; while truncated arguments like:

"No chalk is glass, and all glass is frangible, so . . ."

might constitute a good exercise in drawing the proper conclusions from stated premises.

Section 4: The Exclusive Syllogism

When the major premise of what otherwise appears to be a categorical syllogism is an *exclusive proposition,* we have a special type of argument which merits individual consideration.

Let us remind ourselves at the outset that the exclusive proposition, e.g.,

"Only men are rational"

makes *two* assertions:

(1) Men are rational and
(2) No other beings are rational.

The first of these assertions is *indefinite;* it may mean "all," but formally we can only be sure of "some." (It happens that "*All* men are rational," but when we say "Only females are mothers," we mean that "*Some* females are mothers," not all. The form "Only *a* is *b*," then, justifies our saying only "Some *a* is *b*," nothing more.)

The second assertion ("No other beings are rational") is the same as:

"No non-man is rational"

and this assertion is in turn the partial contrapositive of, and therefore identical with:

"Every rational being is man."

It follows that when I say:

> "Only a is b" (Only men are rational)

I mean:

> "*Some* a is b" (At least some men are rational)
>
> and
>
> "*Every* b is a" (All rational beings are men).

Let us now consider an example of an exclusive syllogism:

> Only x is z
>
> Y is z
>
> ∴ Y is x.

At first, this looks like an instance of an *undistributed middle*, but on closer consideration we can see that the syllogism is perfectly valid; for the major premise:

> "Only x is z"

means:

> "Every z is x"

and this means that the middle term ("z") is distributed once, and the conclusion formally correct.

On the other hand, the *apparently valid* form:

> Only x is z
>
> Y is x
>
> ∴ Y is z

is really invalid; for "Only x is z" implies merely:

> "*Some* x is z"

and with this for major premise, we have an *undistributed middle*.

The exclusive form thus has the effect of reversing subject and predicate in the major premise. When the major premise is:

> "Only M is P"

it should be understood as:

> "Every P is M"

and when the major is:

> "Only P is M"

it should be understood as:

> "Every M is P."

Once this transposition is made, the ordinary rules of the categorical syllogism apply.

Exclusive propositions may also be employed in *enthymemes* of the second order, where they have an effect similar to that already noted. Thus:

> "Since only females are mothers, this dog must be female"

expresses the syllogism:

> Only females are mothers
> This dog is a mother
> ∴ This dog is a female

and since this in turn is equivalent to:

> All mothers are females
> This dog is a mother
> ∴ This dog is a female

the original enthymeme is perfectly valid.

The *exclusive particle* ("only," "alone") reverses the direction of any premise in which it is employed, and may thereby change the formal significance of an argument completely. This applies, as we shall see, to hypothetical propositions and arguments as well as to categorical. The *negative exceptive* proposition (e.g., *"None but* females are mothers"*) has exactly the same sense as the exclusive, and may be similarly employed in categorical arguments.

SECTION 5: MOODS AND FIGURES OF THE CATEGORICAL SYLLOGISM

Recall that the *proximate matter* of the categorical syllogism is three *propositions*, and the *remote matter* the three *terms* which occur in these propositions. Now the *mood* of a syllogism is:

the arrangement of PROPOSITIONS *according to quantity and quality* (as A, E, I, or O) and the *figure* of a syllogism is:

> *the arrangement of the* TERMS *in the premises relative to the middle term.*

Moods. If we consider first the *mood* of categorical syllogisms, we may say, *a priori,* that there are sixteen possible combinations of premises, since there are four types of categorical propositions. Thus in the premises, the possible moods are (read vertically):

Major Premise: A A A A   I I I I   E E E E   O O O O
Minor Premise: A E I O   A E I O   A E I O   A E I O

The mood written $\frac{A}{E}$, or more frequently AE, means simply that the major premise is an A proposition, and the minor an E proposition. Affirmative indefinite (A_1) and singular (A_s) are considered A propositions; negative indefinite (E_1) and singular (E_s) propositions are regarded as equivalent to ordinary E propositions. (Do *not* make the mistake of classifying *singular* propositions as I or O.)

It is evident that certain of these sixteen possible combinations of premises would violate one or more of the rules of the syllogism. Thus the following moods are invalid, as involving either two negative or two particular premises:

Major: I   I   E   E   O   O   O
Minor: I   O   E   O   E   I   O

The mood IE is invalid, since, with the major premise an I proposition, the major term is undistributed in the premises; and since the conclusion of IE must be negative, the major term must be distributed in the conclusion. The mood IE, therefore, always involves an *illicit major.* Our sixteen possible moods are then reduced to *eight* possibly valid ones:

Major: A   A   A   A   I   E   O   E
Minor: A   E   I   O   A   A   A   I

Four of these valid moods have A for major premise, three others have A for minor premise, and there is one EI sequence.

Figures. The *figure* of a categorical syllogism is determined by the position of the middle term in the major and minor premises. Here there are just *four* possible combinations:

1. M is the subject of the major premise and the predicate of the minor premise. (*Sub-Prae*)
2. M is the predicate of both major and minor premises. (*Prae-Prae*)
3. M is the subject of both major and minor premises. (*Sub-Sub*)
4. M is the predicate of the major premise and the subject of the minor premise. (*Prae-Sub, Indirect 1*)

The four figures are then schematized as follows:

1. Sub-Prae	2. Prae-Prae	3. Sub-Sub	4. Prae-Sub
M P	P M	M P	P M
S M	S M	M S	M S
S P	S P	S P	S P

The fourth figure (*Prae-Sub*) is not regarded by the logicians in the Aristotelian tradition as a *distinct* figure, but simply as an *indirect statement of the first figure*. Since the fourth figure always concludes indirectly—e.g. "Some mortal is man" instead of "Every man is mortal"—there is merit in the traditional view that we should speak of only *three proper figures,* and an indirect first figure. Two valid moods in the fourth figure (called "FESAPO" and "FRESISON"), however, do *not* appear to be merely first figure syllogisms concluding indirectly, but rather *valid alternatives* to forms which in the first figure would be *invalid*. There is something, then, to be said for the modern view of the fourth as a distinct figure. In the process of *reduction,* moreover, which we shall shortly be studying, it is *easier* to treat syllogisms in Prae-Sub *as though* they constituted a distinct fourth figure. It seems legitimate to employ a simpler method of reduction, while recognizing that three of the five valid moods in this figure are unquestionably only indirect statements of first figure syllogisms, and that for these three forms at least the more complicated method of reduction advocated by the ancients is a better method. Actually, neither the ancient nor the modern view of this figure seems wholly right, so that any convenient method of reduction may reasonably be employed. We shall adhere to the modern technique only because it is simpler.

Valid Moods in Different Figures. Considering figure and mood together, it becomes evident that not all of the eight valid moods are valid in every figure. Each figure, we shall see, has certain rules of its own which render some moods invalid.

In the *first figure:*

Sub-Prae

M   P

S   M
_____

S   P

there are two rules:

1. The minor premise must be affirmative.
2. The major premise must be universal.

The minor must be affirmative. For if the minor is negative, the major premise must be affirmative and the conclusion negative. In the major premise, then, the major term is the predicate of an affirmative proposition and is taken *particularly,* but in the conclusion the major term is the predicate of a negative proposition and is taken *universally.* This constitutes an *illicit major.*

The major must be universal. Since the minor premise is affirmative, the middle term is not distributed in the minor. Thus, the middle term, which is the subject of the major premise, must be distributed there, making the major premise universal.

Of the eight possible valid moods (AA, AE, AI, AO, EA, IA, OA, EI), only four (AA, EA, AI, EI) satisfy the rules of the first figure. These legitimate moods in the first figure are symbolized in the following mnemonic line, in each key word of which the three vowels indicate respectively the major premise, minor premise, and conclusion:

BARBARA, CELARENT, DARII, FERIO.

In the *second figure:*

Prae-Prae

P   M

S   M
___
S   P

there are likewise two rules:

1. One premise must be negative.
2. The major premise must be universal.

One premise must be negative. Otherwise the middle term is twice predicate of an affirmative proposition, and twice undistributed. It is in the second figure that the fallacy of the *undistributed middle* is most likely to occur.

The major must be universal. Since one premise is negative, the conclusion is negative. The major term is therefore distributed in the conclusion. It must also be distributed in the major premise, of which it is the subject, if we are to avoid the fallacy of the illicit major.

Our eight valid moods are once more reduced to four (EA, AE, EI, AO), symbolized by the mnemonic words:

CESARE, CAMESTRES, FESTINO BAROCO.

The *third figure:*

Sub-Sub

M   P

M   S
___
S   P

is also covered by two rules:

1. The minor premise must be affirmative.
2. The conclusion must be particular.

The minor must be affirmative. As in the first figure, if the minor is negative, the major is affirmative and P is there undistributed.

However, if the minor is negative, the conclusion is negative and P is there distributed. A negative minor premise would thus entail the fallacy of the *illicit major*.

The conclusion must be particular. Since the minor premise is affirmative, S is there undistributed. It follows that the conclusion must be particular, if the fallacy of the *illicit minor* is to be avoided.

Since there is only one of the special rules of the third figure that affects the premises, there are six valid moods in this figure (AA, IA, AI, EA, OA, EI), and the mnemonic words are:

DARAPTI, DISAMIS, DATISI, FELAPTON, BOCARDO, FERISON.

A contemporary Scholastic logician of considerable acumen argues that in the third figure, the middle term may be twice undistributed, and that the two particular premises still yield a valid conclusion.[5]

The following "syllogism" is offered to substantiate this view:

$$\text{Most dogs are gentle} \quad \text{Mp}$$

$$\text{Most dogs are mongrels} \quad \text{Mp}$$
$$\therefore \text{Some mongrels are gentle.}$$

Since, on the supposition that the premises are true, one must also accept the truth of the conclusion, it is argued that this is a perfectly valid form of reasoning.

Perhaps there is implicit here a valid *quantitative intuition*[6] but this is certainly not an acceptable *categorical syllogism,* for in the course of establishing the truth of the major premise we should have to know *already* the truth of the conclusion. Whether or not one knew the truth of the minor premise, provided one knew what is meant by a *mongrel dog*, it would be impossible to know that "Most dogs are gentle" without *actually* knowing that "Some mongrel (at least one) is gentle." There is, therefore, no need to formulate the minor premise in order to know the conclusion. The apparent deduc-

---

[5] John J. Toohey, S.J., *Elementary Handbook of Logic*, New York, Appleton-Century-Crofts, 1948, p. 85.

[6] Many quantitative connections are *valid* without being syllogistically inferred, e.g., that a plane figure has as many angles as sides.

tion, then, of the conclusion from the minor-premise-thought-*under*-the-major is purely spurious, and there is no genuine categorical syllogism. We have already seen that an enumerative universal cannot give rise to a genuine inference (above, p. 49). There is no reason to suppose that an enumerative pseudo-universal, or enumerative particular, can do so; and every argument of the type:

> Most M's are P
> Most M's are S
> ∴ Some S is P

must rest upon enumeration. The relations between two particular propositions of this type constitute an interesting problem, but it is nevertheless absurd to conclude that they permit us to form a valid categorical syllogism which violates one of the major rules.

In the *indirect first* or *fourth figure:*

> Prae-Sub
>
> P   M
>
> M   S
> ———
> S   P

there are three special rules, which must be stated in conditional form:

1. If the major premise is affirmative, the minor premise must be universal.
2. If the minor premise is affirmative, the conclusion must be particular.
3. If either premise is negative, the major must be universal.

If the major is affirmative, the minor must be universal. If the major is affirmative, its predicate, M, is undistributed. If the minor is then particular, its subject, M, would be taken particularly a second time.

If the minor is affirmative, the conclusion must be particular. If the minor is affirmative, its predicate, S, is undistributed. A universal conclusion would then cause S to be distributed and this would constitute an instance of the *illicit minor.*

If either premise is negative, the major must be universal. If either premise is negative, the conclusion is negative and P is there distributed. If P as the subject of the major premise is not also distributed, we have an *illicit major*.

The valid moods of the fourth, or indirect first, figure are five: AA, AE, IA, EA, EI, symbolized in the mnemonic line:

BRAMANTIP, CAMENES, DIMARIS, FESAPO, FRESISON.

SECTION 6: REDUCTION OF SYLLOGISMS TO THE FIRST FIGURE

Syllogisms in the second, third, and indirect first (fourth) figure are sometimes awkward, and their demonstrative force is generally not as great as that of syllogisms in the first figure. In the first figure, looked at from the point of view of *comprehension,* P is always placed in or denied to the meaning of M, and M is always placed in the meaning of S; so it is perfectly clear why P must be placed in, or denied to, the meaning of S.

From the standpoint of *extension,* the first figure is even more ideal, for the middle term serves perfectly its role of *intermediate,* being of *lesser* extension than the major term, P, (M is P) and of *greater* extension than the minor term, S (S is M). Most importantly, in the first figure the *Dictum de Omni* or the *Dictum de Nullo* is perfectly verified. A predicate (P) which pertains universally to a certain nature (M), pertains to everything (S) that comes under that nature; or a predicate (P) which is denied universally to a certain nature (M), is denied to everything (S) that comes under that nature. Although each of the other figures is perfectly valid in its own right, and although the second and third figures are specially suited to certain types of argument,[7] they do not permit as immediate an application of the two supreme principles of the syllogism as does the first figure.

In comparing two syllogisms, one in the first figure, and the other its equivalent in some other figure, careful attention shows that the *sequence* is clearer in the first figure, where minor and major terms

---

[7] Since the second figure always concludes negatively, it is suited to the demonstration of *incompatibility* or *impossibility;* the always particular conclusion of the third figure makes it useful for demonstrating contingency or possibility. Cf. J. Dopp, *Leçons de Logique Formelle,* Louvain, 1950, vol. I, p. 148.

have the same role (subject and predicate respectively) in the premises that they have in the conclusion. Consider a syllogism in the third figure, in *Darapti:*

> Every man is mortal
> Every man is biped
> ∴ Some biped is mortal.

This is certainly valid, but its sequence is not as evident as that of the equivalent syllogism of the first figure, *Darii:*

> Every man is mortal
> Some biped is man
> ∴ Some biped is mortal.

What might be called a "natural" second-figure syllogism like:

> CEs No fish is mammal
> A Every whale is mammal
> rE ∴ No whale is fish

is less clear as to sequence than its equivalent in the first figure:

> CEl No mammal is fish
> A Every whale is mammal
> rEnt ∴ No whale is fish

even though the major premise of the first syllogism is closer to the normal mode of utterance than the major of the second.

For the sake of rendering the sequence of any argument we employ as evident as possible, it is useful to be able to express any syllogism in the second, third, or indirect first (fourth) figure by a syllogism in the first figure. The process of *reduction* enables us to do this. The mnemonic lines which we have given to indicate the valid moods of the separate figures also indicate the manner in which syllogisms not of the first figure can be reduced to the first figure. The original form of these remarkably ingenious lines has been modified slightly by the logicians who consider the fourth an independent figure:

BARBARA, CELARENT, DARII, FERIOque prioris;
CESARE, CAMESTRES, FESTINO, BAROCO secundae;
Tertia; DARAPTI, DISAMIS, DATISI, FELAPTON,
BOCARDO, FERISON habet; quarta insuper addit:

BRAMANTIP, CAMENES, DIMARIS, FESAPO, FRESISON.

For the sake of simplicity, we shall adhere to this tradition.[8]

In each line after the first, the first letter of a mnemonic word indicates the mood of the first figure to which this mood should be reduced. Thus *Cesare* reduces to *Celarent, Bramantip* to *Barbara, Disamis* to *Darii, Festino* to *Ferio.* The *vowels* of each mnemonic word reveal, as we already know, the mood. Thus *Disamis* indicates a syllogism in the third figure (*Sub-Sub*), whose major premise is an I proposition, whose minor is an A, and whose conclusion is an I. The following *consonants,* placed in the body of a word, indicate the *operations* which are to be performed to reduce the syllogism in question to the corresponding mood of the first figure:

s: *Simple conversion* of the proposition signified by the *preceding* vowel.

p: *Per accidens,* or accidental, conversion of the proposition signified by the preceding vowel.

m: Transposition (*mutatio*) of the premises; make the minor premise the major, and the major the minor.

c: Reduction by *contradiction.* This is the *indirect* method of reduction *through* (rather than *to*) *Barbara.* It is signified by a *noninitial* "c," and is applied only to *Baroco* and *Bocardo.*

Direct Reduction. One of the syllogisms cited above:

$$\begin{array}{cc} \text{P} & \text{M} \\ \text{No fish is mammal} \\ \text{S} & \text{M} \\ \text{Every whale is mammal} \\ \text{S} & \text{P} \\ \therefore \text{No whale is fish} \end{array}$$

is a syllogism in the second figure, *Prae-Prae.* Its sequence is EAE, so we designate it a syllogism in *Cesare.* The word *"Cesare"* tells us that to reduce this syllogism to *Celarent,* in the first figure, we

---

[8] The original lines were the invention of an English contemporary of St. Thomas, William of Shyreswood. They gave the moods of the indirect first figure as: BARALIPTON, CELANTES, DABITIS, FAPESMO, FRISESO-MORUM, the *first* vowel indicating the *minor* premise, the *second* vowel the *major.*

have to perform only one operation, indicated by the letter "s." This is the *simple conversion* of the E proposition which is our original major premise. Convert the major, and the syllogism reads:

$$\begin{array}{cc} \text{M} & \text{P} \\ \multicolumn{2}{c}{\text{No mammal is fish}} \\ \text{S} & \text{M} \\ \multicolumn{2}{c}{\text{Every whale is mammal}} \\ \text{S} & \text{P} \\ \multicolumn{2}{c}{\therefore \text{No whale is fish.}} \end{array}$$

This new syllogism is in the first figure, *Sub-Prae,* and its mood or sequence is EAE. It is therefore the equivalent syllogism in *Celarent.*
Another syllogism cited in this section:

$$\begin{array}{cc} \text{M} & \text{P} \\ \multicolumn{2}{c}{\text{Every man is mortal}} \\ \text{M} & \text{S} \\ \multicolumn{2}{c}{\text{Every man is biped}} \\ \text{S} & \text{P} \\ \multicolumn{2}{c}{\therefore \text{Some biped is mortal}} \end{array}$$

is in the third figure, *Sub-Sub,* and its AAI sequence indicates a syllogism in *Darapti.* Convert the minor premise accidentally, as the letter "p" indicates, and we have a syllogism in the first figure, *Darii:*

$$\begin{array}{cc} \text{M} & \text{P} \\ \multicolumn{2}{c}{\text{Every man is mortal}} \\ \text{S} & \text{M} \\ \multicolumn{2}{c}{\text{Some biped is man}} \\ \text{S} & \text{P} \\ \multicolumn{2}{c}{\therefore \text{Some biped is mortal.}} \end{array}$$

A third-figure syllogism in Disamis also reduces to *Darii,* but it requires three operations to accomplish this: simple conversion of the major premise, transposition of the premises, and simple conversion of the conclusion. Thus:

Some crow is carnivorous	DIS
Every crow is bird	AM
∴ Some bird is carnivorous	IS

becomes:

Every crow is bird	DA
Some carnivorous animal is crow	RI
∴ Some carnivorous animal is bird.	I

Remember that an "s" or "p" in one of the mnemonic words indicates conversion of the proposition signified by the *preceding* vowel. In *Disamis,* it is the I proposition which is the original major that is to be converted. Where one premise has to be converted and the premises transposed, it is important to perform the conversion *before* the transposition, as otherwise the wrong premise may be converted. Thus in *Disamis, after* the I major is converted, it is transposed to become the minor premise of the syllogism in the first figure, *Darii.*

The direct conversion of a syllogism in *Bramantip* (fourth, or indirect first, figure) is somewhat out of the ordinary. Thus:

Every Sicilian is Italian	BRA
Every Italian is Latin	MAN
∴ Some Latin is Sicilian	TIP

will reduce to *Barbara,* if we transpose the premises and convert the I proposition which was the original conclusion into an A proposition. Thus:

Every Italian is Latin	BAR
Every Sicilian is Italian	BA
∴ Every Sicilian is Latin.	RA

How can we justify this conversion of an I into an A proposition? Two reasons may be given:

1. Since a syllogism in *Bramantip* is really a syllogism in the first figure *concluding indirectly,* the original I conclusion was really the *converse of an A proposition.* If we know that an A proposition has been converted to I, it is legitimate to convert that I back to A. Thus, if I convert "Every man is mortal" to "Some mortal is man," I may legitimately reconvert "Some mortal is man" to "Every man is mortal."
2. When I transpose the premises, I make "Sicilian," which was the major term, into the minor term. That minor term is taken universally in the premise, and it is therefore permissible to take it universally in the conclusion. When we do take this new minor term universally in the conclusion, we make the old I proposition into an A.

A syllogism in *Fesapo* is remarkable, as mentioned previously, in that its immediate equivalent in the first figure is *invalid*. The typical *illicit major* in the first figure:

> Every Communist is antireligious
> No democrat is a Communist
> ∴ No democrat is antireligious

yields a valid syllogism in the fourth figure (*Prae-Sub*), if we transpose the premises and take the *accidental converse* of the original conclusion. Thus:

> FES No democrat is a Communist
> AP Every Communist is antireligious
> O ∴ Some antireligious person is not a democrat.

When this syllogism is reduced to the first figure, it is not reduced to the invalid form, but to *Ferio,* by converting both premises:

> FER No Communist is a Democrat
> I Some antireligious person is a Communist
> O ∴ Some antireligious person is not a Democrat.

It is difficult, in the light of this explanation, to agree that *all* the valid moods of the fourth figure are but *valid first figure syllogisms concluding indirectly*. This seems to hold for *Bramantip, Camenes,* and *Dimaris* (or *Baralipton, Celantes, Dabitis,* as they were originally called), but not for *Fesapo* and *Fresison*. The last two seem to be as distinct from any valid mood in the first figure, as is any syllogism in the second or third figure.

Indirect Reduction. In the process of *direct* reduction, with which we have been concerned so far, we make a second, third, or fourth figure syllogism into a first figure syllogism by changing the position of the middle term. This is accomplished by converting and/or transposing the premises. In the second and third figures, when one premise is an A proposition and the other an O, these techniques cannot be applied to change the position of the middle term. *Conversion* is inapplicable, since, if we convert the A premise, we should have two particular premises, and the O premise cannot be converted. *Transposition* cannot be used, for in the second and third figures it does not change the position of the middle term.

In the moods of the second and third figures, therefore, where one premise is an A and the other an O proposition, *direct* reduction to the first figure is impossible. There are two such moods: *Baroco* in the second figure and *Bocardo* in the third. For these two moods the ancient logicians developed an ingenious method of *indirect reduction* by means of a syllogism in *Barbara*.

Consider the following syllogism in *Baroco:*

> Every intelligent being is responsible
> Some animal is not responsible
> ∴ Some animal is not intelligent.

This syllogism cannot be reduced to the first figure, but we can show by means of a first-figure syllogism that its sequence is valid. This is what the ancients meant by "indirect" reduction.

Let us suppose, then, that someone denies the validity of this syllogism's sequence. To deny the validity of its sequence is to assert that:

> *the premises can be true but the conclusion false.*

And, continued the ancients, the hypothetical opponent of this syllogism in *Baroco* must then be ready to admit that:

> "Every intelligent being is responsible" (the *major*)

and

> "Some animal is not responsible" (the *minor*)

while *denying the conclusion* that:

> "Some animal is not intelligent."

The procedure is then to construct a syllogism in *Barbara* out of the opponent's position, and to show that this syllogism contradicts a truth already accepted by the opponent. This amounts to showing that to deny the sequence of *Baroco* is a *self-contradictory,* and therefore impossible, position.

To construct this syllogism in *Barbara,* we leave the A premise of the *Baroco* intact, but for the O premise we substitute the *contradictory of the conclusion.* (Since the opponent of *Baroco* denies the original conclusion, he must accept the truth of its contradictory.)

When we draw the necessary conclusion from these premises we have:

BAR   Every intelligent being is responsible (A major of *Baroco*)
BA   Every animal is intelligent (Contradictory of conclusion
            of *Baroco*)
RA   ∴ Every animal is responsible.

But the conclusion of the new syllogism is the contradictory of the original minor premise, and the opponent accepted the truth of the original minor. This syllogism thus shows that by accepting the premises and denying the conclusion of *Baroco,* the opponent of this mood must contradict himself by both affirming and denying the O minor premise. It follows that the sequence of *Baroco* must be valid.

An essentially similar procedure is to be followed with regard to a syllogism in *Bocardo,* third figure (*Sub-Sub*):

BOC   Some neurotic is not inhibited
AR   Every neurotic is unhappy
DO   ∴ Some unhappy person is not inhibited.

Our imaginary opponent, who is presumed to deny the validity of the mood, must grant our premises while denying our conclusion. For the O major of the *Bocardo* we substitute the contradictory of the conclusion. We combine this with the A minor, and we have the premises of a syllogism in *Barbara,* describing our opponent's position:

Every unhappy person is inhibited (Contradictory of conclusion)
Every neurotic is unhappy (Original A minor of *Bocardo*).

These premises lead necessarily to the conclusion:

"Every neurotic is inhibited"

which is the contradictory of the major premise of the *Bocardo,* which was accepted by our opponent. Therefore, the denial of the old conclusion while accepting the old premise, leads to a self-contradictory position, and the sequence in *Bocardo* must be valid.

On this ancient method of indirect reduction, *two* comments would seem in order:

1. It does not seem that to *doubt* the validity of the moods

Baroco and *Bocardo* an opponent need *deny* the conclusion while accepting the premises. To question the validity of a certain conclusion is not necessarily to assert the truth of its contradictory, but only to admit its *possibility*. If the conclusion of the syllogism in *Barbara,* which states the opponent's position, is written in the *possible mode,* e.g.,

"Every animal *can be* responsible"

or

"Every neurotic *can be* inhibited"

there is some *conflict* with the previously accepted O premise, but not precisely *contradiction.* The indirect reduction of *Bocardo* and *Baroco* is probably not so rigidly demonstrative, or apodictic, as the ancients seem to have thought.

2. It is simpler to employ *obversion* to establish the validity of *Baroco* and *Bocardo.* In *Baroco,* obvert both premises:

BAR	Every man is free	No man is non-free	FES
OC	Some animal is not free	Some animal is non-free	TI
O	∴ Some animal is not man.	∴ Some animal is not man.	NO

The resulting syllogism in *Festino* can then be reduced directly to the first figure by simple conversion of the major premise. With *Bocardo,* obvert the major premise and conclusion:

BOC	Some ant is not winged	Some ant is non-winged	DIS
AR	Every ant is insect	Every ant is insect	AM
DO	∴ Some insect is not winged.	∴ Some insect is non-winged.	IS

Then, reduce the syllogism in *Disamis* to *Darii* in the usual way. Since the obverse is the *exact equivalent* of a given proposition, the fact that *Baroco* and *Bocardo* can be obverted to *Festino* and *Disamis* respectively shows their validity and their ultimate reducibility to the first figure.

Construction of Categorical Syllogisms. The chief value to be derived from an intensive study of the process of reduction is that it familiarizes us with the structure and workings of the categorical syllogism. If we understand reduction, we can proceed to the exercise of making-up or constructing syllogisms in each of the moods of the second, third, and fourth, or indirect first, figures, and then reducing these to the appropriate moods of the first figure. No exercise can better assure our thorough mastery of the mechanics of categorical reasoning.

To construct a syllogism in *Festino,* for example, we first schematize the figure and mood:

$$\begin{array}{ll} \text{No P is M} & \text{FES} \\ \text{Some S is M} & \text{TI} \\ \therefore \text{Some S is not P.} & \text{NO} \end{array}$$

Then, we may choose some convenient O proposition—preferably a *true* proposition, for which one can offer some reason, such as "Some flying animal is not bird"—as conclusion. With the conclusion chosen, we have two of the three terms of the syllogism:

$$\begin{array}{l} \text{No bird is M} \\ \text{Some flying animal is M} \\ \therefore \text{Some flying animal is not bird.} \end{array}$$

With the selection of an appropriate middle term, say "mammal," the syllogism in *Festino* is complete:

$$\begin{array}{ll} \text{No bird is mammal} & \text{FES} \\ \text{Some flying animal is mammal} & \text{TI} \\ \therefore \text{Some flying animal is not bird.} & \text{NO} \end{array}$$

Now convert the major premise, as the "s" in *Festino* directs, and the result is *Ferio* in the first figure.

A syllogism in *Datisi* would be schematized:

$$\begin{array}{ll} \text{Every M is P} & \text{DA} \\ \text{Some M is S} & \text{TIS} \\ \therefore \text{Some S is P.} & \text{I} \end{array}$$

Choose an I proposition for conclusion, e.g., "Some intelligent being is mortal," and substitute the minor and major terms indicated:

$$\begin{array}{l} \text{Every M is mortal} \\ \text{Some M is intelligent being} \\ \therefore \text{Some intelligent being is mortal.} \end{array}$$

Possible middle terms would be "animal," "organism," "man," e.g.,

Every organism is mortal	DA
Some organism is intelligent being	TIS
∴ Some intelligent being is mortal.	I

Convert the minor premise to effect the reduction of this syllogism in *Datisi* to *Darii* in the first figure.

To construct a syllogism in *Felapton*, schematize the mood in the third figure, and select an O conclusion:

No M is P
Every M is S
∴ Some S is not P (Some sea-animal is not fish).

Substituting the major and minor terms, we get:

No M is fish	FEL
Every M is sea-animal	AP
∴ Some sea-animal is not fish.	TON

Any of the following would do for middle term: "whale," "porpoise," "oyster," "lobster." Then convert the minor premise accidentally, as the letter "p" indicates, and a syllogism in *Ferio* results.

The first three moods of the fourth figure are clearly first-figure syllogisms concluding indirectly. Therefore, in constructing syllogisms in *Bramantip, Camenes,* and *Dimaris* we should select *indirect* propositions for conclusions. In the case of *Bramantip* and *Dimaris,* take an ordinary A proposition, like "Every animal is mortal," and convert it to "Some mortal is animal," to obtain the conclusion. For *Camenes,* convert an ordinary E, like "No fish is invertebrate," to "No invertebrate is fish," and construct the syllogism with this as conclusion. Some may find it easier to construct syllogisms in *Barbara, Celarent,* and *Darii,* and then to transpose the premises and convert the conclusion of each to yield *Bramantip* (or *Baralipton*), *Camenes* (or *Celantes*), and *Dimaris* (or *Dabitis*). Thus we may construct *Dimaris* schematically as follows:

Some P is M
Every M is S
∴ Some S is P (Some mortal is intelligent)

and, selecting "organism" for middle term, we have:

> Some intelligent being is organism   DIM
> (I)   Every organism is mortal   AR
> ∴ Some mortal is intelligent   IS

which is the same as the following in *Darii,* concluding indirectly:

> Every organism is mortal
> (II)   Some intelligent being is organism
> ∴ Some intelligent being is mortal.

Whether we reduce (I) to (II), or derive (I) from (II), the fundamental relation remains the same, and this holds for *Bramantip* and *Barbara,* and *Camenes* and *Cesare* as well.

Syllogisms in *Fesapo* and *Fresison,* however, are different, since an O conclusion cannot be converted. These must be constructed as moods which are independent of any valid first-figure syllogism, and reduced to the first figure by conversion of both premises. We may illustrate the construction and reduction of a syllogism in *Fesapo:*

> No P is M
> Every M is S
> ∴ Some S is not P (Some sea-animal is not fish).

We may choose for middle term any term which can be denied universally of "fish," provided this term also stands universally for a kind of sea-animal. "Crustacean," "mollusc," etc., would do, e.g.:

> No fish is lobster   FES
> Every lobster is sea-animal   AP
> ∴ Some sea-animal is not fish.   O

In *Fesapo* the conclusion is indirect in the sense that a term which was a predicate in the premise is now a subject, while a term that was a subject is now a predicate. But, this conclusion remains unchanged when we reduce to *Ferio* in the first figure:

> No lobster is fish   FE
> Some sea-animal is lobster   RI
> ∴ Some sea-animal is not fish.   O

The same may be said for *Fresison.* By converting both premises we make the minor term a subject in the premise as well as in the conclusion, and the major term a predicate, but the conclusion itself remains unchanged. The student will note that the sequence is much clearer in *Ferio* than in *Fesapo* or *Fresison*. The latter seem, nonetheless, to be independent moods, though awkward and seldom used.

SECTION 7: THE HYPOTHETICAL SYLLOGISM

Hypothetical reasoning is not as fundamental as categorical reasoning. It is, nevertheless, an independent form which cannot be reduced to the categorical, and which can be used in many situations where the categorical forms of reasoning are awkward or inapplicable. The syllogism which expresses hypothetical reasoning is in no sense a mere variant of the categorical syllogism. On the contrary, it has its own modes and rules which are completely different from the categorical. The hypothetical syllogism may be defined as:

an argument whose first premise is a sequential proposition, one member of which is affirmed or denied in the second premise, and the other member of which is CONSEQUENTLY *affirmed or denied in the conclusion.*

There are several things to note about this definition:

1. Because the hypothetical syllogism transforms a propositional sequence into a syllogistic sequence, or deduction, only those propositions which contain a sequence can form its basis. *Copulative* propositions assert no necessary sequence between their members, and, therefore, do not enter into hypothetical syllogisms.

2. In the hypothetical syllogism, there is, in the strict sense, no major or minor premise, since there is no major or minor term. We call the hypothetical proposition which is written first the *major premise,* but it is only speaking *analogically* that we do so. By the same token, the second statement in the hypothetical syllogism is called the *minor premise,* not because it contains the minor term or subject of the conclusion, but because it is *thought under* the first statement, and in that respect is analogous to the true minor premise of the categorical syllogism.

3. Since the sequence expressed by the hypothetical syllogism is between *enunciations* none of the rules of the categorical syllogism, which govern valid sequences between terms, apply to it. In a hypo-

thetical syllogism, for example, there may be more than three terms, both enunciations may be negative, and the minor may be negative while the conclusion is affirmative; all this without invalidating the sequence in any way.

4. The particular rules of a hypothetical syllogism depend on the character of the sequence asserted by the "major" premise. Since there are three major types of sequential propositions, there are just three types of hypothetical syllogisms, each with its own special rules. These are:

> 1. The Conditional
> 2. The Disjunctive
> 3. The Conjunctive

which we shall examine now in some detail.

The Conditional Syllogism. Since the conditional proposition which forms the basis of this syllogism states only that *if* one thing is true, another necessarily follows from it:

> "If a is b, a is c"

there are just two possible legitimate forms of the conditional syllogism:

> *Antecedent   Consequent*
> If a is b,   a is c
>
> But a is b
> ∴ a is c
>
> *or*
>
> *Antecedent   Consequent*
> If a is b,   a is c
>
> But a is not c
> ∴ a is not b

Since the antecedent necessarily implies the consequent, it follows that if the antecedent is true, the consequent is true. The antecedent being true, so to speak, makes the consequent true. In like manner, if the consequent is not true, the antecedent cannot be true; for if the antecedent were true, it would make the consequent true.

It is thus perfectly correct to argue:

> If Peter is man, Peter is material
> But Peter is man
> ∴ Peter is material.

It is likewise correct to say:

> If Lucifer is man, Lucifer is material
> But Lucifer is not material
> ∴ Lucifer is not man.

It would, however, be *incorrect* to argue:

> If Peter is man, Peter is material
> But Peter is not man
> ∴ Peter is not material

although the antecedent implies the consequent, the denial of the antecedent does not logically entail the denial of the consequent. Even though the antecedent is false, some other condition may make the consequent true. In the example cited, we might suppose that *Peter* is a *dog*. Even though it is true that "Peter is not man," we can see that it by no means follows that "Peter is not material." The premises in this case would be true and the conclusion false: a sure sign of a *formal fallacy*. This fallacy, which occurs in the second or minor premise, is known as:

> *denying the antecedent.*

The other fallacy which may occur in the minor of the conditional syllogism is called *positing* (affirming) *the consequent*. Thus:

> If Peter is man, Peter is material
> But Peter is material
> ∴ Peter is man.

Assuming once again that "Peter" is a "dog," the premises would be true and the conclusion false. The formal fallacy occurs because the truth of the consequent does not necessarily imply the truth of the antecedent, since some condition other than the antecedent may be making the consequent true.

The only other fallacies which may occur in the conditional syllogism attach to the *conclusion*. These are the fallacies of *quality*, where a member is denied instead of affirmed or *vice versa*. Thus:

> If Peter is man, Peter is material
> But Peter is man
> ∴ Peter is *not* material

which is an instance of the *conclusion denying the consequent* when it obviously should affirm it. Another example is:

> If Lucifer is man, Lucifer is material
> But Lucifer is not material
> ∴ Lucifer *is* man

where the *conclusion posits the antecedent*, when it should deny it. Consequently there are four possible fallacies in the conditional syllogism, although the last two are rare and, as it were, accidental:

Fallacies of the Conditional Syllogism.

In the *minor:*   *Denying the antecedent*
              Positing the consequent
In the *conclusion:*   *Positing the antecedent* (where the minor has denied the consequent)
              Denying the consequent (where the minor has affirmed the antecedent).

The entire theory of the conditional syllogism may be summed up in a sentence: *To affirm the antecedent is to affirm the consequent; to deny the consequent is to deny the antecedent; but to deny the antecedent is not to deny the consequent; and to affirm the consequent is not to affirm the antecedent.*

As with the indefinite proposition in the categorical syllogism, the exclusive particle ("only" or an equivalent) has the effect of *reversing the direction* of a conditional proposition, i.e., the apparent antecedent is really the consequent, and vice versa. The proposition:

"Only if a is b, is a c" (Only if a being is female, is it a mother)

does not necessarily mean:

"If a is b, a is c" (If a being is female, it is a mother)

but rather the reverse:

> "If a is c, a is b" (If a being is a mother, it is female).

When this type of *exclusive conditional* occurs as the major premise of a syllogism, we should reverse its enunciations and eliminate the "only," to determine its true antecedent, and its true consequent. We can judge the syllogism by the same rules as any other conditional syllogism. The following is an instance of *positing the consequent:*

> Only if a thing is real, is it sensible
> Intelligence is real
> ∴ Intelligence is sensible

while the following apparent instance of *denying the antecedent* is, in reality, perfectly valid:

> Only if a thing is real, is it sensible
> The ghost of Banquo is not real
> ∴ The ghost of Banquo is not sensible.

Certain conditional propositions resemble those A propositions whose reciprocals are true. Thus, the propositions:

> "Every man is rational animal,"
> and
> "If today is Monday, tomorrow is Tuesday"

resemble each other *materially* in that both remain true when reversed. It is also true that:

> "Every rational animal is man,"
> and that
> "If tomorrow is Tuesday, today is Monday."

These material factors, however, do not alter the formal principles governing either the categorical or the conditional syllogism. A categorical syllogism like this:

> Every man is rational animal
> John is rational animal
> ∴ John is man

is, of course, *formally invalid. Materially,* however, it is not entirely unacceptable, since the major premise can also be written:

Every rational animal is man

and if we substitute this for the original major, we have an argument which is valid in every respect. A *conditional syllogism* like the following is essentially similar:

If a being is man, that being is rational animal
But this being is rational animal
∴ This being is man.

Formally, this conditional syllogism *posits the consequent,* and is simply incorrect. If the original antecedent and consequent are reversed, as they can be by reason of the *content* or *matter* of the proposition, a valid syllogism results:

If a being is rational animal, that being is man
But this being is rational animal
∴ This being is man.

Such a syllogism should be classified "formally invalid, but materially *capable* of being formulated validly." The same is true for a syllogism like:

If today is Tuesday, tomorrow is Wednesday
But today is not Tuesday
∴ Tomorrow is not Wednesday.

As it stands, this is an instance of *denying the antecedent,* but it is more than the truth of the conclusion that makes this argument sound so plausible. The conclusion does not follow from the major *as given,* but the *reciprocal* (or *reverse*) of the major is also true, and the conclusion *does* follow from that. Thus:

If tomorrow is Wednesday, today is Tuesday
But today is not Tuesday
∴ Tomorrow is not Wednesday

is valid both formally and materially. A syllogism cannot be formally invalid and materially valid, since material validity implies formal correctness as well as truth of content. It is possible, however, for a syllogism to be formally invalid but, by reason of the *material reversibility* of its major premise, *materially validATABLE*. Such are the two syllogisms cited above.

The conditional syllogism is very useful in reasoning about *particulars,* and for this reason it is employed more frequently in everyday reasoning than the categorical syllogism. Matters of everyday experience do not lend themselves readily to universal formulations or generalizations, and without these latter we cannot have a categorical syllogism. (Recall that unless at least one premise is *universal,* the categorical syllogism is invalid.) It is probably because it does not require any universal enunciations that the conditional syllogism plays so large a part in what might be called *practical* thinking.

For example, I might be curious to know whether a friend had come to visit me while I was away from home. If I endeavored to reason on the basis of whatever particular facts were available to me, my reasoning would be most likely to take the conditional form:

> If Peter had been here, he would have left a note
> But no note was left

or

If Peter had been here, there would have been tire-tracks in the driveway
But there are no tire-tracks in the driveway

or

If Peter had been here, our neighbors the Taylors would have seen him
But the Taylors did not see him.

Where categorical syllogisms can be constructed about such matters, the task is rather formidable and the product likely to be cumbersome and implausible. The conditional form, on the other hand, is quite simple, and seems to be the *natural* mode of reasoning about particulars. Propositions like the following are often the major premises of reasoning in various practical interests:

If I buy now, when prices are high, I shall probably have difficulty in unloading at a profit later.

If the burglar left no fingerprints, he probably wore gloves.

If my partner opens with a two-spade bid, he has at least a four-honor count in his hand.

If this painting were an original Renoir, the dealer would be asking a higher price.

If this soldier had taken atabrine regularly, he would not manifest the symptoms of malaria.

If the cotton crop is poor, the price of dress goods is bound to rise.

If the surgeon insists upon a local anesthetic, Lindsey must have some sort of respiratory complaint.

The particular and quasi-necessary connections of everyday experience can be nicely expressed in the conditional form. The student will better appreciate the simplicity of this mode of expression, if he attempts to state the equivalent of each of the major premises above in the categorical form.

The Disjunctive Syllogism. A good deal of reasoning, both theoretical and practical, involves analysis of possible alternatives. For this, the *disjunctive* (and the complementary *conjunctive*) propositional form provides a natural point of departure.

Recall that the disjunctive proposition asserts in effect that:

"It must be one or the other" (A is either b or c).

Provided the disjunctive proposition is the major premise of a syllogism, the conditions for a valid inference are realized where

the minor denies one member of the disjunction.

Due to the necessity for *at least one* member to be true, if we deny one in the minor, we must affirm the other in the conclusion. By denying one we affirm the other, and the primary figure of the disjunctive syllogism is called *Tollendo Ponens* (affirming by denying). This figure has two moods, the particular mood being determined by which member of the disjunction is denied in the minor:

Tollendo Ponens

(a) A is either b or c
But a is not b
∴ A is c.

(b) A is either b or c
But a is not c
∴ A is b.

If the major premise of a disjunctive syllogism is *formally perfect,* i.e., of the type:

"A is either b or non-b"

two figures are possible. For, since the members of a formally perfect disjunction are explicitly contradictory, this proposition asserts not only that one or the other must be true, but (by implication) that *both cannot be true.* Therefore, we may go not only from the denial of one to the affirmation of the other, but also from the affirmation of one to the denial of the other. The formally perfect disjunctive thus can satisfy the conditions of valid inference in the *two* figures:

1. By *denying* one member in the minor, and affirming the other in the conclusion (*Tollendo Ponens*), as above.

2. By *affirming* one member in the minor, and denying the other in the conclusion (*Ponendo Tollens*).

Since the minor may affirm either part of the disjunction, or deny either part, in each of these figures of the formally perfect disjunctive, we may have two valid moods. Thus:

Tollendo Ponens

(a) A is either b or non-b	(b) A is either b or non-b
But a is not b	But a is not non-b
∴ A is non-b	∴ A is b.

Ponendo Tollens

(a) A is either b or non-b	(b) A is either b or non-b
But a is b	But a is non-b
∴ A is not non-b	∴ A is not b.

The laws of obversion show that the two figures are perfectly equivalent, but this is true only where the two members of the original disjunction are explicitly contradictory. Where the disjunctive proposition is *materially* perfect, but not formally perfect as in:

"The world is either contingent or self-explanatory"

there is only one formally valid figure, *Tollendo Ponens.* Formally, the following syllogism must be declared invalid:

> The world is either contingent or self-explanatory
> But the world is contingent
> ∴ The world is not self-explanatory

though, by reason of its content, it seems to make eminent sense. The most important rule of the disjunctive syllogism is that

the minor premise must deny

one member of the disjunction. The only exception to this rule is where the major premise is a formally perfect disjunctive, for then to affirm one member is the same as to deny the other. We would therefore designate the syllogism above "Invalid, minor affirms." Knowing the materially perfect character of the major premise, however, we might transform it into a *conjunctive* proposition:

> The world cannot be both contingent and self-explanatory

and this can become the basis for a valid *conjunctive syllogism:*

> The world cannot be both contingent and self-explanatory
> But the world is contingent
> ∴ The world is not self-explanatory.

Or again, knowing the major to be materially perfect, we would know that "contingent" and "self-explanatory" are *equivalently contradictory*, and we could therefore legitimately proceed from the affirmation of one to the denial of the other. Thus:

> The world is either contingent or self-explanatory
> But the world is contingent (= non-self-explanatory)
> ∴ The world is not self-explanatory.

Or lastly, we might transform the materially perfect disjunctive major into a formally perfect disjunction:

> "The world is either self-explanatory or non-self-explanatory"

which yields a valid inference even though the minor affirms one member of the disjunction. But the syllogism must be transformed in some such fashion before it can be designated *valid.*

The only other formal fallacy to which the disjunctive syllogism is subject occurs when the *conclusion denies instead of affirming* or (in the case of the formally perfect major where the minor affirms) when the conclusion *affirms instead of denying*. This is an infrequent and, as the examples should show, an implausible fallacy:

Either you study or you fail
But you do not study　　　　　(Fallacy: *Conclusion should affirm*)
∴ You do not fail.

Truth is either useful or non-
　useful
But truth is non-useful　　　　(Fallacy: *Conclusion should deny*)
∴ It is useful.

Where the disjunctive major is *imperfect,* the fallacy of the *minor premise affirming* is particularly flagrant, for then the inference can be justified neither on formal nor material grounds. Thus:

　　Either you study or you fail
　　But you study　　　　　　　(Invalid: *Minor affirms*)
　　∴ You do not fail.

or

　　Either you study or you fail
　　But you fail　　　　　　　　(Invalid: *Minor affirms*)
　　∴ You do not study.

The disjunctive syllogism has considerable rhetorical value, and is frequently employed in political and other debate. A speaker may combine disjunctively his own proposal with one that his audience or his opponent does not wish to accept. Then, rejecting the unwished for alternative, he can with considerable persuasive force advance the alternative that he proposes, as in the following (imaginary) argument:

Either we forsake the principle of national sovereignty, or we surrender all hope for a peaceful world. But the prospect of another war is abhorrent to every thinking man, and inconceivable in view of the destructive power of the atomic bomb. If, then, we would not see our children slaughtered and our cities annihilated, there is but one alternative: We must surrender a measure of our national sovereignty.

In the criticism of disjunctive arguments, formal principles have only a limited application. The principal concern of the critic should be with the material validity of the major premise. Granted that the argument is formally valid, the material logician must ask: Is the disjunction complete? Or is some *tertium quid,* or third alternative, possible? If it is, then the whole structure of the disjunctive argument topples.

In those matters, too, where the difference between extremes is *by imperceptible degrees,* as between persons who are "intelligent" and "unintelligent," or "sane" and "insane," the disjunctive mode of reasoning is generally inappropriate. Popular thinking tends to create absolute, or nearly absolute, dichotomies between "good men" and "bad men," "normal" and "abnormal," "black" and "white," and to make such dichotomies the basis for disjunctive or conjunctive reasoning. It is easy enough to think that a man *"must be either* intelligent or unintelligent," or that a person *"cannot be both* sane and insane," but since these extremes can only be defined rather arbitrarily and relatively, arguments based on such premises do not fit actual situations very well, even though they may be formally valid.

The Conjunctive Syllogism. Since the conjunctive proposition asserts that its two members

cannot both be true

the conditions for a valid inference are present when a conjunctive major premise having been asserted,

the minor affirms one member of the conjunction.

A typical conjunctive like

"You cannot be both soldier and sailor"

says you can't be *both;* it does not mean that you must be *either.* In the basic figure of the conjunctive syllogism, then, *the minor must affirm,* and there will be two moods, depending on which member of the conjunction is affirmed in the minor. Thus:

Ponendo Tollens

    a) You cannot be both soldier and sailor
       But you are a soldier
       ∴ You are not a sailor.

  b) You cannot be both soldier and sailor
   But you are a sailor
   ∴ You are not a soldier.

Unless the two members of the major are explicitly contradictory (thereby constituting it a *formally perfect conjunctive*), the corresponding examples in *Tollendo Ponens* (minor denies) are invalid:

Ponendo Tollens (invalid)

  a) You cannot be both soldier and sailor
   But you are not a soldier
   ∴ You are a sailor.

  b) You cannot be both soldier and sailor
   But you are not a sailor
   ∴ You are a soldier.

Ponendo Tollens (valid, major formally perfect)

  a) A being cannot be both mortal and non-mortal
   But this being is not mortal
   ∴ This being is non-mortal.

  b) A being cannot be both mortal and non-mortal
   But this being is not non-mortal
   ∴ This being is mortal.

If the major is formally perfect, the two moods in *Tollendo Ponens* are also, of course, valid. In this case, and in this case only, the conjunctive syllogism has *four* valid moods.

  As with the disjunctive, a formal error may occur in the *conclusion*, if the conclusion affirms instead of denying; or, in the case of the formally perfect major and the denying minor, if the conclusion denies instead of affirming. These are more or less *grammatical* fallacies, and unlikely to occur in actual argument, as the following examples should make clear:

  You cannot be both soldier and sailor
  But you are a soldier (Invalid: *conclusion should deny*)
  ∴ You are a sailor.

A being cannot be both mortal and non-mortal
But this being is not mortal   (Invalid: *conclusion should*
∴ This being is mortal.   *affirm "non-mortal"*)

(Notice that a negative statement may be the *affirmation* of a negative member, and an affirmative statement the *negation* of a negative member.)

Unless the minor is universal, a *particular* conjunctive proposition like

"Some man cannot be both rich and honest"
or
"Everyone cannot be both competent and modest"

cannot give rise to a valid conjunctive syllogism. Since the major is restricted, there is no guarantee that it applies to the instance cited in the minor. A syllogism like the following:

Not all statements can be both profound and clear
This statement is profound
∴ This statement is not clear

should be designated "invalid, conjunctive major particular." A *singular* conjunctive, on the other hand, may form the basis for a perfectly valid syllogism, if the same individual thing is referred to in the minor. The following syllogism is thus formally valid:

This statement cannot be both profound and clear
But this statement is profound
∴ This statement is not clear

however questionable the truth of the major premise may be.

The precisely complementary character of the disjunctive and conjunctive forms makes it easy to confuse the valid forms and fallacies of one with the valid forms and fallacies of the other. Recourse to the following table should minimize the tendency to confuse the two.

Valid Disjunctive Forms	*Valid Conjunctive Forms*
1. Minor denies and conclusion affirms (*Tollendo Ponens*)	1. Minor affirms and conclusion denies (*Ponendo Tollens*)

Valid Disjunctive Forms	*Valid Conjunctive Forms*

2. Minor affirms and conclusion denies
   (*Ponendo Tollens:* valid *only* where major formally perfect)

2. Minor denies and conclusion affirms
   (*Tollendo Ponens:* valid *only* where major formally perfect)

Disjunctive Fallacies	*Conjunctive Fallacies*

1. Minor affirms
   (Exception: Permissible where major formally perfect)

1. Minor denies
   (Exception: Permissible where major formally perfect)

2. Conclusion denies
   (Exception: Permissible where major formally perfect and minor affirms)

2. Conclusion affirms
   (Exception: Permissible where major formally perfect and minor denies)

3. Conclusion affirms
   (Fallacious only if major formally perfect and minor affirms)

3. Conclusion denies
   (Fallacious only if major formally perfect and minor denies)

4. Major premise particular

Section 8: Chain Arguments

Important and difficult conclusions can seldom be arrived at by a single syllogism. Such conclusions may require a series of deductions so related that the conclusion of the first becomes a premise of the second, the conclusion of the second a premise for the third, and so on. In philosophy and mathematics, these *chain arguments* may achieve a forbidding degree of complexity, compounding many syllogisms, of various kinds and variously abbreviated, to arrive at a single conclusion like:

"The square on the hypotenuse of a right triangle is equal to the sum of the squares on the other two sides"

or

"A finite distance is infinitely divisible but not infinitely divided."

We shall be concerned only with elementary forms of the chain argument, viz., the *polysyllogism* and the *sorites*, and a related form, the *epicheirema*.

The Polysyllogism. This is the chain argument in its simplest form. For example:

> Every divisible living thing is corruptible
> Every organism is a divisible living thing
> ∴ Every organism is corruptible
> Every animal is organism
> ∴ Every animal is corruptible
> Every man is animal
> ∴ Every man is corruptible.

This is simply a series of syllogisms in *Barbara,* so related that the conclusion of the first becomes the major premise of the second, and the conclusion of the second the major premise of the third. The only abbreviation is that the intermediate conclusions are not repeated. If each of the syllogisms involved is valid, the polysyllogism is valid. If any one of the constituent syllogisms is invalid, the chain, of course, is worthless. Thus, if in the example given we substitute for the final minor a universal negative statement like:

> "No plant is animal"

and then go on to conclude:

> "∴ No plant is corruptible"

we have a patent instance of an *illicit major*. For the simple polysyllogism there are thus no special rules. Apply the ordinary rules of the categorical syllogism to each of the syllogisms involved, and determine the formal validity of the whole accordingly.

The Sorites. This is a specially abbreviated form of syllogistic chain, in which certain premises are omitted, and in which certain others may be transposed to render the sequence more obvious. The simple sorites has two forms, the *Aristotelian* and the *Goclenian*. The *Aristotelian,* or classic, form resembles a series of indirect first (or fourth) figure syllogisms. In it the predicate of the first proposition becomes the subject of the second, the predicate of the second the subject of the third, and so on. Thus:

The Aristotelian Sorites

$$\text{Every } \overset{S}{\text{triangle}} \text{ is a } \overset{M_1}{\text{polygon}}$$

$$\text{Every } \overset{M_1}{\text{polygon}} \text{ is a } \overset{M_2}{\text{plane}}$$

$$\text{Every } \overset{M_2}{\text{plane}} \text{ is a } \overset{M_3}{\text{magnitude}}$$

$$\text{Every } \overset{M_3}{\text{magnitude}} \text{ is a } \overset{P}{\text{quantity}}$$

$$\therefore \text{Every } \overset{S}{\text{triangle}} \text{ is a } \overset{P}{\text{quantity}}.$$

Since the first proposition in the series contains the subject of the conclusion-to-be, it is the minor premise, while the next to last proposition is the major. The conclusion unites the subject of the first premise with the predicate of the last, and this conclusion is not drawn until the chain is complete. The sorites contains as many syllogisms as there are middle terms, or as there are propositions less two. In the Aristotelian sorites, it will be noted, the middle terms show an *increasing* extension or universality from first to last premise.

One can see the advantages of this kind of arrangement if the argument is a very long one. Let us suppose that a mathematical demonstration has twenty steps. If each of these steps is expressed in a complete syllogism, sixty propositions will be required for the argument. The sorites form permits the expression of the same reasoning in twenty-two propositions, a considerable economy.

Though the Aristotelian sorites is not found in the writings of Aristotle, it was the only form discussed by logicians till the close of the 16th century. At that time, the logician Goclenius suggested an alternative form which has since borne his name. The Goclenian sorites resembles a first figure syllogism, and exhibits a descending series of middle terms, the first of which is the subject of the first premise and the predicate of the second, the second of which is the subject of the second premise and the predicate of the third, and so on. The first premise contains the predicate of the conclusion-to-be, and is thus the major premise, while the last premise is the minor. Thus:

The Goclenian Sorites

M_1 P
Every magnitude is a quantity
M_2 M_1
Every plane is a magnitude
M_3 M_2
Every polygon is a plane
S M_3
Every triangle is a polygon
S   P
∴ Every triangle is a quantity.

The *Aristotelian* sorites can be broken up into a series of formal syllogisms, such that the conclusion of the first becomes the *minor* premise of the second, and so on. Thus, we might transform the example given:

Every polygon is a plane
Every triangle is a polygon
∴ Every triangle is a plane
Every plane is a magnitude
Every triangle is a plane
∴ Every triangle is a magnitude
Every magnitude is a quantity
Every triangle is a magnitude
∴ Every triangle is a quantity.

It is possible then to determine whether or not the constituent syllogisms are valid or invalid, and to judge the sorites accordingly.

The *Goclenian* sorites can be transformed into an ordinary polysyllogism simply by drawing the conclusion from the first pair of premises and making this conclusion the major premise of the next sequence, and so on. For the example given the polysyllogism is:

Every magnitude is a quantity
Every plane is a magnitude
∴ Every plane is a quantity
Every polygon is a plane
∴ Every polygon is a quantity
Every triangle is a polygon
∴ Every triangle is a quantity.

From this we can see that the Goclenian sorites is simply a *polysyllogism in which no conclusion is drawn till the last premise is stated,* so that it, too, can be adjudged valid or invalid by simply applying to it the rules of the categorical syllogism.

Though the sorites can be thus reduced to the form of a series of ordinary categorical syllogisms, it is possible to formulate two rules for the sorites as such, whether Aristotelian or Goclenian. These are:

1. Only one premise may be particular—the one which contains the minor term.
2. Only one premise may be negative—the one which contains the major term.

If more than one premise is negative, or more than one premise particular, obviously no conclusion can be drawn (see Rules 5 and 8 of the categorical syllogism, pp. 145, 146).

If a premise is particular, it must be the premise which contains the minor term (the S of the conclusion). In the Aristotelian sorites, this is the first premise; in the Goclenian, it is the last. If any other premise is particular, one of the syllogisms in the sorites has an *undistributed middle.*

If a premise is negative, it must be the premise which contains the major term (the P of the conclusion). In the Aristotelian sorites, this is the last premise; in the Goclenian, it is the first. If any other premise is negative, we have an instance of an *illicit major* term. The student may verify these rules by constructing a sorites which does not adhere to them. An illicit major or an undistributed middle is certain to result.

In extended demonstrations the sorites is, as we have indicated, a valuable form. Its complexity, however (especially that of the Aristotelian sorites), makes it a favorite vehicle for material fallacies. It is a form in the employment of which the beginner in logic should exercise great caution. In most cases, it is on the whole simpler and safer to employ several syllogisms when constructing arguments, and, when given a sorites to be judged, to break it down into the simple syllogistic form.

The Epicheirema. This form is closely related to the sorites. It has the appearance of a categorical syllogism, one of whose premises is a *causal proposition.* (Occasionally, *both* premises may take the causal form.) Since a causal proposition denotes an *enthymeme,* and an enthymeme a syllogism, the epicheirema is in reality at least *two* syllogisms, one of which is abbreviated. Consider the following very simple example:

> Every man is mortal
> Every Hindu is man since every Hindu is rational
> ∴ Every Hindu is mortal.

Here it is the *minor* premise which is the conclusion of another syllogism. This form resembles the *Aristotelian* sorites and can similarly be broken down into syllogisms:

> Every rational being is man
> Every Hindu is rational
> ∴ Every Hindu is man
> Every man is mortal
> Every Hindu is man
> ∴ Every Hindu is mortal.

If the causal proposition is in the *major* premise, the epicheirema resembles a *Goclenian* sorites.

> Every man is mortal because every man is organism
> Every Hindu is man
> ∴ Every Hindu is mortal.

Explicating this, we have:

> Every organism is mortal
> Every man is organism
> ∴ Every man is mortal
> Every Hindu is man
> ∴ Every Hindu is mortal.

Plainly, this is an ordinary polysyllogism. If the third proposition is omitted (thereby not drawing any conclusion until the end of the argument) we have a simple Goclenian sorites. The epicheirema, therefore, is easily reducible to forms with which we are already familiar. It should be a simple matter to make explicit the syllogism contained in the causal proposition, and to verify that each of the constituent syllogisms contains no formal fallacy.

Chain arguments are not limited to the categorical mode, but may combine conditional, disjunctive, and conjunctive forms with it. The famous Aristotelian-Thomistic argument for the existence of a Prime Mover, or first cause of change, is a classic example of the chain argument which begins *categorically* with a statement of fact and a statement of principle to which a proof is appended, develops *disjunctively* the two apparently possible alternatives and finally demonstrates *conditionally* that only one of these alternatives is ontologically possible. Philosophy and mathematics, as we have said, make extensive use of such complex forms. Sometimes, these arguments are fallacious, but they are of limited interest to the formal logician, since the fallacy (if any) is seldom formal. The student who can analyze an extended argument into its component sequences is equipped to deal formally with any reasonings of this type.

SECTION 9: THE OBLIQUE SYLLOGISM

The *oblique syllogism* is often implied in arithmetical and similar forms of reasoning, but it is seldom made explicit. For this reason, the precise nature of those modes of reasoning which imply it is often misunderstood. The oblique syllogism derives its name from the fact that one of its terms is (in Latin) in an *oblique* case, i.e., a case other than the nominative. It differs logically from the direct or ordinary categorical syllogism, in that it does not simply identify two terms in virtue of their identity with a third term. Instead, a certain *relation* (which is what the oblique case indicated) which applies to one term is simultaneously inferred to apply to another term with which the first term has been identified. In the following example the relation is italicized and designated by the letter "r":

$$\begin{array}{cc} \text{M} & \text{P} \\ \end{array}$$
My father is a lawyer
$$\begin{array}{ccc} \text{S} & \text{r} & \text{M} \\ \end{array}$$
Every child of mine is a *grandchild of* my father
$$\begin{array}{ccc} \text{S} & \text{r} & \text{P} \\ \end{array}$$
∴ Every child of mine is the *grandchild of* a lawyer

or

$$\begin{array}{ccc} \text{r} & \text{M} & \text{P} \\ \end{array}$$
Every *upholder of* tyranny is unjust
$$\begin{array}{cc} \text{S} & \text{M} \\ \end{array}$$
But totalitarianism is tyranny
$$\begin{array}{ccc} \text{r} & \text{S} & \text{P} \\ \end{array}$$
∴ Every *upholder of* totalitarianism is unjust.

The perspicacious reader will note that in the oblique syllogism it is not necessary for the middle term to be universal. The quantity of the middle term is in this form unimportant, since it is not the universality of the middle term, but the fact that it is *modified by a relation,* that justifies the inference. The major and minor terms, however, come under the ordinary rules of the categorical syllogism, and cannot be broader in the conclusion than in the premises.

Aside from the possibility of an illicit major or minor, formal fallacies in the oblique syllogism are exceptional. The principal concern of the logician in judging an oblique syllogism is to know whether *the relation involved is transitive,* i.e., to know if it can logically pass from one term to another. In the following example, the relation "world's greatest" is obviously *intransitive,* and the sequence therefore *materially invalid:*

$$\overset{\text{M}}{\text{Every physicist is a}} \overset{\text{P}}{\text{man}}$$

$$\overset{\text{S}}{\text{Einstein is the}} \overset{\text{r}}{\textit{world's greatest}} \overset{\text{M}}{\text{physicist}}$$

$$\therefore \overset{\text{S}}{\text{Einstein is the}} \overset{\text{r}}{\textit{world's greatest}} \overset{\text{P}}{\text{man.}}$$

Modern logicians have explored extensively the principles governing the transitivity of relations and have thereby added an important chapter to material logic. It is unfortunate that by and large modern logicians have not understood the importance of the oblique syllogism as a bridge between what they call the "predicational logic" of Aristotle and modern *relational* logic. This has led to errors in modern *formal* logic, because it has led many thinkers to regard certain *relational arguments* (which really involve the oblique syllogism) as entirely nonsyllogistic in character.

An outstanding example is the so-called *a fortiori* argument, in which the conclusion unquestionably follows logically, while the argument itself seems to have *four terms.* For instance:

> B is greater than C
> A is greater than B
> ∴ A is greater than C.

The classical logician insists that this argument as it stands is invalid since it has four terms. Modern logicians insist, on the other hand, that since the conclusion does follow, this must be a valid nonsyllogistic deduction. There is merit in both contentions. *As a syllogism,* this argument is invalid, yet it is difficult to see how anyone could accept the premises and reject the conclusion. The paradox is overcome, however, if we recognize that the *a fortiori* argument is actually a shorthand statement of *two* valid syllogisms, one of which is *oblique.* Putting the argument in proper form, we should say:

$$\text{Everything } \overset{r}{\textit{greater than}} \text{ that which is greater } \overset{M}{\text{than C is itself}}$$

$$\overset{P}{\text{greater than C}}$$
$$\overset{S}{\text{But B}} \text{ is greater } \overset{M}{\text{than C}}$$
$$\therefore \text{ Everything } \overset{r}{\textit{greater than}} \overset{S}{\text{B}} \text{ is greater } \overset{P}{\text{than C}}$$
$$\overset{M}{\text{Everything greater than B}} \text{ is greater } \overset{P}{\text{than C}}$$
$$\overset{S}{\text{But A}} \text{ is greater } \overset{M}{\text{than B}}$$
$$\therefore \overset{S}{\text{A}} \text{ is greater } \overset{P}{\text{than C.}}$$

Although the explication of the *a fortiori* argument is rather cumbersome, it shows the consistency of this form with the general principles of the syllogism. The student should endeavor to follow the pattern of this explication, and should essay one or two examples on his own. Thereafter, the *a fortiori* argument should offer him no particular difficulty. Let us consider one more example:

> Mexico is north of Panama
> The United States is north of Mexico
> ∴ The United States is north of Panama.

If asked to judge this argument *as a syllogism,* we should be forced to say "invalid, *logical quadruped.*" It can be easily converted into two syllogisms, however, one *oblique* and one *direct,* and both valid. Thus:

$$\text{Everything } \overset{r}{\textit{north of}} \text{ that which is north of } \overset{M}{\text{Panama is itself}}$$

$$\overset{P}{\text{north of Panama}}$$
$$\overset{S}{\text{But Mexico}} \text{ is north of } \overset{M}{\text{Panama}}$$
$$\therefore \text{ Everything } \overset{r}{\textit{north of}} \overset{S}{\text{Mexico}} \text{ is north of } \overset{M}{\text{Panama.}}$$

$$\text{Everything north of Mexico is north of Panama} \quad {}^{M} \quad {}^{P}$$

Everything north of Mexico is north of Panama

But the United States is north of Mexico

∴. The United States is north of Panama.

The system is simply to make the relationally modified term in the original conclusion the basis of the major premise of an oblique syllogism. To this we add the *first* statement of the *a fortiori* argument, and draw the obvious conclusion. This constitutes our oblique syllogism. The conclusion of this oblique syllogism thereupon is made the major premise of the direct syllogism. Added to it is the *second* statement of the *a fortiori* argument. This combination leads logically to the original conclusion, and the explication into valid syllogistic form is complete.

The oblique syllogism can always be expressed in direct form. For example:

This book is a classic

Every student *enjoyed* this book

∴. Every student *enjoyed* a classic

can be expressed directly:

Every person who enjoyed this book enjoyed a classic

Every student enjoyed this book

∴. Every student enjoyed a classic.

As Maritain notes, however, the *same movement of the mind* is not expressed in the direct as in the original oblique syllogism.[9] The direct syllogism identifies two terms simply on the basis of their identity with a middle term *taken universally* once; in the oblique syllogism the middle term, which need not be universal, serves simply as one ground of a transitive relation. The essential part of the inference is the passage of this relation from the middle to the major (or in some cases to the minor). Consequently, the oblique syllogism constitutes a distinct, though not irreducible, mode of inference.

[9] *Op. cit.*, p. 252.

There remain certain forms of deductive argumentation which we have not considered at length—for instance, the *dilemma*. Such arguments, however, combine forms which we have already studied. Their chief interest arises in the *material factors* that govern their validity or invalidity, so that there is little need to discuss them in an introductory course in *formal* logic. If the student has mastered the forms of the categorical syllogism and the nature of the various kinds of hypothetical statement, he should never be without principles by which he can estimate the formal validity of any deductive argument.

LOGIC EXERCISES

Introduction

1. Define logic in general.
2. How does logic differ from all other sciences?
3. For what sort of thinking is a thorough grounding in logic necessary? Why is not common sense sufficient for that purpose?
4. When the scientist philosophizes, what error is he prone to commit?
5. What is meant by *natural logic,* and what is its relation to *acquired logic?*
6. What is meant by saying that logic is a *liberal art* as well as a *speculative science?*
7. Give an original example of an incorrect syllogism whose premises and conclusion are true.
8. Give an original example of a correct syllogism whose premises and conclusion are false.
9. Give an original example of a syllogism which is both correct and true.
10. What is meant by *major,* or *material, logic?*
11. Distinguish between induction and deduction. Where is *incomplete induction* important, and what are its limitations?
12. Assuming the following form as typical of incomplete induction, take an argument derived from a chemistry or biology text and recast it in the proper inductive form:

    M_1, M_2, M_3, M_4, etc. without exception are P
    But the universal standing for M_1, M_2, M_3, etc. is S
    ∴ Every S is P.

13. What are the two aspects under which deduction must always be considered?
14. How does *deductive inference* involve *judgment?* When do we judge?
15. What simpler mental operation does judgment always involve?
16. Since logical thinking must always be communicated by language, why not say that logic is the study of language?
17. Outline the six general topics to be treated in this course.

Chapter 1

1. Is simple apprehension our first source of knowledge? Explain.
2. What is meant by internal sensation? Give examples.
3. When can intellect be said to begin functioning?
4. How does human *intellection* differ from animal *intelligence?*
5. Define simple apprehension.
6. How is *simple apprehension* distinguished from *judgment?*
7. Distinguish between *simple apprehension* as an *act*, and *simple apprehension* as the *product of an act*. Give some synonyms for both.
8. Show in detail how the concept of "brutality" or "honesty" or "residence" differs from any image that might accompany that concept.
9. Why do many people confuse *concepts* with *visual images?*
10. Name two functions of the image relative to the concept.
11. Is it always necessary to have images when we have concepts? Explain.
12. If the *judgment* does not unite *images,* what does it do?
13. Isn't it possible for a very vague image to be universal? Explain.
14. Can a simple apprehension be false? Explain.
15. What do we mean by *notes* in logic?
16. What is meant by the *comprehension* of a concept?
17. What is the relation of the *comprehension* to the *essential definition?*
18. Identify the numbered portions of the following as A. *proximate genus;* B. *ultimate genus;* C. *remote genus;* D. *generic difference;* E. *logical species;* F. *specific difference:*

		1
	2	Substance
Material		3
	4	Body
Living		5
	6	Organism
Sentient		7
	8	Animal
Rational		9
		Man

19. Distinguish between *specific property* and *descriptive characteristic* of "man," and give some examples of each.

20. Give the *essential comprehension*, some *generic properties*, and some *descriptive characteristics* of "sheep," "lion," "antelope," "ant," "house fly," "zinnia," "streptococcus," "mushroom."

21. Identify the numbered portions of the following as in 18:

	1
2	Quantity
Continuous	3
4	Magnitude
Two-dimensional	5
6	Surface
Plane	7
8	Plane
Enclosed	9
10	Enclosed Plane
Rectilinear	11
12	Polygon
Three-sided	13
	Triangle

22. Give the essential comprehension and some specific properties of "Parallelogram," "square," "circle," "ellipse."

23. What is meant by the *extension* of a concept?

24. Does extension have a real, or only an ideal, existence? Explain.

25. If man were the only actually existing animal, would the extension of "man" be greater than, less than, or equal to that of "animal"? Explain.

26. Why *must* extension and comprehension vary inversely?

27. Distinguish *abstract* from *concrete* concepts in terms of the notions of "being" and "state of being."

28. Mention three *concrete* terms which are "abstract" in the popular sense.

29. If every direct concept is abstract, how can we justify speaking of certain concepts as *concrete?*

30. Classify each of the following as concrete or abstract:
concreteness, immaterial (substance), hexagon, beauty, octogenarian, polygon, materiality, abstract (notion), sixteen, twenty-fourth (man), possibility, blue (book), blue (funk), horse, friendly (person), friendly (gesture), amity, angelic (being), soul, disgust, thickness, divine (nature), color, circle, quantity, hair-do, sob, chemistry, vague (impression), Minotaur, proof, boundary, decisive (victory), action, merchandise, sensation, pneumonia, fool, voice, scream, ear.

31. What do we mean by the *singulars* of a concept?
32. Distinguish between *collective* and *divisive* concepts.
33. Classify each of the following as *collective* or *divisive:*
    chain, newspaper, royal flush, trio, playing card, organism, octave, love, piano, spectrum, bouquet, green, brick wall, book, task force, sailor, battalion, baseball, symphony.
34. Why is every direct concept *in itself* universal?
35. What is the real meaning of a "particular concept"? "Singular concept"?
36. Distinguish the "singular *concept*" from the "singulars *of* a concept."
37. Distinguish the *enumerative* from the *genuine* universal.
38. What is meant by a *term?* Distinguish *terms* from *syncategorematic words.*
39. What does the term express *immediately*, and what *mediately?*
40. To what three kinds of existence does a term relate?
41. What is meant by the *univocal* term? Besides technical terms, what other kind is usually univocal?
42. Distinguish between *analogous* and *equivocal* terms. Give examples of three terms which can be *both* analogous and equivocal, and illustrate the different meanings.
43. Decide whether each of the following terms is primarily *univocal* or not. If the term seems *analogous* or *equivocal*, specify which it seems to be primarily, and exemplify your answer:
    loaf, blanket, hairpin, fair, maid, plane, sweet, lemon, lucubrate, fungo, heavy, box, cigarette, atomic, abstract, ring, rude, sensation, chemistry, scientific, speculative, immoral, ion, personality, salt, bond, piano stool.
44. Select a paragraph from a newspaper editorial or political statement and underline each term which is possibly analogous or equivocal. Decide whether each of these terms is *used* univocally, or whether the force of the argument at all depends on the ambiguity of any term.
45. Take a stanza of poetry or a short poem—a stanza of Keats' *Ode on a Grecian Urn* or *Ode to a Nightingale* or any of Shakespeare's sonnets, for example—and underscore all the analogous terms. How much of the esthetic quality of the verse depends on these terms? Are any of these terms "loaded"?
46. Is a change in *supposition* a change in *meaning?* Explain. Does a term *in itself* have any supposition? Why?
47. Take the term "cow" and use it in each of the three main types of supposition.

48. Outline the rules for determining whether the subject-term of a given proposition is in *real, logical,* or *material* supposition.
49. Must a subject-term in real supposition stand for an actually existent being? Explain.
50. Determine the supposition of the subject-term in each of the following propositions:

  a) Man is studied by psychology.
  b) The centaur is vertebrate.
  c) Red is one-syllabled.
  d) Four is greater than two.
  e) The animal is the one sentient organism.
  f) Man is rational.
  g) Man is a concrete concept.
  h) My direct concepts are universal.
  i) Beauty produces intellectual pleasure.
  j) The dog is quadruped.
  k) A square circle is impossible to conceive.
  l) The fish is a type of vertebrate.
  m) Justice is abstract to the second degree.
  n) *Pendennis* is a work by Thackeray.
  o) Dog is a substantive.
  p) Every direct concept is abstract.
  q) My soul is my own.
  r) Some woman is intelligent.
  s) This cobalt is a rare specimen.
  t) Minus five is less than minus four.
  u) Dachshund means badger dog.
  v) Six is twice three.
  w) Intersecting parallel lines are paralloids.
  x) Man is the expression of a concrete concept.
  y) A temperature of minus 200 degrees centigrade is very cold.

Chapter 2

1. Define judgment. What does the judgment unite or separate?
2. What is wrong with this definition of judgment: Judgment is the perception of the identity or non-identity of two terms or concepts?
3. Explain what is meant by the enunciative proposition.
4. Is there any verbal difference between enunciative and judicative propositions? How do they differ?

5. Which are more frequent, enunciative or judicative propositions?
6. How many mental acts are there in a judgment?
7. Define each of the "parts" of the judgment. Of the judicative proposition.
8. Give two examples of sentences which are not propositions.
9. Distinguish the *subject-term, copula,* and *predicate-term* of the following:

   a) Out of deference to your wishes I am going to reconsider his application for renewal of his contract.
   b) Often is his gold complexion dimmed.
   c) Nor is my ear with thy tongue's tune delighted.
   d) All I have is a voice to undo the folded lie.
   e) Not in all instances is this true.

10. What are the *matter* and *form* of the proposition? To what do these correspond in the judgment?
11. Put each of the following propositions in logical form:

    a) Curiosity killed the cat.
    b) Fire burns.
    c) Who pays the piper calls the tune.
    d) Ordinary caution would have prevented the disaster.
    e) Each man kills the thing he loves.
    f) The ambassador delivered a message to the premier.
    g) Friends have all things in common.
    h) Beauty passes.
    i) I hope you are feeling well.
    j) Pop goes the weasel.

12. How do *categorical* propositions differ from *hypothetical?*
13. What determines the *quantity* of a proposition?
14. What *quantifying particle* is *always* a sign of universality? What words are sometimes signs of universality, and sometimes signs of particularity?
15. Distinguish between singular and particular propositions.
16. Which of the two following arguments might represent a genuine inference? Why?

Every book in this library was written by a literate person
Silas Marner is a book in this library
∴ *Silas Marner* was written by a literate person.

Every book in this library was a gift from Carnegie
Silas Marner is a book in this library
∴ *Silas Marner* was a gift from Carnegie.

17. What is meant by the *quality* of a proposition?
18. Give two examples of indefinite propositions which are *equivalently universal,* and two examples which are not.
19. How may *indefinite* and *singular* propositions, which are ordinarily *taken as universal,* be distinguished from explicit universal propositions?
20. What is the one proper form of the *explicit universal negative* proposition? What is the character of the copula in this proposition? Explain.
21. Using "x" for subject and "y" for predicate, write out the *five* forms of the O proposition.
22. Is the proposition "Some man is animal" true or false? Explain.
23. Give two examples of *abstract singular* propositions, and two examples of *abstract indefinite* propositions.
24. Exemplify each of the *circumstantial quantifiers.*
25. Classify each of the following propositions as A, E, I, or O. (If you wish to use subscripts to denote indefinite, singular, or circumstantially quantified proposition, you may do so.)

    A (1) Every animal is mobile.
    A (2) Every disease is non-incurable.
    A (3) All heathens are not immoral.
    E (4) No snake is inedible.
    I (5) Effort is not always rewarded.
  IO (6) Not every knock is a boost.
    O (7) Gold is a precious metal.
    I (8) Most politicians are corruptible.
    O (9) Some ignorant person is not stupid.
    E (10) Rationalizations are never reasons.
    E (11) All hope is not lost.
    I (12) Sometimes too hot the eye of heaven shines.
    I (13) Some doubt is praiseworthy.
    I (14) The isosceles triangle has its base angles equal.
    A (15) Fifteen is the square root of two hundred and twenty-five.
    I (16) Justice is no easy ideal.
    E (17) All who are not concerned are requested to leave.
    O (18) Cancer is not incurable.
    O (19) Not every nonresident is excluded from protection.
    O (20) None who are unintelligent are expected to succeed.
    O (21) Under certain conditions not to tell the truth is permissible.
    O (22) Some non-x is y.
    A (23) This x is y.

I(24) Not all x is non-y.
O(25) That x is not y.
o(26) Some non-x is not non-y.
I(27) X is non-y.
O(28) Some that are not x are y.
E(29) All x is not non-y.
I (30) X is not non-y.
I(31) Few x are y.
A(32) All that is not x is y.
A(33) All non-x is non-y.
O (34) Not every non-x is y.
E(35) X is never y.

26. Distinguish *modal* from *assertoric* propositions.
27. Give three alternative ways of writing "must be" and "cannot be."
28. Show the parallel between the O proposition on the one hand, and the particular impossible (PI) and particular contingent (PC) propositions on the other.
29. Classify each of the following propositions. If assertoric, classify as A, E, I, O, using the subscripts "i," "s," and "c" where appropriate. If modal, classify according to both dictum (if any) and mode, as UN, PI, Imp, N, UC, P, etc.

    (1) Some must succeed.
    (2) Not all can fail.
    (3) None need remain.
    (4) All cannot win.
    (5) Every man can do his best.
    (6) Truth must be upheld.
    (7) Men sometimes profit by experience.
    (8) Not all need wait.
    (9) No one can deny this.
  (10) Men can never be perfect.
  (11) Some restraint is desirable.
  (12) Every child must be disciplined.
  (13) Not all can be expected to have patience.
  (14) Some cannot be trusted.
  (15) Not all x can be y.
  (16) Intelligence cannot be acquired.
  (17) No non-x can be non-y.
  (18) Every x need not be y.
  (19) All that cannot be x is y.

(20) X must be non-y.

(21) Everything that is not x must be y.

(22) X must be non-y.

(23) Not everything that can be x is y.

(24) This x must be y.

(25) X need not be y.

(26) No x need be y.

(27) None that can be x is y.

(28) Some x can be non-y.

(29) This x is no y.

(30) X is not always y.

30. What is meant by a hypothetical proposition?

31. What are the two major divisions of hypothetical propositions? What is the basic form of sequential proposition?

32. Exactly what does the conditional proposition assert, and what does it *not* assert?

33. The consequent of a conditional proposition is implicitly in the necessary mode. Explain.

34. Give an original example of:

   a) a true conditional proposition whose members are false;

   b) a false conditional proposition whose members are true;

   c) a true conditional proposition whose members are true.

35. What is the *copula* in "Unless the seed die, it will not bear fruit"? How else might this be said?

36. Are "wherever" and "whenever" equivalent to "if"? Explain.

37. Is a proposition beginning with "if" always conditional? Explain.

38. Exactly what does a disjunctive proposition assert?

39. Can both members of a true disjunctive proposition be true? Can both be false?

40. Distinguish between perfect and imperfect disjunctive propositions, and give an example of each. Give an example of a *formally* perfect disjunctive.

41. Reduce each of the following disjunctive propositions to *two* or *four* conditional propositions, according as it is an imperfect or perfect disjunctive:

   a) A thing is either colored or without color.

   b) A being is either mortal or not man.

   c) A thing is either extended or not material.

   d) A man either tries or he does not succeed.

   e) A is either b or c.

f) X is either non-y or z.

g) X is either y or non-y.

42. Similarly reduce each of the following propositions to two or four conditional propositions:

   a) A nation cannot be unprepared and secure.
   b) You cannot be both performer and spectator.
   c) A door cannot be both closed and ajar.
   d) A geometrical figure cannot be both plane and solid.
   e) A cannot be both b and c.
   f) A cannot be both b and non-c.
   g) A cannot be both b and non-b.

43. In the conjunctive proposition, what manifests the necessity of the sequence? How does the conjunctive differ from the conditional and disjunctive in this respect?

44. How are copulative *propositions* distinguished from *sequential* propositions? Under what conditions is a copulative proposition false?

45. What is the difference between a proposition like "Sodium and chlorine are chemical elements" and one like "Sodium and chlorine compose common table salt"?

46. Why is a proposition like "This picture is well painted but a masterpiece" somewhat lacking in sense?

47. Does the proposition "Only fools are in favor of war" say that "*All* fools are in favor of war" or that "All in favor of war are fools"?

48. Reduce each of the following *exponible* propositions to the *pure copulative* form:

   a) Every man except Adam was once a child.
   b) Justice alone is worth fighting for.
   c) None but the good die happy.
   d) Man as animal is teachable.
   e) Because truth is worth while, it is difficult.
   f) Every a except b is c.
   g) X alone is y.
   h) C as b is o.
   i) Only p is q.
   j) Since q is r, q is s.
   k) None except a is b.
   l) None except x need be y.
   m) Every a except b must be c.

n) Only x can be y.

o) A as b cannot be c.

49. Distinguish between *contrary, contradictory,* and *subcontrary* propositions. What is the most extreme form of opposition? What is the perfect form of opposition? Why is this?

50. Construct a *square of opposition,* using X and Y for S and P. Granted any one of the propositions in the square as true or false, give the corresponding status of each of the other propositions.

51. Construct an analogous square for the *modal* proposition.

52. In the *octagon* of opposition for the *quantified modal* proposition, how many *contraries* are there? Granted that the universal necessary (UN) proposition is *true,* what is the status of the remaining seven propositions in the octagon?

53. What is the subcontrary of "Money is not valued everywhere"? What is the contrary of "People always want more than they have"?

54. Give the contradictory of each of the following propositions. Give the contrary or subcontrary, if the proposition has any.

   (1) Some crow is white.
   (2) All men are not intelligent.
   (3) No onion is sweet-smelling. *E*
   (4) Every ape is irrational.
   (5) John is not here. *E*
   (6) You never can tell. *E*
   (7) Age must be respected. *E*
   (8) No moron is a logician.
   (9) Every pedant is a bore.
  (10) Homicide is not always murder.
  (11) Some criminal is not reformable. *o*
  (12) Now it can be told.
  (13) Indifference cannot right wrongs.
  (14) All mistakes must be rectified.
  (15) No race can be superior in all respects.
  (16) No child need go hungry.
  (17) All cannot receive this saying.
  (18) The submissive person is always insecure.
  (19) Not all need go.
  (20) Under certain conditions we can achieve certainty.

55. Why do we employ the "may not be" or "may be" forms in opposing the *consequent* of a *conditional proposition?* With

regard to which member of the *disjunctive proposition* do we employ these forms? Why is it unnecessary to use these forms in contradicting the *conjunctive proposition?*

56. In the modal proposition "need not be" is contradicted by "must be" and "can be" by "cannot be." This is not the case in the disjunctive and the consequent of the conditional proposition. How are these forms there contradicted?

57. Give the contradictory of each of the following propositions:

   (1) If the dog is hungry, he will howl.
   (2) If all remain, all must take the consequences.
   (3) If man is naturally free, he need not be a political slave.
   (4) Either we avoid war or civilization is lost.
   (5) You cannot be just and indifferent to racial prejudice.
   (6) All who do not obey the law are guilty.
   (7) Some nonhuman is not insensitive.
   (8) Neither one of these teams need win.
   (9) Men have greater strength, but women are braver.
   (10) Peter and Paul were Apostles.
   (11) Peter and Paul were not cousins.
   (12) Some man need not serve.
   (13) All anger is not wrong.
   (14) No nonbeliever is non-miserable.
   (15) Man as animal is selfish.
   (16) No man can pursue both riches and honor.
   (17) Every love except spiritual love is transitory.
   (18) None but the evil are truly miserable.
   (19) The weariest river somewhere meets the sea.
   (20) The moon is not a planet.
   (21) None of the students is exceptionally intelligent.
   (22) Only a hero would have done it.
   (23) Not all who are called respond.
   (24) Never have I seen such ignorance.
   (25) The world is either contingent or self-explanatory.
   (26) Unless you study, you will fail.
   (27) Some people are always complaining.
   (28) You can lead a horse to water, but you can't make him drink.
   (29) No man is infallible, and every man must be selfish.
   (30) Some truth must be upheld, and no truth need be doubted.
   (31) Either a man must work or he need not expect to live.

(32) Either some must sacrifice or all can be enslaved.
(33) Unless all must come, some must be foolish to do so.
(34) Truth is the object of the intellect.
(35) All a cannot be b.
(36) No a is b.
(37) Every a must be b.
(38) No a need be b.
(39) Some a is b.
(40) Some a can be b.
(41) Some a need not be b.
(42) No a can be b.
(43) All a need not be b.
(44) Some a is not b.
(45) If a is b, a must be c.
(46) If a is b, all a need not be c.
(47) If a is b, some a can be c.
(48) If a is b, all a cannot be c.
(49) Unless a is b, some a can be c.
(50) Unless a cannot be b, a is c.
(51) Either some a must be b or some a can be c.
(52) Either all a cannot be b or not all a need be c.
(53) Every a cannot be both b and c.
(54) A is b and c and d.
(55) Some a must be b and all c cannot be d.
(56) No a need be b and no a can be c.
(57) All a can be b but all a cannot be c.
(58) Neither need a be b nor can c be d.
(59) A as b can be c.
(60) Every a except b is c.
(61) Only b is c.
(62) No a except b can be c.
(63) A as b must be c.
(64) Some a can be both b and c.
(65) Although a is b, a is c.
(66) Because a is b, a is c.
(67) Since a is sometimes b, c is not always d.
(68) A is b.
(69) This a is not b.
(70) Whenever a is b, a is c.

58. Give the formal reason why the predicate in an affirmative proposition is taken universally.

59. How should each of the following propositions be represented by means of circles?

   a) Every fish is vertebrate.
   b) Every triangle is a three-sided polygon.
   c) Some animal is intelligent.
   d) Some man is a soldier.

60. Give the formal reason why the predicate in a negative proposition is taken universally.

61. Use circles to represent each of the following propositions:

   a) Some man is not tall.
   b) No circle is polygon.
   c) Some man is not a sailor.
   d) Justice is not expediency.

62. Why do the laws regarding the distribution of the predicate-term not apply strictly to the singular term?

63. Why is it incorrect to place a sign of quantity before the predicate of any proposition?

64. Are *conversion, obversion,* and *contraposition* forms of *immediate inference?* Just how are these operations to be understood?

65. Convert each of the following:

   a) No dog is intelligent.
   b) Every mammal is warm-blooded.
   c) Every man is rational animal.
   d) Some polygon is triangle.
   e) Some food is not wholesome.
   f) Some man is a carpenter.
   g) This politician is corrupt.
   h) John hears a noise.
   i) Sacco is not guilty.
   j) The boxer punches his opponent.
   k) No plant has sense organs.
   l) No non-a is non-b.
   m) This a has no b.
   n) All a is not b.
   o) Some non-x is y.

66. Obvert each of the following:

   a) Some nonhuman is not insensitive.
   b) Some fish is not edible.

c) No learned man is unfortunate.

d) Some criminals are not unabnormal.

e) Some man is just.

f) Every Caesar has his Brutus.

g) Each man claims his own.

h) Every a is b.

i) Not every a is b.

j) No non-a is non-b.

k) Some a is not non-b.

l) All that is not a is b.

m) None that is not a is non-b.

n) This a does not lack b.

o) All that is a is not b.

67. Give the partial contrapositive of each of the following:

a) No man is angel.

b) Every flower has a stamen.

c) Some wine is intoxicating.

d) Some zeal is not commendable.

e) Some unimaginable things are not impossible.

f) Every defeat is not avoidable.

g) No nonbeliever is non-miserable.

h) Some nonhuman is not insensitive.

i) Some people who are not educated are not unintelligent.

j) No fish are unable to swim.

k) Every dishonest person is untrustworthy.

l) Not all inedible things are tasteless.

m) Every non-Aryan is non-inferior.

n) Every a is b.

o) No x is y.

p) All y is not non-x.

q) No non-x is y.

r) Some non-x is non-y.

s) Some non-y is not x.

t) All that is not x is y.

68. Give the full contrapositive of each of the following:

a) Every sheep is ruminant.

b) Some triangle is not isosceles.

c) Every x is y.

d) Every non-b is non-a.

e) Some x is not y.

f) No x is y.

69. What is meant by the *reciprocal* of an A proposition? What by its *inverse?* What is the relation of the reciprocal and the inverse to each other? To the original A proposition?

70. Granted the truth of the first proposition in each of the series below, designate the succeeding propositions as consequently *true, false,* or *doubtful:*

A. (1) Every neurotic is inhibited.
    (2) No neurotic is inhibited.
    (3) No neurotic is uninhibited.
    (4) No uninhibited person is neurotic.
    (5) Some neurotic is inhibited.
    (6) Some neurotic is not uninhibited.
    (7) Some inhibited person is neurotic.
    (8) Every inhibited person is not neurotic.
    (9) Every inhibited person is non-neurotic.
   (10) No inhibited person is neurotic.
   (11) Every uninhibited person is non-neurotic.
   (12) Every inhibited person is neurotic.
   (13) Some uninhibited person is non-neurotic.
   (14) Some non-neurotic is uninhibited.
   (15) Some neurotic is uninhibited.

B. (1) All moral actions are intelligent.
    (2) All unintelligent actions are nonmoral.
    (3) Some moral actions are not intelligent.
    (4) Some moral actions are unintelligent.
    (5) No moral actions are unintelligent.
    (6) All intelligent actions are moral.
    (7) No intelligent actions are nonmoral.
    (8) Some intelligent actions are moral.
    (9) All nonmoral actions are unintelligent.
   (10) No nonmoral actions are intelligent.
   (11) No unintelligent actions are nonmoral.
   (12) All unintelligent actions are moral.
   (13) Some moral actions are intelligent.
   (14) Some moral actions are not unintelligent.
   (15) No intelligent actions are moral.

C. (1) Every x is y.
    (2) Every x is non-y.

(3) Every y is x.
(4) Every y is non-x.
(5) Every non-x is y.
(6) Every non-x is non-y.
(7) Every non-y is x.
(8) Every non-y is non-x.
(9) Some x is y.
(10) Some x is non-y.
(11) Some y is x.
(12) Some y is non-x.
(13) Some non-x is y.
(14) Some non-x is non-y.
(15) Some non-y is x.
(16) Some non-y is non-x.
(17) Some x is not y.
(18) Some x is not non-y.
(19) Some y is not x.
(20) Some y is not non-x.
(21) Some non-x is not y.
(22) Some non-x is not non-y.
(23) Some non-y is not x.
(24) Some non-y is not non-x.
(25) No x is y.
(26) No x is non-y.
(27) No y is x.
(28) No y is non-x.
(29) No non-x is y.
(30) No non-x is non-y.
(31) No non-y is x.
(32) No non-y is non-x.

Chapter 3

1. Define deductive reasoning and give its *proximate* and *remote* matter.
2. Distinguish between *consequent* and *sequence*. What sort of sequence does an invalid syllogism have?
3. What is the *form*, or specifying principle, of the syllogism?
4. Define *major* and *minor terms*, *major* and *minor premises*.
5. What are the four principles upon which categorical deductive reasoning is based? How do we know these are true?

6. Distinguish between the *terminological, quantitative,* and *qualitative* rules of the categorical syllogism.
7. What does a *logical quadruped* lack?
8. Show how the terms "liberty," "democracy," "science," "practical," may give rise to quadrupedal arguments.
9. Can a term be validly broader in the premises than in the conclusion? Illustrate.
10. If the conclusion is negative, what term must be universal?
11. In what way do the *illicit minor* and *major* and the *undistributed middle* resemble the *logical quadruped?*
12. If the premises are true and the conclusion false, what is indicated concerning the syllogism?
13. Show why EI and AO *sequences* must yield a particular conclusion.
14. Why can no conclusion follow from an OI *sequence?*
15. Designate each of the following syllogisms as *valid* or *invalid,* and if invalid, state the fallacy:

(1) No valid syllogism has an undistributed middle
This syllogism does not have an undistributed middle.
∴ This syllogism is valid.

(2) No gentleman is vulgar
Some politician is vulgar
∴ Some politician is not a gentleman.

(3) All wild canaries are migratory birds
All wild canaries are songsters
∴ All migratory birds are songsters.

(4) Every dictator nominated himself
The President nominated himself
∴ The President is a dictator.

(5) Not to vote is to neglect your duty
Not to register is not to vote
∴ Not to register is to neglect your duty.

(6) Not to give to charity is selfish
To pay the landlord is not to give to charity
∴ To pay the landlord is selfish.

(7) No American is a slave
Every slave wants freedom
∴ Some who want freedom are not Americans.

(8) All Bronxites are Easterners
All Easterners are Americans
∴ Some Americans are Bronxites.

(9) Every a is b
Every b is c
∴ Every c is a.

(10) No man is impeccable
He is man
∴ He is not impeccable.

(11) Every communist is anticapitalist
No member of the N.A.M. is a communist
∴ No member of the N.A.M. is anticapitalist.

(12) Every absolutistic creed is undemocratic
Religion is an absolutistic creed
∴ Religion is undemocratic.

(13) All birds fly
All geese fly
∴ All geese are birds.

(14) All who are not guilty are innocent
He is not guilty
∴ He is innocent.

(15) Every Nazi is a racist
No democrat is a Nazi
∴ Some democrat is not a racist.

(16) Every mystery is a religious belief
The whereabouts of the fleet is a mystery
∴ The whereabouts of the fleet is a religious belief.

(17) Every d is e
Some f is e
∴ Some f is d.

(18) No cat has nine tails
Every cat has one more tail than no cat
∴ Every cat has ten tails.

(19) Man is studied by psychology
Hopkins is man
∴ Hopkins is studied by psychology.

(20) The animal is the one type of sentient being
Every wolf is animal
∴ The wolf is the one type of sentient being.

(21) Every cow is cloven-footed
Every cow is ruminant
∴ Every ruminant is cloven-footed.

(22) No a is b
No b is c
∴ No c is a.

(23) No a is b
Some c is a
∴ Some c is not b.

(24) Nothing is better than liberty
Prison life is better than nothing
∴ Prison life is better than liberty.

(25) All gold is metal
Something that glitters is not gold
∴ All that glitters is not metal.

(26) All that glitters is not gold
Aurum glitters
∴ Aurum is not gold.

(27) All who are not educated are ignorant
You are ignorant
∴ You are not educated.

(28) Food is necessary to life
All candy is food
∴ Candy is necessary to life.

(29) No spiritual substance is gaseous
The body is not a spiritual substance
∴ The body is gaseous.

(30) Man is studied by psychology
The white rat is not man
∴ The white rat is not studied by psychology.

(31) No dog is invertebrate
Jeff is a dog
∴ Jeff is not invertebrate.

(32) No informed man is a bigot
Some college professor is a bigot
∴ Some college professor is not an informed man.

(33) What can be perceived sensibly is true
The existence of the soul cannot be perceived sensibly
∴ The existence of the soul is not true.

(34) All the angles of a triangle equal 180 degrees
A is an angle of a triangle
∴ A equals 180 degrees.

(35) John is taller than Kevin
Kevin is taller than Anthony
∴ John is taller than Anthony.

16. Put each of the following enthymemes in syllogistic form and state whether it is valid or invalid:

a) Since this is a triangle, it must be a polygon.
b) Because everything thinkable is finite, God is not thinkable.
c) Since every canary sings, that bird must be a canary.
d) A plant, being a living thing, must possess a vital principle or soul.
e) Since this syllogism has a negative minor, it cannot be in the first figure.
f) This man is intelligent, so he does not read comic books.
g) Since no material thing can act upon itself as a whole, the intellect cannot be material.
h) Since this man hates his fellow man, he cannot love God.
i) You cannot say that all Southerners are democrats, for all democrats believe in equality.
j) This speaker is a Red, since he criticizes free enterprise.
k) Since all valid scientific theories have been confirmed experimentally, the principle of indetermination must be a valid scientific theory.
l) No honest man would support this proposal, but this politician is untroubled by scruples.
m) This Senator is a supporter of democracy, since he opposes socialism.
n) He has never helped me, so I feel no obligation toward him.
o) Joan of Arc must have been a schizophrenic, since hearing voices is a well-attested peculiarity of schizophrenics.

17. Determine whether each of the following arguments is valid or
    invalid:
    a) Only fools believe this
        You don't believe this
        ∴ You are no fool.
    b) Since only organisms are mortal, man must be an organism.
    c) Only a is b
        C is b
        ∴ C is a.
    d) No one but a zany would behave in that fashion, so I've
        come to the conclusion that Smithers is not quite bright.
    e) No person of mature development attempts to push other
        people around, so this hoodlum can never have grown up.
    f) Only M is P
        Every S is M
        ∴ Every S is P.
    g) Only ruthless people become millionaires, and Spofford is
        anything but ruthless, so he'll never be a millionaire.
    h) Anxiety is too disruptive of adjustment to be regarded as a
        defense mechanism.
    i) Since pleasure only follows upon the attainment of the object
        of desire, it cannot be itself the object of desire.
    j) Without stable habits there can be no personality in the
        strict sense, so the infant who has lived only a short time
        cannot be said to have personality in the strict sense.

18. Why is the mood IE always invalid?
19. In the first figure, why must the minor be affirmative?
20. In the second figure, why must the major be universal?
21. In the third figure, why must the conclusion be particular?
22 Reduce each of the following syllogisms to the appropriate mood
    of the first figure:
    a) Every mammal is warm-blooded
        No fish is warm-blooded
        ∴ No fish is mammal.
    b) No fish is invertebrate
        Every mollusc is invertebrate
        ∴ No mollusc is fish.
    c) No gentleman is vulgar
        Some politician is vulgar
        ∴ Some politician is not a gentleman.

d) Some crow is carnivorous
Every crow is a bird
∴ Some bird is carnivorous.

e) Every mad dog is vicious
Every mad dog is a domesticated animal
∴ Some domesticated animal is vicious.

f) Every man is organism
Some intelligent being is not organism
∴ Some intelligent being is not man.

g) Some insect is not useful
Every insect is animal
∴ Some animal is not useful.

h) No needy man is rich
Some needy man is a miser
∴ Some miser is not rich.

i) All Bronxites are New Yorkers
All New Yorkers are Americans
∴ Some Americans are Bronxites.

j) Every polygon is rectilinear
No rectilinear figure is an ellipse
∴ No ellipse is a polygon.

k) Some triangle is isosceles
Every isosceles figure is polygon
∴ Some polygon is triangle.

l) No democrat is a bigot
Every bigot has a closed mind
∴ Some persons having closed minds are not democrats.

m) No giant has a pituitary deficiency
Some persons having a pituitary deficiency are Texans
∴ Not all Texans are giants.

23. Construct syllogisms in *Camestres, Festino, Baroco, Datisi, Felapton, Bocardo, Bramantip, Camenes, Dimaris,* and *Fesapo,* and reduce each to the first figure.

24. Define the hypothetical syllogism. Can the argument of an hypothetical syllogism always be as well expressed by a categorical syllogism?

25. Summarize the rules of the conditional syllogism in one sentence.

26. What fallacy may occur in the *conclusion* of the conditional syllogism?

27. On *formal* grounds, determine the validity or invalidity of each of the following. If invalid specify the fallacy.

  a) If there are no controls, prices will rise
  But there are controls
  ∴ Prices will not rise.

  b) Only if there are no controls will prices rise
  But prices will not rise
  ∴ There will be controls.

  c) If today is Monday, tomorrow is Tuesday
  But today is not Monday
  ∴ Tomorrow is not Tuesday.

  d) If today is Monday, tomorrow is Tuesday
  But tomorrow is not Tuesday
  ∴ Today is not Monday.

  e) If a is b, a is c
  But a is not c
  ∴ A is not b.

  f) If a is b, a is not c
  But a is not c
  ∴ A is b.

  g) If a is not b, a is c
  But a is not b
  ∴ A is c.

  h) Only if a is b, is a c
  But a is not b
  ∴ A is not c.

  i) Only if we work hard, do we succeed
  But we will work hard
  ∴ We will succeed.

  j) If a disease is hereditary, it is not contagious
  But tuberculosis is contagious
  ∴ Tuberculosis is not hereditary.

  k) If x is y, x is z
  But x is not y
  ∴ X is z.

l) If the conference does not succeed, war is inevitable
But the conference will succeed
∴ War is not inevitable.

m) If wishes were horses, beggars would ride
But beggars do not ride
∴ Wishes are not horses.

n) Only if x is y, is x z
But x is not y
∴ X is z.

o) Only if this fellow were a fool or a fraud would he make this proposition
He is obviously not a fool and he makes this proposition
∴ He is a fraud.

28. Determine the validity or invalidity of each of the following arguments:

a) A metal is either naturally liquid or not mercury
But this metal is not naturally liquid
∴ This metal is not mercury.

b) A metal is either naturally liquid or not mercury
But this metal is naturally liquid
∴ This metal is mercury.

c) The universe is either contingent or self-explanatory
But the universe is not self-explanatory
∴ The universe is contingent.

d) Either we visit the dentist or have trouble with our teeth
But we visit the dentist
∴ We will not have trouble with our teeth.

e) A is either b or not c
But a is not c
∴ A is not b.

f) It is either raining or not raining
But it is raining
∴ It is not raining.

g) A is either b or c
But a is not b
∴ A is c.

h) X is either y or non-z
But x is not z
∴ X is not y.

i) X is either y or non-y
But x is y
∴ X is not non-y.

j) A man either tries or he does not succeed
But this man succeeds
∴ This man tries.

29. Why is disjunctive reasoning often inapplicable to actual situations? Can you see why the tendency to overwork the disjunctive form in argument has been labeled "a two-valued logic"?

30. Determine the validity or invalidity of each of the following:

a) A nation cannot be unprepared and secure
But this nation is not unprepared
∴ This nation is secure.

b) A nation cannot be unprepared and secure
But this nation is secure
∴ This nation is not unprepared.

c) A geometrical figure cannot be both plane and solid
But the spherical triangle is not plane
∴ The spherical triangle is solid.

d) An animal cannot be irrational and man
But this animal is irrational
∴ This animal is not man.

e) A feeling cannot be both pleasant and unpleasant
But this feeling is unpleasant
∴ This feeling is not pleasant.

f) No man can be both schizophrenic and normal
This man is not schizophrenic
∴ This man is normal.

g) Everybody can't be both charitable and prudent
He is charitable
∴ He is not prudent.

h) A cannot be both b and non-b
A is not non-b
∴ A is b.

i) X cannot be both y and z
X is y
∴ X is not z.

j) An animal cannot be lacking in freedom and not governed by instinct
But man is not governed by instinct
∴ Man is not lacking in freedom.

k) You cannot sow the wind and not reap the whirlwind
You sow the wind
∴ You do not reap the whirlwind.

l) You cannot strengthen Europe successfully and not build up German military power
You oppose building up German military power
∴ You oppose strengthening Europe.

31. Determine the validity or invalidity of each of the following:

a) Every divided nation is insecure
Every oligarchy is a divided nation
∴ Every oligarchy is insecure
Every dictatorship is an oligarchy
∴ Every dictatorship is insecure
No democracy is a dictatorship
∴ No democracy is insecure.

b) No contingent being is uncaused
Every changing thing is contingent
∴ No changing thing is uncaused
Every material thing is changing
∴ No material thing is uncaused
Every chemical element is a material thing
∴ No chemical element is uncaused.

c) No democrat is a racist
Every racist is a breeder of hate
Every breeder of hate is a public menace
Every public menace should be imprisoned
∴ No democrat should be imprisoned.

d) Every Communist favors State ownership
Not every Socialist is a Communist
Every agrarian is a Socialist
Every farmer's commune is agrarian
∴ Some farmer's commune does not favor State ownership.

e) Every happy man is just
No just man is lacking in prudence
Every man lacking in prudence is intemperate
Every intemperate man is unworthy of respect
Every man unworthy of respect is discontented
∴ No happy man is discontented.

f) All statements of what ought to be are nonscientific since
they cannot be answered by investigative methods
Logical positivism contains many statements of what ought
to be
∴ Logical positivism contains many statements which are
nonscientific.

g) All self-contradictory positions are meaningless
Logical positivism is a self-contradictory position since it
affirms as valid the philosophical statement that no philosophical statement is valid
∴ Logical positivism is meaningless.

h) No believer in democracy is intolerant
Every intolerant person is unchristian
Every unchristian person is practically irreligious
Every practically irreligious person is unhappy
∴ No believer in democracy is unhappy.

i) Every bigot is intolerant
Some college professor is a bigot
∴ Some college professor is intolerant
No uninformed person is a college professor
∴ Some uninformed person is intolerant.

j) Some man is idiot
Every idiot is lacking in responsibility
Every being lacking in responsibility is incapable of evil
intent
No being incapable of evil intent should be punished for
wrongdoing
∴ Some man should not be punished for wrongdoing.

32. Put the following arguments in proper syllogistic form:

a) X is less than y
Z is less than x
∴ Z is less than y.

b) Peter is taller than Tony
Tony is taller than I
∴ Peter is taller than I.

c) It is not as far from New York to Pittsburgh as it is from New York to Chicago
It is not as far from New York to Philadelphia as it is from New York to Pittsburgh
∴ It is not as far from New York to Philadelphia as it is from New York to Chicago.

d) Nihilism is worse than communism
Communism is worse than socialism
∴ Nihilism is worse than socialism.

33. Are the following oblique syllogisms valid or invalid? If invalid, is the fallacy *formal* or *material?*

a) Every badminton player is an active sportsman
Essick is the most talkative badminton player in seven states
∴ Essick is the most talkative active sportsman in seven states.

b) All bigotry is unchristian
Some clergyman is a defender of bigotry
∴ Some clergyman is a defender of what is unchristian.

c) Every sister of mine is the aunt of my children
My children are but two
∴ Every sister of mine is the aunt of but two children.

d) My individuality is dependent on my self-concept
But my self-concept is intangible
∴ My individuality is dependent on an intangible.

e) Equality is a right guaranteed by the Constitution
But every infringement of equality is unjust
∴ Every unjust act is an infringement of a right guaranteed by the Constitution.

f) Every perception is a conscious awareness
No simple sensation requires a perception
∴ No simple sensation requires conscious awareness.

g) All discriminatory legislation is unconstitutional
Some Congressman supports discriminatory legislation
∴ Some Congressman supports what is unconstitutional.

INDEX